CONN SMYTHE

If You Can't Beat 'Em
in the Alley

CONN SMYTHE

If You Can't Beat 'Em in the Alley

with Scott Young

PaperJacks LTD.

Markham, Ontario, Canada

A CANADIAN

PaperJacks

One of a series of Canadian books
by PaperJacks Ltd.

CONN SMYTHE: IF YOU CAN'T BEAT 'EM IN THE ALLEY

McClelland & Stewart edition published in October, 1981
Paperjacks edition published October, 1982

ISBN 0-7701-0231-X

Chapter One

There were advantages to living all my life in the city where I was born. For one, I was never very far from reminders of my beginnings, such as they were. Within sight of Maple Leaf Gardens, just across the parking lots (and over a few signboards) to the east, is the house where my parents lived in rented rooms when I was born. It was 51 McMillan Street then, now called Mutual. When I built the Gardens thirty-six years later I thought of buying the house and using the space to park my car. I didn't, so that reminder of starting out poor was with me every day for life. Even thirty years later when I sold the Gardens part of the deal was that I would be provided with offices there for life, with a secretary, car, and driver. It was an arrangement that the eventual owner, Harold Ballard, lived up to although with an occasional grumble.

Other places from my boyhood I didn't see as often. One day in the summer of 1980, when I was eighty-five, I went to one of them. I'd been to the chiropractor, I think, or the acupuncturist, both of whom I visited regularly to help ease the pain I'd had ever since being hit in the lower back by a bomb fragment during a German air attack near Caen in 1944. When I came out I said to my driver, Mike Walsh, "Mike, take me out to Scarborough." He knew where I meant. We headed east along Eglinton between the rows of shopping centres and factories and apartment buildings where fields and farms had been when I was a boy. Near Markham Road, I got out with my cane and limped over to where I could look down a bank beside the railroad track. I used to run down that bank almost every day. There was a certain time when a train would pass that spot and some friend of my father who worked for the railroad would throw off a newspaper. It was my job to be there when the paper landed. I would scramble down the bank and then take the paper home to dad.

The house we lived in then had advantages (or some might say disadvantages) that a lot of people wouldn't mind today. We paid no rent and no taxes, because we were squatting there, although with the owner's permission. We had no telephone and no bills for electricity, water, sewage, or heat. We had no electricity. Water came from a pump in the yard. Not far from the back door was the privy, a one-holer. We could usually scrounge enough wood for the round stove in the kitchen that provided what heat we had, as well as cooking our meals. In winter one of my chores was to heat a pail of water on the stove each morning before school. I'd go out and pour it down to thaw out the pump and get enough water for the day. There was also a chicken house where I used to throw my oatmeal porridge to the chickens every morning I could do it without getting caught. In summer I would play in the open fields with other kids from Scarborough School Section No. 9. In winter it was skating and sliding.

We got the place free because it and two or three other empty ones nearby were owned by a member of the Theosophical Society, to which my father belonged. He was a very gentle man, a vegetarian, and although he thought most of the time that he wasn't making many yards with me about theosophy, he did better than he thought. After he died in 1947 I joined the society and paid my dues each year. The doctrines are based on the Hinduistic and Buddhistic beliefs that a person's status in life is based on his deeds in a previous incarnation. Dad didn't make a full-scale theosophist out of me, but maybe I am, in my heart. One of their beliefs in particular – as ye sow, so shall ye reap – seems logical to me. I do believe that if you do good, you get back good; and if you do bad, you'll get bad back. Believing that, I've always felt that it didn't make much sense to weight the future against myself by doing a lot of bad things. I've been rude to people, blasted people, but I always did so only when I believed it was for their eventual good. Anyway, my father lived by theosophy and in a way our free house in Scarborough was supporting evidence. At a time when he was down on his luck, a theosophist friend said to him, "Go and live in that house of mine in Scarborough. I'll be happy just having someone in it and looking after it." Which he did for about four years, from when I was six until I was ten. Then dad got a job as a reporter with the old *Toronto World* and we moved back into the city.

I don't remember the place where I was born near the Gardens, 51 McMillan. I was only two when we left there and moved to the first place I do remember. It was then called North Street, but now is part of Bay, the first two blocks south of Bloor. Bloor was not quite out in the sticks then but certainly wasn't the business street it is today. Our house, one of a row, was No. 18, across the street and a little south of where La Scala restaurant now stands. I didn't know until later that the reason we moved to North Street was that my father's business, A.E.S. Smythe and Company, cement dealers, with offices at 157 Bay, had gone under. You could look it up. The company name is in large bold type in the 1897 Toronto city directory, but in 1898 isn't listed at all. Moving to our end of North Street was a step down. All that I know of his income in those days was that he made a little money editing a magazine called *The Lamp*, for the Theosophical Society. He wrote a little, free-lance, and worked in construction, too. Our closest neighbours were working people, meaning poor, but the upper end of the street was different. Close to Bloor was a church, big houses, rich people. They had horses and carriages and one family, the Arnoldis, had a pony cart.

Not that there was any caste system that I remember. But if there was a party for kids at the rich end of the street, or even if I was just asked in for milk and cookies, I noticed that not all the adults were mothers or fathers, like at our end. I was meeting my first cooks and nannies and men-servants.

Our place couldn't have been substantially built. There was a hole in one wall halfway up the stairs where I had hit it with my baby bottle while protesting being carried to bed. In winter I remember huddling with my father and sister in front of the tiny fireplace, with a screen behind us to keep the heat from getting away. Mary was five years older than I, and my father's favourite.

The two short blocks of North Street in those days had only one intersection, at Czar Street, now called Charles. There was a vacant lot or two. We also played on the street, which was a rough macadam. A ditch and a gravel walk were between the road and the houses. I mentioned one family at the other end, the Arnoldis. Frank Arnoldi, Q.C., the father, was a powerful lawyer in the city then. His son Bay was my childhood hero. He was a championship boxer at Upper Canada College and later at Royal Military College in Kingston, and was worth a little boy's hero-worship. When I was only about five, Bay had a new BB gun, an air gun that fired pellets. One day he let me hold it. I saw a workman across the street bending over, giving me a large target. I fired. Bullseye! The workman, roaring with rage, ran across the street through the horse-drawn carriages and delivery wagons. Bay grabbed the gun back. He was big even then. The workman demanded to know who had shot him.

"Well, you can see who is holding the gun," Bay said.

The man might have killed me, but he didn't feel like tackling Bay.

We lived near the Arnoldis for only those few years from 1897 to 1900 or so, but for some reason the family befriended me from then on. An uncle of Bay's got me my commission in the First World War. Bay commanded a regiment in that one. In the Second, Bay, by then Colonel F. F. Arnoldi (I don't know where the nickname Bay came from), helped me get my own command, the 30th Battery, which I later took overseas.

What I remember from those days are only scattered fragments of childhood, the scenes more than the details. Automobiles were a rarity when I lived on North Street, but traffic was heavy with carriages and pony carts. The hot-rodders of the time were light delivery wagons, always going full speed as grocery and butcher boys careened through the slower traffic to make deliveries throughout the city. I wasn't conscious then that my mother, who people called Polly but whose maiden name was Mary Adelaide Constantine, drank too much. She was English, short, plump, pretty, and carefree. I loved her. What I have as a sense of fun comes from her. She and my father were a terrible mismatch. They were married in the late 1880's on a boat bringing them to Canada, she from England and he from Ireland, and I never remember them living together for more than a few months at a time. He was seven years older but that wasn't the problem. He was gentle, quiet, teetotal, a vegetarian, and a theosophist. She . . . wasn't. Two or three times she left and went home to England, sometimes bringing jolly friends back with her. When she was around and things were tough, sometimes father would be the one to leave. In today's world, the marriage probably would have ended quickly in separation or divorce, but I have warm memories of them. I loved them both and mother especially, but dad too, gave me lots of love in return.

When I was five, in 1900, I started to kindergarten at Wellesley School, a few blocks south of us on the south east corner of what is now Wellesley and Bay. On one of my first days in kindergarten a boy put up his hand and asked to go to the toilet. Then another. Then a third. Maybe they gave me the idea. But suddenly I really had to go. When I put up my hand the teacher said, "No! No more!"

I couldn't, or at least didn't, hold it. I peed on the floor, which was slanted, and the stuff ran down and formed a pool under the teacher's feet. She was furious, but I stood up for my rights. "I told you I had to go!" I said.

The route to and from kindergarten was full of fear for me, because we had to pass St. Michael's College. Religion was very bitter in those days. The Knights of Columbus, Catholic, celebrated St. Patrick's Day; the Orangemen, Protestant, July 12. But those were just the *big* fighting days. All year when Protestant and Catholic kids came together there would be fights. Sometimes coming out of school we little kids would run east all the way over to Yonge before turning north and cutting back toward home on Czar Street; we were scared to death of being attacked by the Catholics if we went the short route north past St. Michael's.

Still, the greatest fight I ever saw was one day going home from school when a fight started between three St. Mikes' kids. One fought the other two up a lane and then along street after street, always with his back to the wall, or he never would have been able to hang on. It was a lesson I didn't forget: if you looked after your rear, you could keep going. It works in fights, war, business. Getting home, or getting to school, often was that kind of adventure. We were afraid not only of the fights. In our ignorance, we sincerely believed that if we were captured by the priests, we'd never be seen again alive. I've always thought the Catholics have it pretty easy – do anything they like, then confess, and be forgiven. It's the opposite of, "as ye sow, so shall ye reap." I *know* that there is no such thing as being forgiven.

About the time when I was ready to move from kindergarten to Grade One, things must have been particularly bad between my mother and father, because at first when he and I moved to Scarborough my mother stayed in the North Street house. I think my sister was with her, too, at first, but later she came to Scarborough. Mary and I didn't get along. I felt she was butting in, her first Christmas out there in 1902. This was my dad and I wanted him to myself. I made a scene, threw things, cried, fought her and dad. But under it all I was deeply disappointed, even shattered, being sure that my father loved Mary more than he did me. The truth is, I never shared things well with anybody, all my life. I have some children and grandchildren who – well, everything they have they'll share with others. I never had that feeling. I would give something freely, didn't mind giving it, but nobody was going to take it away from me, or just move in and use it. Perhaps it's the kind of a feeling that an only child has, when suddenly it isn't the only child. I've had daughters of my own since and I know how a father can feel toward a daughter; and I learned as well that sons can be different, sometimes prickly, fighting back, causing trouble. Anyway, I was desperately jealous of Mary and the way dad treated her that one Christmas. All in all, my memories of Mary are not good. Once in Scarborough she tattled on me for throwing my porridge and milk in with the chickens, getting me in trouble. The reason I couldn't eat the stuff was that at the farm where we bought milk the cows ate a lot of turnips, and the milk tasted like turnips. It was straight from the cow, not pasteurized. I just had an instinct that it was bad for me. Mary drank it all the time and when we were still living there she developed a terrible goitre, a swelling of the thyroid gland at the front and side of the throat, and fairly common in those days. Right or wrong, I always figured she got it drinking all that raw milk. Anyway, I didn't drink the milk and I stayed healthy, while her goitre got so bad that when she was twelve she had to be taken to the hospital. She died there on May 22, 1903.

I was eight then. My father took Mary's death very hard. From then on until I was a man, it was mostly just the two of us living together, although a year or two after Mary died my mother brought from England a woman friend who stayed with us one winter. I don't know where my mother was but one night, complaining about the cold, this friend tried to get my father to go to bed with her to keep her warm. He wouldn't. Then she tried me. I declined as well.

Where mother was living then I'm not sure, but in 1905 when I was ten, dad and I moved into a single room at 12 Bond Street, just above Queen, where St. Michael's Hospital is now. Our first room was on the second floor and cost $1.50 a week. It was warm in winter, because a stovepipe ran through it from downstairs. There were a lot of other people in the house and only one bathroom, but that wasn't so bad. Most of the other people only bathed on Saturday nights, so we could pick almost any other day of the week.

Dad could walk to work in a few minutes to the *World* office at 83 Yonge Street. And he was happy, writing about everything under the sun. Although the *World* was chronically short of money, and skipped many a payday (once later dad had eighteen weeks back pay coming to him), we still made out all right.

Dad would be away a lot at night because the *World* was a morning paper. He decided to put me into a private school as a boarder – St. Alban's Cathedral School on Howland Avenue, a block above Bloor in the district between Spadina and Bathurst. It closed down a few years later but there's another school there now, St. George's. I made a pretty good contribution to help St. George's get started in 1964, but in 1905 Dad had to scrape hard to get the fees of $50 a year. I sometimes ponder the result. On North Street I'd known people who had more than I did. In Scarborough everybody had seemed pretty well in the same boat; none of us had much. But in St. Alban's I was again the poor boy, and by then was old enough to know it. I think maybe that hating so much to be the poor boy then gave me the urge not to be poor, the sooner the better. I didn't covet what others had, but I hated what I was, that my clothes weren't as good as the others had, that when there was something to buy I might be able to spend a nickel while the other fellow spent fifteen cents. I didn't *mind* him having fifteen cents, but I wanted fifteen cents, too. I wanted to be in the class where I loaned a bicycle, not borrowed it. Compared to them, I felt like the smell behind a motor car. A lot of good people went to St. Alban's. Cecil Cowan's mother used to come with lovely parcels of food that we'd all share. The mother of a boy named Davidson gave me the first pair of good skates I ever owned. I remember them well. We went to play hockey at Upper Canada College one day. After playing, we walked back down Poplar Plains Road. It was a pretty long walk and we sat for a while on a mound of snow, talking and resting. When we got up to go we were talking and laughing and somehow I left my skates.

When I ran back later they were gone. I never felt so badly about losing something in my life.

And talk about other people's parents and their beautiful parcels. One of the last times I saw my mother, on her feet, she came into the church where the choir was practising. She had on a fat and frowzy looking straw hat and was carrying a paper bag. She looked half-stewed. We were all up there in the front of the church when I saw her coming down the aisle. The other boys saw her about the same time I did. You sure couldn't miss her. One of them said, "Gee, who's this old bird coming?"

I hadn't thought it out in advance. I just said it, bang. "It's my nanny," I said.

I'm glad to get that lie off my chest after all these years. I've been ashamed of it ever since. But there's a contradiction in the shame, because it saved me a lot. Poor kids are easy to put down, by kids who aren't poor. It wasn't that I didn't love her – it was something else. She could make great cookies and the bag was full of them. I shared them around and my friends enjoyed them. It gained me a lot of stature to have a nanny who could bake like that, but if I'd owned up to her being my mother it would have been something very different.

Someone once suggested to me that my denial of my mother was something like the Bible story of Peter denying Jesus Christ, and I suppose that could be. But if Peter was in a choir and Jesus came down the aisle plastered, maybe Peter would have said he didn't know him that time, either.

A year later my mother wound up in Toronto Western Hospital, the same one in which my sister had died. I was never told exactly what was the matter with her, but drinking and not looking after herself were parts of it. There was always some kid at St. Alban's who would lend me a bike to ride down and see her. One time I bought her a package of ju-jubes. When I stood beside the bed and gave it to her she burst into tears. She couldn't help it, she said. I was her little boy and was so kind, bringing her ju-jubes. I don't remember seeing her after that. She died. I don't remember anything about her funeral except that I was not there when she was buried alongside my sister in the cemetery at St. Margaret's Church in Scarborough. The gravestone showed that she died on October 18, 1906, when she was thirty-eight and I was eleven. Memories of what drink did to her made me pretty well an abstainer for life. On special occasions I have had a glass of champagne, or a sip of it; seven times from Stanley Cups my hockey teams won. But it was soon after mother died that someone noticed that I had never been christened. I was old enough by then to protest against my registered name of Constantine Falkland Cary Smythe. I insisted on plain Conn and got my way.

The matter of being poor, and of always trying to do well in competitions, sometimes made me take some shortcuts. I needed a little money now and again. Dad rarely gave me any unless he approved of what it was going to be spent on. Yet he cared nothing for money himself, never seemed to know what was in his pockets, so sometimes if his pants were over a chair in the room on Bond Street I'd go through them and take a little. Then once at St. Alban's during a service there was an accident with the collection plates, and silver was rolling all over the place. When we in the choir went to help pick it up, I tucked some away under a rug where I could get it later. Some of my experiences then, knowing that a poor kid will do anything to get his hands on some cash once in a while, made it possible for me to understand why some other poor people do what they do.

I remember also one time a few years later I won a competition at the Ernest Thompson Seton camp in New York state. Various youth organizations both in Canada and the United States used to pick boys to attend the camp. I'd been sent by the Toronto Central YMCA. Once in the Seton camp there was a competition between six of us that involved trailing a deer (we were supposed to be Indians, I think) through some woods just by looking for deer tracks and other signs left by someone who had gone ahead. The idea was to track the deer until one of us found it (a stuffed dummy) and shot it with a bow and arrow, to win the competition.

I've been lucky all my life, but I was just learning that then. At the start of this competition, my shoelace came untied. By the time I fixed it, the others had run on ahead and disappeared. I ran in the direction they'd gone. In a few minutes I thought I heard them over to one side, so I ran that way and what do you think? I burst into a clearing. There was the dummy deer not ten feet away. I hadn't seen a track or a clue, but I'd got there first. I drew my bow and arrow, shot – and missed. So I found the arrow in the bush, carried it back, and plunged it into the dummy's heart by hand. Then I yelled for the others. There was nothing in the rules that said a guy couldn't be just plain lucky, so I won the competition.

My father was a tender man, not like me at all. The only time I saw him get desperately angry was when we were at the theatre – at the *World*, he was theatre critic, music critic, book critic, you name it, he did it – and at some touching or emotional part, a man nearby started laughing. Dad stood up and I thought finally I was going to see him slug someone. He couldn't stand to see something he thought was nice, destroyed.

He tried to teach me to appreciate many of the better things of this world, tried to make something different of me than what I am, but when he found he couldn't do that, he didn't stop me going along the road that was more my natural one. I was interested in games, sports, athletics – and he helped me in that because newspapermen got passes to everything. I could go to any game, free of charge. I couldn't have gone otherwise. He was the one who first interested me in racing. If there was something special doing at the old Woodbine track (now called Greenwood), he'd be down there doing the colour story – for instance, at the King's Plate in 1907, the first one I remember, when Kelvin won for Ambrose Woods and paid big. When I won that race (by then called the Queen's Plate) with Caledon Beau in 1958, a colt I'd bred on my own farm, I remembered those days fifty years earlier when father would take me to races with him. He would write in the press box. I would carry his stories back downtown on the streetcar and deliver them to the *World* office. He said the reason the *World* sent him to the track was that he had a son who would be messenger boy and run the copy back downtown for nothing.

In those days, my early teens, we were together a lot, although there were some places I didn't go, like the Legislature (he covered that, too, sometimes). He was a good newspaperman. I've often told other newspapermen that they'd be better if they had some of my father's ethics.

But he could also write. I used to clip his stories and paste them in books. Not long ago I came across one column he used to write in *The Sunday World*, called "Crusts and Crumbs," by Albert Ernest Stafford, the byline he used. He was taking a shot at someone in a connection not important here, but it read this way:

It is astonishing how dogmatic people can be about matters which they have never taken any pains to study. We meet men every day who will lay down the law in the most arbitrary manner on subjects about which they are a century or two behind the age . . . asserting, and what is worse, insisting on other people accepting, ideas that were abandoned about the same time as the flat earth and the geocentric universe. And the less opportunity these people have had to study and for getting real knowledge, the more dogmatic they are. Ill bred children are always opinionated.

I find that rather graceful. Many a modern columnist has made a good living with a lot worse, and none that I've ever met had the kind of guts he showed one time in 1910 when there was an argument about a development around Ashbridge's Bay. He had researched thoroughly for his stories, but because of politics his own paper's editorials took a position that father strongly disagreed with. Furious, he went down the street to an opposition paper, the *Telegram*, and wrote a blast that the *Telegram* ran as a front-page editorial. The *World* didn't fire him for it. The publisher only said to him, "Why didn't you write that for us?"

Thirty-odd years later I went down and told Joe Atkinson of the *Toronto Star* some scandalous facts about wasted time in training our troops for overseas. He wouldn't print it because the *Star* was a Liberal paper, and the government was Liberal. But he did send Gregory Clark to check it out. A few weeks later Atkinson told me that, if anything, I'd been too easy on the Army – but the *Star* still wouldn't print the story. I ran into Clark on a train platform about that time and challenged him for lack of guts. I told him he knew the truth, why didn't he take it to some paper that would print it, as my father had? We had hot words. He wrote me a note the next day telling me to sell my peanuts, he'd sell his papers. But I must have got to him. He didn't speak to me for twenty years after that.

If my father could hear me holding him up as an example, he would turn over in his grave. When we were together I was always trying to prove him wrong. When he switched from being a reporter to being an editorial writer, of course he didn't really need facts any more and could be like all the rest of them, long on theory and short on practice. Even today I read editorials with dad in mind. One of the last things he tried to sell me, many years later, was that Stalin had the right idea. Never mind all the Russian people that got murdered, the *theory* was right. Editorial writers never seem to mind whether the blooming thing they're touting will work. Even in the room on Bond Street when I used to clip dad's stories and paste them in a book, where nobody ever read them again, I would argue with him. Later we disagreed on his editorials. And once I laid a little trap for him. We moved a lot. Every time we moved, we had to take an increasing pile of books with us. From Bond Street we moved across Yonge to 125 Simcoe, the Strathy Building, above a bank. A couple of years later we moved to 50 Gerrard Street East into the Ellington Apartments, getting a little more space. But our next move, to 85 Bleecker, was the first time he had a room all to himself with wall to wall books that I was pretty sure he never read after the first time. I stretched a thread along one shelf. A year or so later I said we should get rid of some of the books, they took up too much space, he never read them.

"Of course I read them!" he said.

I showed him the thread, undisturbed.

Yet in trying to develop me as a person, he did a lot of the right things. When I was thirteen, the *World* ran a circulation-getting contest for its delivery kids, the prizes being trips to England. When it came time for the winners to go most of them were girls and he was considered the ideal moral person to be the chaperone. He took me along with him. I met my relatives for the first time; my aunt in Manchester, my mother's sister, who was good to me then and later, when I went over as a soldier. On that same trip he took me to meet his people in Ireland. My grandfather, James Smythe, had given me a book called *Tom Brown at Oxford* a few Christmases earlier but I'd never even seen a picture of him. He had some terrible disease. At meals he'd eat a spoonful of food, and half of it would come right back up into a basin he kept beside him, between him and me. It sickened me. I asked my Dad not to make me sit beside grandfather at meals as I couldn't stand it.

"Haven't you got any manners?" he said.

"I've got better manners than my grandfather," I said. "I wouldn't shoot up stuff right into his face like he does into mine."

But he made me sit there anyway. I'm still that way, squeamish about people who can't control themselves, through disease or whatever. Many years later when I was doing all I could to raise money for crippled children, some people had the idea that I was the ideal benefactor, that these kids would crawl up on my knee, and love me, and I'd cuddle them, but that wasn't true. What I could do was raise money to help them, but to watch them struggling to eat, or be fed, lacking control to do it right – I just don't have a strong stomach. I don't want to be there.

Chapter Two

My grandfather Smythe had been a choirmaster and a good musician. I know dad would have been happier if I had taken up a baton instead of a hockey stick. He didn't put any tangible obstacles in the way of me playing games, but he never bought me any sports equipment either, even at Christmas, and never came to watch me play, even later when I was getting to be pretty well known. That hurt me more when I was younger. Afterwards, I came to ignore it. I was just not the kind of son he would have chosen, if he'd had the say. In one book of verse he published in 1891, *Poems Grave and Gay* (Imrie and Graham, Toronto), there is one that might have been a wistful laying out of his hopes for the kind of son he'd like to have. A father and son are standing by a window, looking at the stars and talking.

Bob is a small philosopher;
I am the sire of the tender sage,
And half expect him to make a stir
Out in the world when he comes of age . . .

It wasn't my kind of stir that he had in mind, I'm sure, but if you think of a man hoping for a tender sage and getting me instead, I suppose he would deserve a certain amount of sympathy. He must have had a premonition, because when I was born I was registered as Constantine Falkland Cary Smythe, and you can't get Bob out of that.

Another poem, quite different, he wrote about my sister Mary after she died. It was published in a volume called *Garden of the Sun* (Macmillan, 1923) and is called "Before The Burial." One line reads, "Little daughter, only twelve," and the poem reflects not only his grief but belief in her reincarnation:

When thy soul shall walk the earth
Clothed anew in mortal birth,
May I follow through the spheres
Worthy of thy love and tears!

I understood that grief better myself more than forty years after Mary's death when my own youngest daughter died tragically. But as a boy wanting my father's love, wanting to be first in his heart, I would have settled for him cheering from the sidelines when I played the games that gave me a chance to be somebody. His love for Mary did affect my life in another way. After my mother died and there were just the two of us left, he had other close women friends. But by then I didn't get hurt as often or as deeply as I had when I was only six or seven. I had got used to the idea that with him, sometimes I came second to somebody else. We loved one another but he had his life and I mine, part of mine being that I was so attracted to sports. Still, I have always thought there is an advantage to having an Irish sire and an English dam. Those races enjoy the contest. I always have. You have to enjoy, to be any good.

For me, organized sports began when I was ten. I was too small to be in the St. Alban's cadet corps, but the cricket team needed a combination scorekeeper and water boy. I wanted the job more than anyone else, so I got it. When I finally did begin to play, I felt I was always the worst player on every team. But as long as I was better than the next best one who didn't make the team, the last cut, I was happy. I knew that without size or strength I had to make it on hard work. Over the next ten years or so, it was amazing how often I was a team captain without being anywhere near the best player; just because I wanted it so much. There were extra duties in being captain that others didn't want to be bothered with, but I loved. It meant being in charge, telling the others we had to practise at such and such a time, you play right wing and I play centre, and so on.

It was the summer of 1908 when dad took me to England and Ireland. Travel in those days, of course, was by ship and rail, and took time. That June I had passed the Grade Eight examinations at St. Alban's, and when we returned to Canada late in the year I had missed the first term of high school. So I was nearly fourteen when I was enrolled as a boarder at Upper Canada College. My father obviously couldn't afford it. I used to bring in the money for my fees myself, sometimes by the week. One day when I was standing in front of the registrar's desk unfolding crumpled paper money and putting dimes and quarters and nickels into little stacks, I glanced up and saw that the registrar had tears running down his cheeks. I don't think he cried any when the Heintzmanns or others among my rich classmates sent in their fees.

I hated Upper Canada College. I hated the new-boy duties, fagging (running errands, doing odd jobs) for seniors. It seemed an unjust place to me from the first. They made me serve a full year of the new-boy stuff; I had entered just after Christmas, so I had the rest of that school year and the first half of my second year to be at every senior's beck and call. I recognize that Upper Canada College discipline has helped produce some of the finest Canadians in many fields. But my firsthand opinion was that it also produced a lot of skunks. Years later I insisted that my own two sons, Stafford and Hughie, go there, simply because I knew from my own experience that once a boy had gone to Upper Canada he would never again be in awe of great family names, money, power, or social standing. He would know that although a good private school like UCC might produce the best, it also can produce the worst. Stafford hated it as much as I did, and eventually dropped out to finish high school at Runnymede Collegiate; but Hughie did well, winning three awards for excellence. I think he pushed on to win three because I had won only two and he wanted to be better than I was.

But he and Stafford didn't have the poor-boy thing to cope with. When I was there, two or three other poor kids and I would run together like mice, admiring the moneyed people, practically saluting when we were allowed to share the fantastic food parcels that would come from some boy's mother, delivered by the chauffeur.

Still, the place did have its value to me. Hockey was just starting the week I arrived, and I was chosen captain of the Lower Flat hockey team. That suited me fine. It gave me a grip on something. When we were on the ice, I was top man. What I said, the others did. It was becoming more and more ingrained in me that I was as good as anybody; that I could have their kind of life if I tried hard enough. We played ten games that winter, eight wins and two ties, and our team picture – the first time I ever had my picture in the paper –. was in the rotogravure section of the *Sunday World* that spring. Dad working there probably didn't hurt any, but I gazed a lot on that photo of eight boys (seven regulars and one spare) with me sitting in the middle where it read: C. Smythe, capt.

I weighed 112 pounds then and my hair was very fair, almost white. But that didn't make me the white-haired boy to the masters. One morning I skipped Sunday School and went to see my father at his room on Simcoe Street. I didn't think it was any great sin to go and I thought I'd got away with it until one day soon after, our housemaster called me in. There were a bunch of hockey sticks in his room. I thought, boy, he's going to give me a new stick!

"Pick one out," he said.

I did and then he took it from me, hefting it.

"Now bend over," he said.

When I did he whacked me with the hockey stick, a hell of a blow, and told me I was getting it because I had missed Sunday School. I thought it was a rotten Upper Canada trick, and still do.

The autumn after my mid-winter arrival, I tried for the rugby football team but never made better than about third-string. The word that, "Smythe's no good at football" came in handy a couple of years later.

After a year and a half at Upper Canada dad put three and three together: I hated the place; it cost more than he could afford; and I was old enough at fifteen that I wanted more freedom. So he okayed my move to Jarvis Collegiate. Jarvis Street was a lot better then, lined with huge houses. The Masseys (whose sons went to private schools, needless to say) lived only a few doors from the school. One son, Vincent, was to become Canada's first Canadian-born Governor General; and another, Raymond, the famous actor. I didn't even know they were alive then. At Jarvis I met Harvey Aggett, a good athlete who was on all the school teams I was on. We became almost inseparable. His father had a big plumbing business. Because my own home was sometimes rather empty, my mother gone, I spent as much time at the Aggetts as I did at home. Harvey, who I called Wreck, could often borrow the family Cadillac, a big touring car that made the two of us a rather attractive item to the girls. Their family belonged to the Balmy Beach Canoe Club so we often paddled there. In the next two years Wreck and I played on hockey, rugby football, and basketball teams for Jarvis. In my second year, we had an exhibition rugby football game booked with Upper Canada. By then I was first-string at Jarvis, one of those big 120 pound fullbacks. When Upper Canada heard that I was a starter they decided Jarvis couldn't be much good. They put out their second team against us. We led them about 65-0 when they decided to call it quits.

I was getting to be not a bad scorer by then. I spent hours on the basketball courts at the Central YMCA, learning to shoot baskets from different corners. It wasn't very good for my scholastic work, but was great for basketball. I wasn't big enough to get the ball away from other players and down the court, but if somebody would get it to me I could put it in. I played hockey the same way, hanging around the nets waiting for someone to get the puck to me. We won the city schools championships in both basketball and hockey in the spring of 1912, my last year, and the previous autumn we should have won the city schools rugby football championship, too. We had four or five football players who went on to play senior with the Toronto Rowing and Athletic Association, and Toronto Argonauts. Also, two or three later played for Varsity. Anyway, we were good and we knew it. Too well. We would play Harbord, Riverdale, all the other schools, and beat them by thirty-five or forty points, while Parkdale, the next best team, would only beat them by a point or two. When the final game came against Parkdale we got all dressed up in our sweaters with the big J in front, and paraded in open cars past the school, everybody cheering, on the way to the game. We were sure we would win by a mile. I got hammered on the opening kickoff. Nothing went right from then on. Near the end we were three or four points behind when they lined up almost on their goal line, and fumbled. Wreck Aggett fell on the loose ball in the end zone. It would have been the winning touchdown except that he looked up, grinning all over his face – and let the ball squirt loose. They fell on it. The two points we got for a safety touch weren't enough. It was the first but not the last time I found that you never should figure you've got a championship won, until you've beaten the other guy.

Reg Hopper, a Jarvis team-mate who was a pillar of the Ontario

Society for Crippled Children many years later, remembered something else about that season. When we were playing Malvern Collegiate, Reg dove for a loose ball at the same time that one of the Malvern stars, Dave McIntosh, tried to kick it. Unfortunately he kicked Reg's head instead.

Reg said, "When I came to there was the damnedest fight going on all around me and you know who started it and was in the middle of it . . . You, Connie."

I remember the Parkdale game for something good as well, however. Some girls at Parkdale who called themselves the Nights of Gladness were always involved whenever there was a school dance or party, as there was after that final game. I knew one of them slightly but there was another I wanted to know, as soon as I saw her. They say there is no such thing as love at first sight, not love that lasts, but there was for me. When I managed to get introduced to her I liked her even better. Her name was Irene Sands and she was beautiful to me and not only beautiful but good, in a way hard to explain. I wasn't quite seventeen and she was a little younger. It just seemed that from the moment we met we talked the same language. She was small, the right size for my five feet seven. She said she'd go to a movie with me. I used to skip school almost every Wednesday to go the the matinee at Shea's where they had all the great vaudeville acts of the time, Jack Benny and the rest, and our first date was one Wednesday at Shea's.

When I found that Irene lived in the Spadina area, I was sure she was rich and lived in one of those Spadina mansions above College. I didn't want her to know how little I had. Then one night she let me take her home and it was wonderful. She and her father lived above his store at 340 College, not far from Spadina, but certainly not in the rich part. It turned out that she thought the same about me as I did about her; that maybe she wasn't in my bracket as far as money and family were concerned. I've never been so relieved in my life as I was, climbing those stairs to their little place above the store. There was never anyone else in my life from that time on.

I was getting sick of school by then. My marks were good enough that I was going to pass Grade Twelve without writing the final exams, so I wanted to quit as soon as the hockey season was over. Dad wanted me to go on to university, but there was a lot of publicity then about the future of the clay belt in northern

Ontario, with lots of land open for homesteading, and I was determined to be one of the pioneers and make my fortune. We battled and I was only seventeen but I refused to listen to him. Finally he said, "All right, go!"

I have an old notebook headed: March 15, 1912, account of Conn Smythe, Lot 13, Concession 4, Clute Township, northern Ontario. It records that I paid homesteading dues of fifty cents an acre for one hundred and fifty acres, spent $63.78 to clear two acres, $23.35 for logs to build my house, $22.50 for lumber, $27.80 for furniture, $5.00 to rent a team of horses, and other costs for nails, roofing, hinges, windows, and so on, for a total of $288.00. That spring and summer I worked like a dog. When we were carrying logs I always seemed to have the heavy end. I'd be so tired every night I could hardly eat. But by mid-summer my house was finished and I decided to go back to the city for a few days and see Irene. We were at the old Woodbine track out Queen Street East when I heard that big fires had swept through my area. Then a telegram came. The fire had burned all I'd done, the house, furniture, and everything.

I told dad I wasn't going back. He said, "Oh, there's a quitter in the family!" I said, "Oh, no, there isn't. I'll give it to you. If you think it's so goldarn good, go on up there yourself."

He didn't, but I guess there was more to my decision than just the fire. I hadn't known how much I would miss the city, Irene, the shows, the company, the games, and other sights to be seen. I couldn't see myself grubbing for a living in the bush, ever again. To do better, I enrolled in civil engineering at the School of Practical Science, which the University of Toronto's engineering faculty was called then. I was short of money for fees because I was on the outs with my father, wasn't working, and still had $288 tied up in the homestead. But I figured somehow I'd get the fees.

Ever since Upper Canada College I'd been doing a bit of betting on the races. At Upper Canada I'd roomed with Hendrie Hay, a nephew of the Hendrie family that owned horses, and had won a few on his tips. In the late summer of 1912 when the races were at Hillcrest, a gang of us who'd been at Jarvis and were going on to university, we hoped, went out there a lot, getting in using my father's passes. It was great to watch racing on those half-mile tracks – excitement and bookmaking and always tips going around. Not a race that there wouldn't be three or four fellows who would come up and give you the inside information on which horse was going to be held back, or whatever. Anyway, I got to believing that all the races were fixed, and when the bunch of us started comparing notes about what desperate shape we were in for our university fees we thought, well, fixing a horse race would be the simplest way to get even.

One friend, Goldie Levy, knew a lot of jockeys. He had an idea of how it could be done. "We'll pick a race where only about four horses have any chance," he said. "Then we give each of the jockeys on the top three horses a $50 ticket on the fourth one. That's all we have to do – you don't ask them to pull their horses, or anything – just give them the tickets."

I thought, well, this is high finance right off the bat. The rest of us were Wreck Aggett, Dago Morton, Squib Walker, Cecil Richardson, and Stoney, the undertaker. Picking the race was important. It took us days but finally we found a good filly named Miss Menard running against three good colts and some bad ones and knew she would be a good price. We put up the funds. But then just before the race Goldie was looking very thoughtful and finally said, "You know, you can make absolutely sure of this if you send a $50 ticket down to the starter."

So we put another $50 on Miss Menard and Goldie went down with it to the starter but just as we were about to put up our own bets on Miss Menard, Goldie came tearing back and said, "Geez! It's all off! I'm going to be ruled off the turf! The starter can't be fixed!" And he added "Not only did he refuse to take the ticket, he said he's going to leave our horse at the post!"

We had the money we were going to bet on Miss Menard, so we went around and bet on the favourite. Sure enough, up goes the barrier and I remember Cec Richardson, aptly describing the start.

"My God," he said, "there's Miss Menard – twat to the wire." The starter had done exactly as he said he would, let the race go with her facing backward. There she was, coming around last all the way. The three jocks we'd given the tickets to, they were running one, two, three, and when they came into the stretch they all just went wide, right to the outside fence, taking everybody in the field with them except Miss Menard, who was too far behind to go with the crowd. She came around on the inside and won the race and we didn't have a quarter on her. Not one five cent piece. But then Goldie remembered the $50 ticket on Miss Menard that the starter wouldn't take. So we just broke even. That was the only time that I had anything to do with a fixed race. It sure taught me a lesson. I have heard many times since about races being fixed but at no time have seen any evidence of it being done. There are so many imponderables, or even improbables. Like with Miss Menard. If she hadn't been held at the post she probably would have been swept wide with all the rest and something else would have won.

All of which made me a sadder but wiser man when dad came up with my university fees somehow and a lovely part of my life began. I got into inter-faculty football and when winter came I made the Varsity Intercollegiate Junior hockey team. By exam time in the spring I had pretty well planned what I was going to do next.

I still had the homestead, but now with a chance to sell. A carpenter friend of dad's who had a shop on Church Street, another theosophist, had a son at loose ends who let his father talk him into at least going up to see my place. My diary, which I faithfully kept for seven or eight months in 1913, shows that on April 23, a Wednesday, I wrote my last exam, Dynamics ("poorest of my exams, but expect to pass on whole"), went to the Princess Theatre to see "Quaker Girl," ate with dad at a cafeteria, and then, "Wreck came down with auto," and took me to the station, where I caught a train for Cochrane at 5:30 p.m. Two days later I went by railroad speeder to my lot ("got soaked"), where the carpenter's son offered me $250 for it. I accepted, walked back to Cochrane, and caught a train to Toronto. I got there on Sunday, April 27. "Met Irene. Walked home with her. Stay for tea." And on the next day, Monday, April 28: "Went down to city hall. Got job in Mr. Overend's surveying party as chainer at $9 per week . . . went out to Waverly Road in morning and Logan in afternoon. Bed, 10."

So there I was in April, 1913, only 18 but with $250 in my pocket, a $9-a-week job, and the world looking good. Later that summer another fire went through the Cochrane area. The carpenter's son had rebuilt my cabin. He tried to escape the flames by getting into a little stream. He boiled to death there. When I heard of it, I knew that could have been me in the boiling stream if I hadn't been lucky. Instead, all that summer I worked for the city, watched baseball, shows, vaudeville, and chased around with Wreck in the Aggett's Cadillac. When summer was over Wreck and I took a train north for a holiday, fishing and shooting partridges, getting back in time for classes to start in September.

Irene used to come to all the games, football and hockey, and that winter was a good one. I was named captain of the Varsity Juniors and we played in the Ontario Hockey Association Junior series as well as Intercollegiate. In March of 1914 we beat Frank Selke's Berlin team in the Ontario semi-final before meeting Orillia in the two-game, total goals final. Orillia had some great players, but we beat them 4-3 in the first game, in Toronto. It must have been a good night for hanging around the net because if you look up the record you'll find that the worst player on the team, Conn Smythe, scored all four Varsity goals. We went to Orillia for the other game of the total-goals home and home series, sure that we'd put on a big show and win it all. We never saw the puck all night. They murdered us 10-3. I got one goal, which gave me thirty-three for the season, in fifteen games. I was beginning to make my first mark, in hockey.

That summer I worked as a timekeeper for the C.N.R., helping build the Brock Avenue subway. When the war started later in the summer and I got back to school, three or four of us from second year engineering went down Bay Street to enlist. The recruiting office for the Princess Patricia's Canadian Light Infantry was in the downstairs of the old *Mail* newspaper building. There were three big old sergeants in there with huge mustaches and campaign ribbons from right back to the South African War. They looked me over. I was nineteen and looked about fifteen.

"What do you want in here?" one asked, finally.

I said I wanted to enlist.

"No children allowed in this battalion," he said. "Go home and see if you can grow some hair on your face."

That cooled me out some, but at the time Canada lacked training facilities for the huge numbers of men trying to enlist. Many of the ones accepted then had previous service with British units or the Canadian Militia and I hadn't even been in school cadets. Still, I had a feeling my time would come. Back at university I tried for the rugby football team. It was a great one that year. In Raymond Massey's book about his own boyhood (he was a year younger than I), he calls that Varsity team of 1914 the best the university ever had. Varsity only lost one game that year, an exhibition against the Carlyle Indians from the United States, with the great Jim Thorpe. Massey named me among the stars of that team. I wasn't. A lot of people promote me from time to time, and it's nice, but I always prefer to be promoted when it's the truth. At Varsity that year I was never better than third-string.

But after the football season, we got our junior hockey team together again and in March of 1915 made it to the Ontario finals again – this time against Selke's Berlin Union Jacks. Berlin later was re-named Kitchener, but at the time, the largely German-born players took an awful ride from fans elsewhere. The team name, Union Jacks, was an attempt to overcome some of that. Anyway, the home crowds in Berlin weren't any too respectful of us, either. In that first game of the home and home, I came out of it with my fair hair stained brown from tobacco juice that people would spit at me every time I got near the boards.

It was quite a game in other ways. The goal umpire stood right behind the net in those days. Selke always said that any goal umpire who wasn't worth two goals to his home team (one for the home team, and one disallowed for the opposition), should be fired. People he had hired were robbing us so openly that twice in the first period Berlin goal umps were ordered out of the game by the referee.

There was another little matter. Wreck and I had bet every cent we had on Varsity to win. The money was being held by a man who said that if we won, he'd meet us later at the Walper Hotel with the cash. Without much time left, we were down 7-5. I scored two goals in the last few minutes to make it 7-7 and protect our investment, but couldn't get the winner. Then we went down to the Walper to get our money back. The man wouldn't give it to us. He insisted we had bet we would win. There was quite a crowd around listening, among them Wreck's father, John Aggett. He was about five feet six or so and was death on gambling, but this was different. He couldn't push his way into the middle of the argument so he jumped up on a chair. He had a good voice. "If this boy's money and my boy's money aren't paid back right away," he roared, "the crown attorney will be here in ten minutes." Out came the money.

With the tie, it all came down to the second game of the series, two nights later in Toronto. On that night of Thursday, March 11,

1915, four thousand, seven hundred people came by car and trolley and on foot to the Mutual Street Arena. The game was as close as the first one, but with one big difference.

In those days of seven-man hockey, substitutions were not allowed. If someone got hurt, or had to retire for any reason, the other team had to drop a man, too. The score was 3-3 late in the second period when one of their men, Irvin Erb, broke a skate and had to go off. Our coach came to me, as captain, and said, "Who do we take off?"

"Me," I said.

He protested, "The captain can't come off."

I'd taken a big body check about then. I was groggy. I insisted, so I came off.

We didn't do so well against them, each playing six men. We each got another goal before the end of the period, making it 4-4. It was still tied 4-4 in the third when something happened that Selke later called the biggest boner of his life. His brother-in-law, a Canadian featherweight boxing champion named Bert Ayerst, came to him and said to be sure not to put Erb back on the ice. "Without Smythe out there, Varsity isn't the same team," he said. (I'm quoting Selke, not me).

Anyway, Selke always was a suspicious fellow and that was his downfall. Sometimes in those days if the home team got ahead the timer made the clock go faster. We weren't ahead, but Selke was standing right behind the timer instead of being at his own bench. Someone at the bench produced another pair of skates for Erb. Without Selke there to tell Erb to stay where he was, Erb put on the borrowed skates and jumped over the boards. That meant I could jump on, as well. Back at seven-man hockey, we scored five goals. I got two of them, to go with one I'd scored in the second period. The 9-4 score gave us the Ontario Junior championship and although it had never been done before for a Junior team, we were given Varsity letters as a reward. I still have mine, someplace.

By then, in mid-March of 1915, the university looked like an Army camp, with tents on the campus, marching bands, recruiting speeches almost every day. I celebrated with Irene after the final game, and told her that the whole team was going to enlist, including me. We'd been talking about it for weeks, and had decided that win or lose in the hockey final, we were going to get in uniform right away.

The following Monday nine of us from the hockey team went down to join up in two artillery outfits that were recruiting. By the end of the day I was Gunner C. Smythe, 25th Battery, Canadian Field Artillery, and one of the papers ran our pictures – the ones of Wreck and me looking even younger than we were, because they used shots taken at Jarvis with the big J showing. Two others in that bunch were George (Squib) Walker, a pal of mine who later became chief scout for the Leafs, and Ed Morton, whom we called Dago because he was short and dark. Nicknames of that sort weren't considered the racist no-nos they are now.

I've heard often how this fellow couldn't get in, or that one was turned down, but in both wars I found that if anybody wanted to get in, he got in. George Walker – we called him Squib because of his size – couldn't see ten feet without his glasses. That day luckily Squib didn't have to do the eye test first. After lunch, we had figured out how he'd pass it. The eye test room was long and narrow and the person being tested had his back to a door with a hole in it. We posted somebody to watch through the hole. When the officer would point to a letter on the chart, our guy would whisper it to Squib, who had very good ears. Maybe the inspector knew it was going on, but maybe he didn't. All he said to Squib was, "Gee, you've got good eyesight."

A funny thing happened to Squib, though, after we moved up near Ottawa to take our training. He was fine with his glasses, which he wore all the time. Each morning on parade our section, the ammunition column, used to form up in front, the other sections behind. One morning an inspection was called and a sergeant told Squib he'd better get rid of his glasses. He went to stash them somewhere. When he got back we had been formed up in a different order. Squib marched up to where he thought we should be, then went along this wrong line peering short-sightedly at people, trying to see if there was anybody he knew.

Right then the officer doing the inspection came in. I've always thought a great deal of that man, whoever he was. He must have sensed something was going on because he turned and left again and waited until Squib found the rest of us in the rear rank and fell in. Then the officer marched up and down the ranks with a special look at Squib, and told us we had a fine outfit. They actually washed Squib out of the first couple of drafts of gunners that went overseas, but he finally made it to France with an anti- aircraft unit later in the war. Someone told me where he was and I went over one afternoon with some food that had come in parcels from home. I was standing there by the guns talking to him when a plane came over. He yelled, "Fire!" They started shooting. I looked up and yelled, "My God, Squib! That's one of ours!"

He said, "Don't worry, Connie. We never hit anything. But if one comes over and we don't fire at it, I'd lose my job."

When we were in Ottawa, five or six weeks after we joined, there was a little story in the *Toronto Telegram* that I kept. It said that "the University men who joined the 25th and 26th Batteries now mobilized at Ottawa and Kingston, are keeping up their sporting interest. Several teams have been organized in both cities to play baseball and other games. In a match at Ottawa yesterday (the clipping is dated April 28, 1915) Lal Saunders pitched for the 25th Battery and Connie Smythe played short. The Artillery team defeated Ottawa College 9-7 . . ." A whole war later when I had my own battery I used to do the same thing – keep the fellows busy playing games while they were training, waiting to go into action.

In Ottawa I ran our unit's canteen and made a little money. Squib was always lucky at dice, crown and anchor, whatever was going, so I'd sometimes finance him. When we moved from Ottawa to Valcartier for advanced training that summer, some of the old vets there had a crown and anchor game going. One night Squib was cleaning them out. But after one last roll of the dice, three sixes that would have won us $192, the proprietors just flung the crown and anchor board – actually, it was a sheet of oilcloth – in the air and ran. They got away because when they threw the oilcloth in the air our money went with it, and we were scrambling around trying to get that back. We did catch them later but had to settle for about sixty cents on the dollar.

My Army career wasn't exactly in high gear, either, at Ottawa or Valcartier. When they lined us up by size, Squib was always at the small end, with either me or Dago Morton next to him. When they were looking for non-commissioned officer material they'd start with the six foot threes at the other end. We little guys were awfully belligerent about it, but still, none of us got stripes.

Then something happened that I thought was a disaster at the time, but turned out lucky. Horses hauled the guns and ammunition in those days, of course. We were in the last stages of our Canadian training, almost ready to go overseas, when a horse stepped on my foot and I wound up in hospital. While I was there, my unit went overseas along with my closest friends. Soon they were in England and I was not. I was very despondent, bored, upset, and angry. I felt I could have gone overseas and let my foot heal there. I proved my mobility, at least to myself, by skipping out of the hospital one morning and going to Montreal for a horse race. When I got back late at night the orderly said, "Where have you been?"

"Never mind," I said. "I'm back."

Apart from that one break, I had time on my hands to write letters. Some were to Irene, and she wrote to me. Another was to dad. I told him about other Varsity people being promoted, some even getting commissions, while I couldn't even make lance-corporal. I guess he thought about who he knew with influence, and hit on our old friends from North Street, the Arnoldis.

In his quiet way, he told Bay Arnoldi that if anyone on that Varsity hockey team deserved to be commissioned, how could the team captain be overlooked? It made sense. Bay Arnoldi's uncle was a colonel, I think in Ottawa. He got things moving. In mid-July, when I'd been four months Gunner Smythe, fit to get back into training with another unit, I was called into the orderly room and paraded in front of an officer.

"There's something here for you I think you'll like," he said, handing me an official-looking letter.

He was right. I did like it. The letter, dated July 17, 1915, was an order for me to report as a provisional lieutenant to the Royal School of Artillery (Field and Horse) at Kingston, for a course starting August 2. All I had to do was pass. That I did on September 11, which a few days later knocked the word "provisional" off my rank and left me just plain Lieutenant Smythe in the 2nd (Ottawa) Battery, 8th Brigade. Six months or so later I was given the big piece of parchment signed at the bottom by Sam Hughes, Minister of Militia and Defence, and at the top by the Governor General, the Duke of Connaught, stating that George V was hereby sending to "our trusty and well-beloved Conn Smythe, gentleman, greeting," and commissioning me as a lieutenant in the active militia. King George V had called me a gentleman. It all came from living on North Street and knowing the Arnoldis. Nobody can tell me that luck isn't important in the world.

But there was more to Kingston. Taking the course at the same time was Gordon Southam, one of the finest all-around athletes in the country. His family owned the newspaper chain that still bears the Southam name, but I looked up to him for other reasons. He was a North American champion at court tennis, had played football on a University of Toronto team that won the Grey Cup a few years earlier, was a good hockey player, had led a Canadian cricket team to England, and was a born leader. He was big and strong and was doing what some well-off men did in World War One – organizing his own unit to take overseas. What he wanted was a Sportsmen's Battery. He already had recruited some, both officers and men, from the Orillia Junior team that had beaten Varsity in 1914. One of his ideas was to get a hockey team together and play in an O.H.A. Senior league while we were training. He knew that we'd be at Niagara-on-the-Lake under canvas for a couple of months, and then move to winter quarters at Exhibition Park in Toronto, where there would be a league to play in.

"Smythe," he said to me one day, "would you be interested in joining my Battery?"

Would I? I said, "I'd give my life's blood to be with you." I knew this was going to be a hell of a hockey team and it would be a good way to put in the time before we went overseas. He had his Battery's officer complement (three besides himself) filled, but had me added as a supernumerary.

Of course, with a lot of these prospects riding on how well I did on my course, I worked hard. Yet one of my fondest memories of Kingston is about a man who didn't. His name was Counsell. I noticed him first one day when the Artillery School introduced us to one of its little toughening-up exercises, a fifteen-mile bareback ride. Men who did it sometimes came back with the seats of their pants soaked with blood. Counsell did it that first day, but the next time when we were getting our horses I saw Counsell hiding in some straw in a stall. He shook his head at me, so I didn't say anything. When we went out, one of the sergeants, probably with an ass as tough as old leather, was wearing Counsell's jacket and taking the ride in his place. When we came back hours later and

Counsell had his own jacket back on and was mingling with the rest of us, someone asked seriously, "Did you enjoy the ride, sir?"

"Wonderful day!" Counsell laughed. "Just wonderful!"

Probably that was one reason why he failed the course. The night when the rest of us were celebrating having passed, he was having a fair amount to drink. One of the other officers was a huge man named McLaglen, a brother of Victor McLaglen who later won an Oscar for a movie called "The Informer." McLaglen was well over six feet, huge, and because he was so big he got away with a lot. One of his little games was to let go a punch, a jab, straight at somebody. He had the uncanny ability to stop the punch so that it never landed, but always knocked the ash off the other man's cigarette. This annoyed people a lot, but he was so big nobody ever did anything about it.

This night McLaglen was there having a drink or two. Counsell was looking at him, obviously plotting something. Finally Counsell got up and said that although he hadn't passed the course, he had learned something in his six weeks here.

"McLaglen," he said. "You stand up there." He pointed to a place along a wall. The big guy stood there grinning. He was smoking a cigar which had a long ash on it. Everybody thought Counsell was going to do the McLaglen trick of knocking off the ash. Instead, he wound up and hit McLaglen with every ounce he had. The cigar went down McLaglen's throat and down he went, too. With one punch, Counsell had become heavyweight champion of the Canadian Army.

We trained our few weeks at Niagara and then route-marched to Toronto with our horses, artillery, wagons, and everything else. It was late in 1915, early winter, time to get our hockey team operating. By then I had done well enough that I'd been taken on full Battery strength, in command of the left section – the gun crews who manned four of our eight eighteen-pounders. They'd been champions with the Hamilton Alerts in football and Orillia in hockey and I was a green twenty-year-old. Those tough nuts in the left section didn't let me get away with much. We had battles that later ended in friendships for life, for those who lived.

In Toronto I was given the job of organizing the hockey team and acting as manager. That meant I had to attend meetings with a lot of experienced hockey men who proceeded, they thought, to

skin me because of my inexperience. There were four Toronto
teams in our O.H.A. Senior group – our 40th Battery, Argos,
Riversides, who had future NHL star Reg Noble as rover, and the
Toronto Rowing and Athletic Association (T.R. & A.A.). All our
games would be played in the Mutual Street Arena, but in each
game one team was named home team, getting the larger percentage of the gate. The other managers knew that crowds generally
were smaller at the beginning of the season before fan interest built
up, and from a money standpoint it was better to be designated the
home team later in the season. I didn't know anything about that,
and they got me to agree to be home team for most of our early
games. The old hockey men, I was told later, laughed at how
they'd put one over on the kid, but the joke was on them.

Twenty-five hundred people for our first game wasn't a bad
crowd; but we were slaughtered 6-1 by Reg Noble and the Riversides. I played centre and the newspapers reported that "Smythe's
weakness on back-checking" had been one factor in the defeat,
with kinder words for Gunner Jack Pethick from Regina who
played defence that day but could play anywhere, and Driver
Lovering Jupp at right wing. That was the last game I played,
deciding to concentrate on getting players out there who were better than I was. We switched goalers for our second game, an
exhibition in Preston, putting in Driver Skid James from Peterborough. We won that one 8-3, and in our second league game
beat T.R. & A.A. 4-3. But on January 15, in our third game, we
started what turned out to be a famous (at the time) rivalry with
the Argos. They beat us 4-3 in overtime, before four thousand
people – and the old-time managers who'd euchred me into the
early home games were beginning to see that they'd misjudged.
Patriotic sentiment in Toronto, plus our good players, were starting to make us crowd favourites. Four days later we beat Riversides and Reg Noble 5-4, before a bigger crowd. Then on Saturday
afternoon we played Argos again. There was a lot of betting on
games then, but the papers later reported there hadn't been much
on this game. Nobody wanted to bet on us against the Argos at
first. Some money did show up after we'd taken a two-goal lead.
We took them to two overtime periods before they beat us again.
Pethick moved up to rover for that game and scored twice.
Everybody in town was talking about those two great overtime

games between the 40th and the Argos and looking forward to the following Wednesday night when we'd play them again.

Then, at the first of the week, Major Southam got orders that we were about to be shipped overseas. It was secret, but he thought I should know this next one against Argos probably would be our last hockey game in Canada. As a minor piece of retribution, this meant that the guys who had conned me in the scheduling weren't going to get the home-team break in gate money from us at all. Anyway, Southam and I were talking in the lobby of the arena before the game when a man named Brenner came along. He was in the steel business, making a pile selling to ammunition factories. I'd seen him around. He was a big bettor.

"Want to bet on your team, major?" he asked Southam.

Southam said he did. I piped up, "I'll bet you, too. I've got a hundred dollars that says we'll win."

"Ah," he said. "I don't want peanuts." He turned back to Southam, who suddenly had a glint in his eye. He didn't like the peanuts crack. He also knew that for various reasons I still had our gate receipts from the last three games in my pocket. He murmured to me, "How much you got in those gate receipts, Connie?" I told him about $2,800. Southam turned back to Brenner.

"How much can you handle?" he asked.

"Anything you've got, major."

Southam turned to me and said, "Give me the twenty-eight hundred, Connie." That kind of blanched Brenner but he put it up. We handed the $5,600 to somebody to hold. In the dressing room I stood up in front of the team: Lieutenant Jack Gooch, Jupp, Pethick, James, Driver Quinn Butterfield, Sergeant Squaw Mac-Nab, and Sergeant Mawk McKenzie and told them that every nickel this hockey team had in the world was riding on this game. That was all they needed. Quinn Butterfield from Orillia scored two goals in the first four minutes. Jack Pethick got another. Then Squaw MacNab. We led 4-0 after the first nine minutes. Butterfield got another before the end of the period, when we led 5-1. Gooch and MacNab scored in the second to only one of theirs. And in the third Butterfield got his final score, giving him four on the night in our 8-3 win. We picked up our $5,600 after the game. Not only that, but the crowd was 6,378, a record, and our lion's share was $1,106, giving us nearly $7,000 in all. The only thing that marred that game was that there was a big fight in the crowd near the end of it and one of our 40th Battery men was badly hurt. People who say that crowds in hockey have only got bad in recent years don't know what they're talking about.

We celebrated so thoroughly that night that a few days later when the league hurriedly re-scheduled a game for us against the Riversides, hating to see such a good meal-ticket leave, we weren't even in it. The papers hadn't exactly spelled it out, but every fan knew what it meant when the *Globe* reported: "Local hockey fans will learn with regret of the inability of the 40th Battery Senior team to finish their schedule. The Battery is leaving Toronto in the near future." We were beaten 4-0 but at the end of the game the whole crowd stood up and gave us three resounding farewell cheers. And when we got to England a few weeks later every man going on leave was given some of our winnings to spend. The rest went to buy sumptuous Christmas dinners for the whole Battery, nearly two hundred men, every Christmas until the end of the war.

We had exactly four days in Toronto after that final game. I spent much of it with Irene. We talked a lot about marriage. I asked her, and we became engaged. But we decided against the kind of marriage that was happening very often in those days – one that only lasted a few days or weeks before the man went off to the war, and maybe didn't come back.

My father had asked me for dinner on the Sunday night, a day after our last game. I'd never introduced him to Irene so I went alone to his apartment on Bleecker Street. He had married again, but Janie, his wife, left us alone after dinner. She and I didn't get along. I remember one thing about that night that I thought was funny. Dad said he hoped that maybe sometime I'd be lucky enough to be fighting next to a certain division that was mostly made up of Irish Catholics.

I protested, "But all my life you've told me, 'beware of the Catholics. Don't have anything to do with them, you know. Don't trust them.' "

"Yes," he said, "but they can fight like hell."

In a sense, that dinner at dad and Janie's place was my twenty-first birthday party, two days in advance. Before we left by train on February 2, the day after my birthday, I received a letter from my father that I have kept ever since. Maybe it tells more about us from his standpoint, as father and son, than I've been able to do justice to.

The World Office Toronto
Tuesday 1st February 1916

My dear boy, I suppose you find it hard to think of yourself twenty-one years ago, but the dear little chap who used to love me so much and put his arms round my neck, and climb up on my knee, and play ball and do all the other little things which you won't think anything of till you have children of your own, are all in my mind. Well, dearie, you are a man now, and your own master, as I have always tried to have you be. I may not have done as well by you as I had hoped, but you are all I could wish in the main things, clean, truthful, honest, brave and generous. I think you will have enough regard for the old days to keep these things in your heart all your life.

I do not know anything about the girl you were talking about Sunday night, but try and be all, in all things, that you can think she would wish you to be. If she is worth anything she will wish the best and highest for you.

You know I do not set much store by wordly possessions. Those who work hardest do not always get the greatest rewards. But no reward worth having or that will afford real satisfaction is to be had without hard work. I am looking forward to a life of great success for you, but success is only to be had on the old hard terms. You are not a shirker and I feel sure you will face the conditions and win the success.

You are going on a high quest now, not for yourself only, but for all the world. I have never bothered you much with religion but I want you to feel that you are all the time in the care of the Master, and that He will be with you in times of difficulty or danger. Even though you stand in the shadow of death you need fear no evil for He will be with you if your heart is turned to Him. I was going to ask you to read the Bhagavad Gita [the famous eighteen chapters of the Hindu Mahabharata, where in the divine incarnation Krishna expounds] and the New Testament sometimes, but I won't ask anything of you. You are a free man and should listen to your own heart as I have done. The Master is there at all times.

There are many friends who will be watching you and caring for you. Our Theosophical people are more interested in you than you perhaps imagine. You won't forget our society for which I have worked so long and which represents so much that is worthwhile. You may be able to comfort many a poor fellow with things you have heard from us.

I wish you could write me every week at least. I will do the same for you. If it is only a card, try not to miss, for we shall be very anxious about you. Try and remember your old friends also in England. They may not be so showy but they are very true and loyal. Your aunt thinks a great deal of you on your mother's account. Try and make her love you for your own sake. You can be very loveable and charming when you please.

The war has interfered with many plans I had for you. You are going to England but not as I had expected. I do not know what another year may bring, but we are all in the hands of the Eternal. I hope you won't think this a sermon or a screed. It is just a loving word from your old Daddy to wish you all the best things in the world and to kiss you goodbye as you go away and leave all the old times behind forever. Don't forget, no one will ever love you better than I do. It makes me all the sorrier that I have such a poor way of showing it.

God bless you dear, now and always. Janie sends her love with mine and she won't forget you.

Love, my dear boy. Your loving Daddy.

Chapter Three

Somebody asked me once whether soldiers talked much about fear of being wounded or killed. I never heard that during World War One. It was always fear that we wouldn't get there. I'll give an example. The man who was hurt in that big hockey game against the Argos was in terrible pain but we all covered for him. He pleaded with us that he didn't want to miss going overseas. It took three men to help him onto the train and later on shipboard, but he died at sea. When I saw the body wrapped in the Union Jack slip into the ocean after the burial service I thought what a terrible tragic way that was to end a life.

But none of us really knew what was ahead. Certainly on the night after my twenty-first birthday when we boarded trains with a lot of other units on a siding in the Exhibition Grounds, heading for Saint John, New Brunswick, and a troopship to England, I didn't know that before my next birthday I'd be crouching in a shellhole in France so afraid that I kept fumbling and dropping ammunition I was trying to load into rifles that I'd picked up from the bodies of soldiers in nearby shellholes.

The thing I feared most was being yellow. I couldn't have stood that. The two qualities I admire most are guts and loyalty. Although to me loyalty is the more important, I've had a lot of both from people I have fought alongside, and worked with, in peace and war. I certainly don't want another war to happen, but I served through two big ones and I'll feel to my dying day that I owe more to the Army than I lost in the years I gave. There were men alongside who would give their lives for me, as I would for them. There was a cause worth fighting for. Figuring out what that cause was, we learned to love our homeland and everything it stood for, or should stand for, and to appreciate how much the people we left behind meant to us.

In my case, there was one other factor. All my life my father had been drumming into me the mystical eastern beliefs of Theosophy. I can give one element of it to you in the official, more or less, version – that a Silent Watcher holds in his hand a mighty cable of golden strands, each strand stretching invisibly to a living being. Dad didn't especially approve of my slangy references to this being as The Man Upstairs, but after missing that second and fatal northern Ontario forest fire, taking the first one as being a warning, I began to notice I was chronically lucky. Afterward, when I was lucky I would tell people, "I got a nudge from The Man Upstairs." Maybe some thought I was kidding, but five times in the next few years I lived, unscathed, when death or maiming was a better than 50-50 chance. Each time it was luck, not guts or planning or intelligence on my part. I simply believe in the existence of The Man Upstairs. Now you know.

We landed at Plymouth, England, on February 14, 1916, and from mid-morning until early darkness, headed east by train until we stepped down at Liphook and marched in a steady drizzle through the dark to the damp huts of our first camp, Bramshott. Obviously the Army wasn't quite ready for us, because a few days later we all got six-day leaves. I took a train to Manchester for a warm welcome from the aunt and uncle I'd met with dad during my 1908 trip, and found a good friend in my cousin Gwen, more my own age. Others who went mainly to London and lived it up came back with lurid tales. I just listened. I was a virgin then, engaged to another one back home, and although I'd already had a couple of close calls I intended us to stay that way until we were married.

Early in March we were issued a few horses, but not nearly enough, so our daily route-marches through the country lanes were on foot, more for the fresh air and exercise than anything else. It was mid-April before we begged, borrowed, or stole enough horses and mules to get on with real training at Witley, an artillery camp about eight miles from Bramshott. There we resumed the same kind of training we'd done in Canada, everything except firing live ammunition.

We were a very close-knit outfit, only five officers and one hundred and forty-four men including non-coms, gunners, signallers, drivers, a veterinarian, and a priest. By then we all knew one another. Captain Bill Wilson from Hamilton was second in command under Major Southam. Of the three lieutenants, Fred Scott was recreation officer, Art Boyd had the right section, and I had the left section. My section had given me a hard time at first, green as I was. But soon we got along fine. We were all competitors. They loved one night exercise, a competition to see how fast gun crews could get into action. Everybody was supposed to be in bed, in pajamas, when the alarm – the "Stand to!" – sounded. Each section was timed from then until it reported all guns manned and ready to fire. The rule stated only that the men had to be in bed, in pajamas. It didn't specify what could be worn under the pajamas. I got a supply of extra big ones. My section wore them over their full uniforms. We won that event by a mile.

One other competition that spring didn't go so well, for me. It was a gymkana, a field day. In one part of it officers raced together in pairs, on horseback, each pair holding one baton between them. My horse was a little thoroughbred I'd picked out personally, very fast; never travelled at anything short of a full gallop. The rest called me the galloper. The other horse, my partner's, wasn't fast enough. I was hanging on to my baton for dear life, practically towing the other rider along, and my saddle got pulled over to one side. When we came to a jump that looked about eight feet high to me I leaned forward in preparation for the horse taking the jump. But he apparently felt his job was to charge right through the middle of the hedge, which he tried. I went over his head and down I came with the horse on top of me. When I staggered to my feet my pants fell down. I couldn't do anything about it because I was trying to hang on to the horse. When people ran up I yelled, "Pull up my pants, for God's sake, in front of all these people!" Then I collapsed.

I broke three ribs in that fall. Funny, both times I went to France to fight, in 1916 and 1944, I had broken ribs. That first time they took me to a hospital in Liphook. I didn't have any pajamas, but a cousin of one of our lieutenants, Fred Scott, was there, and loaned me some. Years later I ran into Scottie's cousin outside of Simpson's store in Toronto and right away he needled me: "Here's a fellow that's supposed to keep his word all the time, and he's a thief!"

"What are you talking about?" I demanded.

"Those pajamas you borrowed! You were supposed to send them back!"

I had, but he'd never received them. I took him into Simpson's and bought him the most expensive pajamas I could find. I didn't want anybody to be able to say I owed him a pair of pajamas ever since the spring of 1916.

Late in May we started out for our first shoot, the whole 8th Brigade fully equipped for active service, making a four-day march to Larkhill Camp on Salisbury Plains. It meant being in the saddle for long stretches, including one that started at midnight and ended in mid-morning. We had a week at Larkhill of live shells and lots of action, then moved back to Witley for what we suspected might be our last few days in England. The King was to inspect us on Dominion Day, July 1, and the rumours were that we were for France soon after.

There was one result of that Royal inspection that might not have been recorded before. All through our training in Canada and England up until then, there'd been one main fear in the Battery: not that we'd get killed, wounded, or taken prisoner, but that we'd get scalp mange, and go bald. The horses had to go through disinfecting pits on a routine basis. All the rest of us used to shave our heads and rub Glover's Mange Cure into our scalps. It smelled awful. Our tents and huts had stunk of mange cure all spring, until that lovely Dominion Day when King George came down to inspect the whole camp.

It was a great sight. Major Southam had outfitted our Battery with nickel-plated stirrups and bits that shone in the sun brighter than those of the other units, who had to spend hours polishing theirs. The horses, decked out with white neckpieces, pulled hundreds of guns by, our eighteen-pounders among them. Then we formed up the square facing the King and somebody called for three cheers.

As the shouts went up, he took off his uniform cap in acknowledgement and we could see that he hardly had a hair on his head! We had a vote in our quarters that night and decided that here was a guy, head of an Empire of six or seven hundred million people, and if he couldn't grow hair we might as well take our chances, too, and not stink out our huts and tents any more. Nobody sold any Glover's Mange Cure to us again.

There was big news from the front late that day, as well. The huge Allied attack along the Somme had begun. We didn't know at the time that the Allies suffered 60,000 casualties that day, wave after wave charging the German lines and getting mowed down. But preparations for our move were stepped up – dipping horses against the mange, preparing wills, storing surplus kit. At dusk on July 12 we moved out, mounted and fully equipped. We were loaded into trains for Southampton, then into boats which sailed on the night of July 13. The next morning we disembarked at Le Havre and made a brave show riding off the docks with all our nickel bits and irons shining, to bed down for the night.

The only trouble was that when we rolled out for inspection in the morning we didn't have a bit or stirrup left. We'd done a fair bit of swapping bad horses for good ones in England, not always with the knowledge of the copyright owners, so we should have been more careful in Le Havre. Other units had admired our nickel-plated gear so much that they had cleaned us out during the night.

The major called us together. "Now, we've just been taught a lesson," he said. "It's part of learning the business. But if we don't have all that gear back here by tonight, there's going to be some casualties in these ranks before we ever get into action."

By the next morning we had all the bits and irons we needed, and a few more, plus a lot of new leather saddles and about twelve extra horses. That was our reception in France, and how we dealt with it.

Right away we were moved by train (forty hommes or eight chevaux per boxcar) into the Ypres salient in Belgium. It was already a famous battlefield. The British had suffered heavy casualties there in the first months of the war, but held on desperately, nobody knowing that the line established then was to stay practically unchanged through the whole war. It was the only place in Belgium the Germans didn't overrun. The British decision to hold Ypres, and to hell with the cost, was because a few miles south was Saint Omer, crossroads to the Channel ports of Dunkirk, Calais, and Boulogne. These were vital supply routes for British, Canadian, and other Dominion troops, who for years held that north part of the front. The Canadian First Division had been sent in to take over one frontage of about four thousand yards in April, 1915 – and ordered not to yield. The trenches before Ypres then were terrible; only two or three feet deep, more like a series of unconnected ditches than a continuous trench system. Parapets were only another two feet high and too flimsy in places to stop a sniper's bullet; while one Canadian Army report said, "the ground where the men stand in firing position (is) . . . paved with rotting bodies and human excreta." Those 1915 Canadians had only a few days to try to improve trench conditions before the Germans launched their first gas attack of the war, causing two divisions of French Algerians on the left flank to break and run, leaving the Canadians dangerously open to attack from that side. Yet the Canadians held. In the first twelve hours or so one Canadian battalion was reduced from eight hundred men to one hundred and ninety-three. In the two weeks of gas, artillery, and infantry attacks that followed, six thousand Canadians were killed, wounded, or missing, and the Ypres salient thrusting out into enemy territory was shortened a little, but still held.

More than a year later we were following a proud Canadian tradition when our advance party, and those of other Third Division units, first moved forward into the salient on July 17. It was a fairly quiet sector then, as good a time as any for troops to go into action for the first time. Members of the 40th at first took regular duties with experienced crews from the 3rd Canadian Field Battery, but then the 3rd moved out and by July 30, we of the 40th were on our own, firing our eighteen-pounders at the German lines. Under occasional machinegun fire and shelling ourselves, we suffered our first casualties and were there for much of the next two months, occasionally out of the line to the nearby town of Wytschaete for a rest, sometimes moving the guns. Everything had to be done at night in the salient because every part of it was visible from the higher ground held by the Germans. I remember one stretch in the line when my bed was a ledge dug out of a bunker wall. Rats used to jump off the floor and land on me looking for a place to sleep. They didn't bother me. They got so much to eat from the dead that they left the living alone. Once a bit of shell fragment skinned the back of my neck. When the Colonel came up the next day he said, "Any action?"

"Well, I got a little scratch," I said, and showed him.

"My God," he said, "Why didn't you report that?" He phoned back to headquarters and said I'd been wounded in action but was staying on duty. That was the first time I made a casualty list and got a wound stripe.

In late September at Wytschaete, I had a hot argument with Major Southam, running afoul of him, as I often do with others, thinking I know so much. I wanted to get promoted and the war seemed very slow and I told him he wasn't running the Battery right. Well, somebody not long ago told me I wasn't running my thoroughbred farm right and I sure blew off, so I can imagine what the major felt like. He was angry and I must have been furious, because I told him to take his coat off and I'd show him. I was all ready when our right section officer Art Boyd grabbed me and got me out of there.

I said, "What are you doing that for? I might have had a crack at him!"

"That would have been your last crack," Art said. "I'd have been at your funeral."

He was probably right. But as it was, within a few weeks the major was dead. I've always felt unhappy about flying off the handle at him, although I was sure I was right at the time.

We kept hearing, from units moving into our area and by war communiqués, about heavy fighting on the Somme. British and Empire divisions made up most of the Allied forces there. They had been badly beaten up. The extent was not known in detail until later – but to push one salient a mile into the German lines, the First Australian and New Zealand Corps (Anzacs) lost 23,000 men in one six-week stretch; the Newfoundland regiment was practically wiped out on the first day, July 1 – 700 casualties. July 1 is still a day of mourning to many families in Newfoundland.

Early in October it was our turn. We were relieved by an Imperial Army Battery from the Somme front, shared wagon lines and talk with them for a couple of days, then set out on the 100-kilometre forced march for the Somme, pushing our horses hard through the mud of autumn as we headed south along the Albert road making about 25 kilometres a day.

Our horses never let us down. We never let them down, either, there or elsewhere, if we could help it. Sometimes that wasn't easy. The Army had some screwy rules. One was the mange dip, all right in itself, but it didn't take into account seasons or local conditions. Our horses were working in the mud all the time. I've seen six-horse teams hauling guns or ammunition wagons through mud that was lapping around their bellies. Two of the worst things for a horse are to be wet and cold. Yet the Army had these big mange-dip pools and the rule was that every horse had to go through one every so often; be led up to the edge, slide in, and plunge out the other side supposedly sterilized against mange. In the cold, even the cold of October, a lot of horses might not get the mange but they'd die of the chills they got from being soaked and chilled. Our men refused to expose good horses to that kind of treatment. What we did was take a few of our oldest and weakest horses through the dip dozens of times, enough to make our count, subbing for stronger horses. In this way we were able to keep the better horses dry and fairly healthy. It was a case of the cure being a lot worse than the disease. Our unofficial system saved many. The old and weak ones that went through many times, died. The stronger ones survived, and on the march to the Somme they dragged our guns along those muddy roads with hardly any rest, on only ten pounds of food a day. My men and I did things like that which could have got us all court martialled, but we weren't going to have our horses slaughtered by some stupid order.

We made it to the Somme in good time and by October 7 were preparing gun pits in support of Canadian positions near the little town of Courcellette, which they'd taken to everybody's surprise in a general attack three weeks earlier all along the front. They hadn't been ordered to take Courcellette; just to take a ruined sugar factory and a system of German trenches in front of the town. But they had been told to take the town if they could do it on their own, without assistance. That meant, it was on their own heads. They did it. I was proud to be from the same country as those men. The Princess Pats overshot their intended launch point at first, and found themselves fixing bayonets and getting ready to charge when suddenly Germans started popping out of dugouts all around, some fighting but most with their hands up. The Royal 22nd from Quebec (the justly famous Van Doos) and the Nova Scotia Rifles took the town itself, and that's where they were when we started moving in with our guns.

Digging our gun positions was bad. Under the topsoil was white chalk that showed up clearly to the Germans on the slope beyond Courcellette. It felt like being at centre ice with no clothes on. I thought they could probably see us for fifty miles. The Germans had been in that place we now held for a long time and had dug positions as deep as forty feet into the chalk, with passages leading up to the surface where their guns were. Down below they had just about every comfort, including complete safety from anything but a direct shell hit.

On the night of October 12 we hauled our guns in, six horses to a gun – a lead team, a centre team, and a wheel team. Two other Batteries were lined up alongside us, so we made up practically one twelve-gun Battery, a big target. Two or three days later we were called upon to do a job of wire-cutting that meant firing for several hours. Three hostile balloons were hanging not far away and evidently observed our gun flashes. Soon after noon on October 15 a German 5.9 gun began ranging on our position and got it, dead on, putting over a heavy strafe that partially buried some of our guns and made it impossible to continue firing. Major Southam ordered us to leave the guns and take cover. He was hurrying along giving the order. I started to run after him when my batman, Gunner Walt Dawson, grabbed me and said, "Come on! Get into this dugout!" I jumped down in to what had been one of the German dugouts. Three dead Canadian officers from the Winnipeg Rifles were in there. One was stabbed, I guess by a bayonet. Another had been shot and had died half-upright with his arms wrapped around a stovepipe. The third was lying in a corner. I guess they'd been there for weeks. The smell was awful. We were still there about twenty minutes later when a sergeant named Moffitt came down the passage and said to me, "You're O.C. of the Battery."

I said, "What's the matter? What do you mean?"

He told me Major Southam had been killed. So had Sergeant-Major Norm Harvie. They'd been caught by a direct shell burst when they were running. I would have been right with them if Walt Dawson hadn't grabbed me and saved my life.

Now, with the position spotted and useless, we and the other Batteries were going to have to get our guns back out. That was the order that came down. Our Captain, Bill Wilson from Hamilton, hadn't been in the forward positions when this happened, but pretty soon he was sent up to take over the Battery from me. Then it was my job to go back for our horses and come back to get the guns. This had to be done at night. There was only one road. The German gunners had it well tabbed. They pounded it all night long. I was never so scared in my life, starting toward the front with our horses and those from the other Batteries along that road with constant shelling going on.

Then I had an idea: why do we have to stay on the road? We just had the horses and empty traces, going up to get the guns. I said, "Why don't we get off the road and cut across country?"

There was some argument that maybe we'd get lost. I wasn't worried about that. My men, Hamilton and Orillia fellows, were used to playing hockey and football and coping with situations as they come up. I knew what I was going to do. "I'll meet you up there," I said.

So the other Batteries came their way, and we came mine. We got there and hooked up to the guns and then just had the one trip back down the road under shellfire instead of one up and one back.

We weren't always so lucky. A little later when we'd moved the guns back up into another position I was leading a change of gun crews to the front when a shell landed among us. I've seen people blown to bits, but the worst is when a man is blown to bits and still is living, suffering terribly. One of our top gunners, Jack Pethick from Regina, star on that hockey team of ours only eight or nine months before, had his guts blown out. They were hanging around him in this shellhole full of mud and water and he was moaning heart-rendingly. We couldn't do anything for him. I groaned to the sergeant – remember, I was only twenty-one then – "This is terrible! What can we do?"

The sergeant said quietly, "Why don't you go up to the head of the line and see if there's anybody hurt up there?"

I went up. When I came back a few minutes later Pethick had been put out of his suffering. I always admired that sergeant for sending me out of the way, and for doing what had to be done, out of kindness, putting a man out of his suffering, although he loved Pethick as much as I did.

It was a long two months on the Somme. It's amazing how tiny one part of a great war can become. In front of Courcellette were three places, sort of redoubts, gun emplacements in the chalk that were supported by trenches. Being Canadians, we had named them Regina Trench, Kenora Trench, and Desire Trench. Regina Trench was taken and retaken four or five times. Once we had a position near it for a forward observation officer. The job there was to watch where our shells were landing. We strung phone lines up to the observation post and called back directions on whether to drop the shells back a little, raise a little, or what.

One day I was sent up before dawn to man the post. There was a hell of a lot of German shelling all that foggy morning, usually the prelude to an attack. My phone line had gone dead, probably hit. I couldn't even phone back to find out whether I was to stay until after dusk, as usual, or come back, so I stayed. The shooting went on heavier than ever. I figured an attack would come any time. I could see men moving in the fog. I hunted around in shellholes and gathered all the rifles and ammunition I could find from the bodies there, and started loading so I'd have something to fire.

That's when I knew I could be as scared as anyone living. I was shaking so much I could hardly put a cartridge in a gun at all. The firing got worse and worse and all of a sudden out of the fog I could see men crouched over moving toward me and I thought, my God, here goes the last of the Smythes and nobody's ever going to know what happened to me. Then about a hundred yards away a man straightened up. He was a Canadian. I sat there for half an hour and congratulated myself on being alive. I was sure right then that I couldn't have killed anybody, but I'll never know. I did know that if I didn't look out, although I might not think I was yellow, I wouldn't be able to act properly when the time came unless I started right then to train myself, be ready at all times to act like a man.

There were always reminders of what could happen, not only death. After the Somme battle wound down late in November, the net result was that the Allies had advanced five miles in nearly five months. The British and Empire divisions had lost four hundred and twenty thousand casualties and the French nearly two hundred thousand. I counted myself lucky to be alive when we pulled out on November 26 and marched back north, hauling our guns and wagons, to take up positions in the Mont St. Eloi area. In a few weeks some of us had our first leaves in England after six months in action, and I saw my old friend Wreck again.

We had kept in touch by mail, his first letter to me from England in September of 1915 talking about Toronto race results he had seen and asking, "How are the ponies running for you? And how is Irene? I'll bet you wore a track from Kingston to Toronto on weekends when you were taking that officer's course." He'd been expecting to go to France soon, but when I'd seen him on leave in England in 1916 he'd been getting frustrated, and his last letter to me, dated December 7, 1916, was still from a camp in Sussex. "Dear Conn, I was sure glad to get your letter the other day but shed many tears when I read that an old friend had her nose in front at a real price and we weren't there with a mitt-full of tickets on her. However, we will give them a ramble some day . . . Hope your luck is still holding. Yours, Wreck." He was up for a commission then, which soon came through. I saw him for a couple of nights in London, but never again.

The rest of the leave in London I spent with a friend from the 38th Battalion – Captain Thain MacDowell – from Brockville. He'd been a football player at the University of Toronto. His nerves were so badly shot right then – shell-shock, they called it – that he couldn't count past ten. Every time we went to the theatre and he was laying out his money, he couldn't get past ten shillings. I'd always have to pay the rest. I told him, "When I go back next time, I'm going to get shell-shocked too."

But I don't know that I'd want to do it his way. At Courcellette he had led his men on an attack that took two trenches on a little mound in front of Regina Trench. That mound was hardly noticeable from any distance but controlled the area. He stayed two extra days there against orders trying to get some brass up to see how useful the position was and decide to hold it. Finally he lost so many men he had to get out. He got the Distinguished Service Order for that, but he was still convinced we'd given up ground we hadn't had to. A few months later he won the Victoria Cross when we were both at Vimy Ridge.

When he and I returned to France from leave the 40th Battery was near Arras in France, not far from the German-held positions at Vimy. It was in that area in February, just after my twenty-second birthday, that I was awarded a Military Cross after incredible luck or, as I prefer to think of it, another nudge from The Man Upstairs, saved my life.

At that time the Canadian Corps was trying something new – sending an artillery officer and a signaller in with an infantry raiding party. I was the first. I volunteered and was attached to the 7th Infantry Brigade, which included the Royal Canadian Regiment, the Princess Pats, the 42nd Battalion of Highlanders from Montreal, and the Cape Breton Highlanders. Early in the morning of February 12, 1917, the infantry went over the top. Its job was to raid German trenches directly opposite, take some prisoners, and get back. I jumped off from our artillery observation post to follow them close behind. With me was a signaller from Brantford, a game little guy named Harry Coutts. He and I moved out with Couttsie carrying the phone and stringing line behind us. The idea was that instead of calling for artillery support from one set position farther back, I would see from close at hand where shelling would do the most good in support of the raid. On my first call I gave the infantry plenty of clearance for our shells, but when the first salvo came over they looked too high to me. I ordered, "Drop two hundred."

Right after I gave that order a lot of white puffs showed right in among the attacking infantrymen just ahead of me! I thought, "My God, I'm killing our own men!" All the infantry ever talked about to an artillery man was that we killed more of our own infantry than we did Germans. That might have been true, I don't know, but when I saw those white puffs I thought, if they're going to get killed by my mistake, I don't want to get back either.

I drew my revolver and ran down amongst the infantry, to find that the white puffs were from German grenades, not my shells at all. Couttsie said later I looked like one of the Keystone Cops, dodging around the grenades, but I was too busy to laugh. I was right in the middle of a battle between the two front lines, until I jumped down into the German trench with my revolver and fired a few shots, hitting two Germans, and then came around a corner, and saw a big German with his rifle up on the parapet. He just had time to look at me when I jammed my revolver in his stomach and pulled the trigger. He slid down into the trench, cursing me in German all the way. I don't know German but I know what he thought of me.

I kept going along the trench and ran into some of the Cape Breton Highlanders. Their officer had had one foot blown off, so again I was acting O.C., for the moment. A couple of the Highlanders had made a little sling so they could carry him. They also had two prisoners as scheduled. We had to fight our way back under fire but I didn't pull my trigger again, as it happened, until we got to our lines safe and sound. Then, just before I jumped down into our trench I turned around, gesturing defiance at the German trenches, pointed my revolver that way and pulled the trigger.

It went click.

I was out of ammunition.

I hadn't fired a shot since the one into the German.

If I'd fired one shot more before I first got into the trench, my revolver would have gone click into the German's stomach. Then I would have got a shot or a bayonet in mine, and would have gone down cursing him in Canadian.

A general named Archibald was there when we came in. He congratulated me and the next day the officer commanding the 42nd Battalion, Major S. C. Norsworthy of the 5th Royal Highlanders of Canada, recommended me for the Military Cross. I've seen the letter he wrote, saying that he wasn't certain what was the correct procedure in recommending an officer of another unit for an award, but was enclosing herewith an AFW 3121 in quintuplicate, signed by himself. I guess the quintuplicate will do it every time. Three weeks later in daily routine orders, under the heading of Awards and Decorations, there were two Military Crosses and one of them was mine. When it was published later in Canada in a list of Military Crosses, my paragraph read: Lieutenant Conn Smythe (Field Artillery) – Organized some men and led them with great dash, thereby dispersing an enemy party at a critical time. Himself accounted for three of the enemy with his revolver.

Not a word about going around for the rest of the action with the revolver empty.

At that time, we were sometimes in the line, sometimes out for a few days rest. But one day the Highlanders to whom I was attached got very annoyed. A Jewish officer from Toronto came in as a replacement. He was Myer Cohen, born on Huron Street. He was wearing a kilt. That was okay, but he got lost coming up and instead of poking around and finding someone to ask, he stood up there practically in No Man's Land and yelled, "Where are you, 42nd Battalion? Where are you?"

With only about one hundred yards between the lines, it was about the worst thing he could have done. When he was pulled into the trench I found that I knew him from a Y camp I'd been to at Lake Couchiching. He was a good lad, with two fine brothers, but he'd sure got off on the wrong foot with the Scotchmen. I talked to him a lot later in our dugouts. He told me how hard he was finding it to make the grade with some of the other officers because of being Jewish. All he wanted to do was make good in the battalion. "Well," I said, "you had an awful bad start."

The others rode him pretty hard. But one night a little later a parcel came in for him, containing a lot of special Jewish food. Some fellow made a disparaging remark about the kind of food it was. Cohen's mother had baked the stuff. He went wild. He cleaned everybody's clock down there in the dugout, all in one go. That made things a little better for him. He fought with the 42nd later at Vimy, and then went on to Passchendaele where he was killed after fighting so bravely that he was recommended for the Victoria Cross. He didn't get it, but being recommended for one is a great honour. He was a game, fine man, as so many of my Jewish friends are, in battle or elsewhere.

After the war, after all the fighting, I went to his parents' place on Huron Street. I just wanted to tell his mother and father something about their son, convey some of my admiration to the parents of a wonderful man. They gave me a cool reception. Whether it was their grief, or whether they didn't think he should have joined up, or whatever, I left rather frustrated.

As I imagine everybody knows, I never got to be a general. I started the First War as a lieutenant and ended the same way; started the Second War as a major and ended the same way. But that didn't stop me from being sure sometimes that I could have done better at planning than the people who were doing it.

That's what had nearly got me into the fight with Gordon Southam, back before the Somme. And it was going to get me into trouble at Vimy, because on March 28 after Captain Bill Wilson had been doing a good job as our Officer Commanding for nearly six months since Major Southam was killed, a section from the 41st Battery was amalgamated with the 40th to form one six-gun Battery. The O.C. from the 41st, a Major named Syre, took command of us, and I didn't like him. Partly this was because of the close spirit we'd had in the 40th ever since we were formed and I didn't like to see Bill Wilson knocked out of the top spot. However, it wasn't all mere resentment of a newcomer. Another officer who came to us at the same time, Lieutenant Monty Clarkson, became a good friend of mine very quickly.

This amalgamation happened just twelve days before the attack on Vimy Ridge. The whole Canadian Corps was there, four divisions, all of us with reinforcements for what we'd lost on the Somme. Of course, a lowly lieutenant on a job like that doesn't get to know much about overall strategy, but the seven-mile escarpment called Vimy Ridge already was as famous a name as Verdun or Ypres. The Germans had dug in at Vimy in 1914, the French had tried to dislodge them in 1915, and by early 1917 the Germans had had two full years to build up a system of permanent trenches, forts, redoubts, dormitories, and passageways.

I never could figure out why in so many places – as in Ypres, Courcellette, and now in Vimy – the Allied positions always seemed to be at the bottom of a hill, the Germans on top. I don't understand it yet.

Allied positions behind this front were centred on the old walled city of Arras. A maze of caves and tunnels ran through the chalk, some used as safe cover to many infantrymen moving up for the Vimy attack. There were something like one hundred and seventy thousand men in the Canadian Corps, with some supporting British units, and on the freezing morning of April 9, Easter Monday, about fifteen thousand assault troops moved into position for the attack on Vimy. What I remember best about the morning of the Vimy attack, the biggest victory in Canadian Army history and the biggest Allied land victory of the war up until then, was that Driver Skin Langton's young brother was on guard duty for my section and when I got up about 4:30, well before dawn, an hour before zero, there he was – sound asleep on the hay.

The barrage that morning started at 5:30 with the bark of a sixty-pounder just behind us. At that signal all our guns opened up and the assault troops went over the top of trenches or charged out of tunnels, some blowing new tunnel exits right into No Man's Land. Our shelling for more than a week, five hundred rounds a day from each of hundreds of guns along the front, had paved the way by flattening German trenches and blowing gaps in the German wire. Our troops had to fight machine guns, grenades, and bayonets for every few hundred yards they advanced, but not much wire.

Later that day we moved the wagon lines forward, closer to the gun positions so that we could signal one another visually. The misty morning had turned to drizzle, sleet, and snow. When I moved the wagons I tried to use a plank road that had been built along there. A Canadian, Major MacKendrick, had had the idea of beating the mud by laying plank roads, something like the old corduroy roads in Canada that the settlers laid through muddy spots and swamps. That morning the theory was okay but the practice wasn't. With the sleet and snow and rain, the planks were so slippery that the horses were plunging around, falling, the wagons slipping right off. So we had to go back to our old business of heading across country. Naturally, nobody had been able to build a boardwalk ten miles behind the lines and see if it would work. Theoretically it was perfect and later plank roads at Passchendaele helped, but it wasn't worth a five-cent piece that day – except that it wasn't long before the first large batch of prisoners came back along the plank road through our gun positions, holding their ears against the thunderous barrage that was going on all around. Some guns had as many as six hundred empty shell cases behind them by 11:00 that morning.

Reports were coming back that the attack was going well, some units ahead of schedule. As the day wore on the Battery settled down to firing on special targets called back from our forward observation points, close to the infantry. We expected any hour to be ordered to bring our guns forward, but it was night before we moved both our guns and our wagon lines. Those not on duty slept in old rat-infested dugouts nearby.

Over the next few days a lot of things are just a jumble.

I do remember one day I was taking ammunition up when a shell landed right between our two wheel horses and split them to either side, dead. Luckily the men weren't hurt. But when I looked at the carnage my first thought was, what'll we do now? Everything looked shattered. But then all the training that we'd done came into play. My men unhitched the two leading teams, hauled the dead horses off to one side, backed up the other two teams, hitched their traces to the wagon, and we were underway again in a couple of minutes, four horses pulling instead of six. I got a lot of credit for that and did not do one lousy thing.

It was a few days later before we moved again. On April 15, the 40th Battery guns were hauled across Vimy Ridge, among the first guns to get there. The infantry had occupied most of the ridge in the first twenty-four hours, then had gone down the other side to drive the Germans out of Vimy Village. In the morning I looked down the other side to where the village of Vimy was. The first line was beyond the railway embankment on the other side but we were still within easy range of the German artillery. There were four crashed British planes below the ridge. They'd been observing for our artillery, doing their job. Then something happened that changed the rest of the war for me, perhaps changed my life.

On April 16, we moved the guns forward into Vimy Village itself. The gun crews dug our pits along one side of a road that ran north from the village square toward a little place called La Chaudière. Battery headquarters were in a deep dugout, where our new major spent most of his time. My job was bringing up ammunition. Our ammo dumps were well to the rear and that trip was no picnic. The only road down the face of Vimy Ridge was as well known to the Germans as the nose on their face. It was like running the gauntlet to get ammunition and rations around one corner called the Devil's Elbow.

The Germans also lobbed a few shells into the village itself, with the square a particular target. On April 20th I made a trip up with ammunition, reported to the major, and heard about plans to move the guns ahead a little to new pits in front of the railway station. Two other lieutenants, Fred Scott and Monty Clarkson, were up there now with a digging party. I left and made my way back under shellfire several miles to load up for another trip. Someone there said there'd just been a call from H.Q. A shell had landed among the pit-digging party. There'd been casualties. They'd been hit when they were coming back across the square. The message was that Scottie and Monty were among the wounded, but that was all.

It probably took me a couple of hours or more to get back to Vimy with my next load. I went straight to the headquarters dugout to see the major.

"Are Scotty and Monty badly hurt?" I asked. "Where are they?"

He looked up. "They're out in the square," he said.

I couldn't believe it. "You mean to say that they've been out there wounded all this time, and you're still sitting down in this dugout?" I yelled.

I hated that man right then.

I went out on the run. Out on the square Scotty was lying quietly, but Monty was moaning. I got hold of Scotty first. He was dead. When I felt in his pocket to get his wallet to send home, one leg dropped right off. Monty Clarkson, who'd been an outside wing for Varsity, was moaning and talking and calling for his mother. I got someone to help get both out but Monty died three r four hours later. They both had been out there for at least the me it had taken me to get back up there. They might not have ied if someone had hauled them in as soon as they were hit. I nought to myself, I don't want to serve in this Battery any more nder a major like that.

I told him that, face to face, and right then I put in for a transfer ɔ the Royal Flying Corps. I know now that I shouldn't have. I hould have known that he wouldn't last long. He was out of there ı a few weeks, replaced by Bill Wilson, but by then I was in the ᴀir Force. I missed those guys, the esprit de corps we had, together ɔ long. There was nothing like this in the Air Force. I would have ᴇen proud to serve under my original captain, who had been pro- ᴀoted major. Bill Wilson, dead now, commanded the Battery for ᴄe rest of the war, as fine a man as ever lived.

Before my transfer came through, though, I had another in my tring of lucky escapes. Most of Vimy Village by then had been ʰelled to the ground. One night I got into one of the wrecked ᴏuses, all the windows knocked out, and had a sleep. When I was kid I used to have one awful nightmare, that I was in a boat ᴏing down, drowning. I was having this nightmare that night, ᴏing down in the water, suffocating, when I came to, to find my ᴀtman, Walt Dawson, forcing a gas mask on me. The Germans ᴀd been firing gas shells and the place was full of it. The shells ᴀrdly made any noise, just a plop. If Walt hadn't come looking ᴏr me I might not have come out of that alive, either. Walt didn't ᴎow where I was, but he'd come searching. Men like him were an ᴎportant part of the Army, to me. There's no way in civilian life ᴎat you get that kind of chance to show a man that you love him, ᴇspect him, want him to keep on living.

In the early summer of 1917 my transfer came through to the ᴏyal Flying Corps, later the Royal Air Force – and I was posted ɔ England for training. Soon after, I first met Billy Barker, who ᴀter was president of the Toronto Maple Leafs and to me the ᴦeatest Canadian flier of the time, which is saying something.

The Air Force had been looking particularly for artillery officers ɔ train as observers. I got high marks on that part of the course, ᴠith my experience. Then six were chosen to take courses as ilots. I was one of the six. Although I didn't care for that – I ᴠanted to stay in the gunnery end of things – I went through the ᴏurse. Before I got my wings, Barker showed up as an instructor.

He took one of our fellows up. When the man came back, his hair practically had turned white. "Nobody go up with that guy ever again!" he advised. From then on, nobody would go up with Barker. He got sore. One day when there was an inspection he took a plane up and flew it right through one of the hangars, in one end and out the other, buzzing some senior officers so that they had to flatten out right on the ground.

When he came down he was told, "You're under arrest."

"All I want to do is go to France," he said. "You say you want volunteers, send me."

They did, but not to France, to Italy. He didn't feel the competition was very good there. He never even counted the planes he shot down on the Italian front, because he didn't figure they were good enough. But while there he buzzed another inspection. That time the King of Italy was ducking with the rest. Barker finally got what he wanted: a posting to the western front. I was on the air field in France when he brought in his squadron there. What warrior. At that time he had the Military Cross with two bars, and the Distinguished Service Order with bar. Late in the final days of fighting in 1918, Barker survived a dogfight that from time to time involved him and sixty German planes. He was wounded in the right thigh, then in the left thigh, then had his left elbow shattered. He fainted twice. Each time, coming to, he found himself being attacked again. He shot down six planes that day and just made it across our lines before he crash-landed full of holes. For that, he won the Victoria Cross. That was the kind of tradition we wanted when we made him the president of the Leafs. It wasn't all we got, but we'll come to that.

By the time of that last Barker dogfight, I wasn't around. I wasn't interested in being a fighter pilot so I'd got back into what did interest me, flying artillery observation planes, specifically a two-seater called the RE8. It also was known as The Incinerator because it had a habit of bursting into flames. We were taught how to side-slip and put the flames out. If you side-slipped too much, a wing might drop off. It was a great feeling to go into the air in a thing like that.

Anyway, I didn't know at first that airborne artillery observers weren't as meticulous as the fellows on the ground. On the ground, you had to be more careful with your calls. Other people could see what was happening. Up in the air, I found to my sorrow that when the flying weather was bad an observer might just yell out a few signals and nobody ever could be sure whether they'd been useful or not. I wouldn't allow that in my airplane. Trying to be too meticulous was my undoing.

By now it was October. The infantry had been fighting bitterly for months pushing the Ypres salient outward toward Passchendaele. We flew every day over that sea of mud and shellholes. The ground was clay, without drainage, and after three years of war was indescribable.

The last day I flew the clouds were low, less than two thousand feet. I shouldn't have been sent up in that weather, or, once up, should have had enough sense to let the observer fake it and then come back and say, "Great shooting."

Instead, I got down below the cloud and was dodging around the enemy observation balloons, so we could see better. My observer was a Roman Catholic, Andrew Ward. We had spent a lot of time arguing about religion. That didn't stop us from being good in the air together. Anyway, when we were hit and my rudder controls shot off, I thought it was a machinegun burst from the ground. My observer's brother, with an Irish outfit on the front, saw it happen and much later told us he thought we were hit from above.

It didn't matter much. I was pumping my feet to try to get control, but couldn't. The engine's torque then took over and put me into a flat spin, so I shut off the engine and put the nose down looking for a place to land. I could see some woods below. They were all shot up, the branches gone, so they were like spikes sticking up. I said, "God, I hope I can miss that – I don't want one of those spikes up my rear end."

Our circles were getting wider and wider. Ward finally tapped me on the shoulder very coolly and said, "What's going to happen now?"

I said, "We've done a lot of arguing about religion, Wardsy. In about five seconds we're going to find out who's right."

His life was in my hands but he never said another word. A stout man, a good man to have alongside. We were low now, being shot at from below, and I got hit in the leg and then in the calf. I remember thinking about fellows who put steel cans under their seats as protection. I wished I had. Finally we were skimming the ground. There was a great big crater in front of us. We slithered across the mud, into it.

We were alive, but we were in No Man's Land. A couple of guns were firing at us. Not far away also there was a man waving at us. I said, "We'll make it." For the next hour and a half or so we went from shellhole to shellhole toward the guy who was waving. Finally, getting close, I said to Wardsy, "You make for him. Get a start. I'll try to distract the others." So he got up and ran. I let him go about forty yards before I started out after him. I think I passed him ten yards later. Then we came to this position where the man had been waving – and he was a German!

I was so mad I just stood on the parapet and cursed him for every kind of a rotten bastard. He pulled out his revolver and shot twice from point-blank range. Another German dove at him and told him to stop, prisoners were better than dead men. When they pulled us down into their trench, I looked at my flying coat. This may sound sort of foolish, but I think I had generated so much force in my anger that no bullet was going to hit me. There were holes in my flying coat on both sides of my chest, and neither of them had scratched me, although my other minor wounds were bothering me some.

I have to give credit to the Germans. They had been in there for six or seven days without relief. Their nerves were shot but they weren't giving an inch. I'd seen shelling on the Somme and at Vimy, but nothing like what our guns were doing to those guys. Yet they were still holding on to those frontline bunkers.

That night they did get relief and took us back and into a big room, a headquarters of some kind, with a lot of officers there to question us. One was General Rupprecht, the Crown Prince of Bavaria. He'd been at the front almost from the beginning of the war. He was the German Army Commander in that area, kind of a nice-looking fellow. Everything went fine until he said he thought he wouldn't make a bad job of running Canada as Governor General.

I exploded, "For God's sake, you don't think you're going to win this war, do you?"

They hustled me out of there like I was shot out of a gun.

Later that night I realized I wasn't any hero. We were sent farther back with only two or three guards. I think we could have overpowered them, but Allied shelling was so heavy that that's all I was thinking about. With the minor wounds I'd got in the air, I wasn't in good shape. For some reason I was thinking, I don't mind being killed if someone sees it happen, but not being obliterated without anybody knowing. I also thought quite a bit of home, knowing that in a day or two I would be listed as missing in a telegram to my father, and then he would go and tell Irene. It did happen that way. I've seen the clippings since – old hockey pictures of me with the words above, Reported Missing, and a few paragraphs about when I had joined up, when I had won the Military Cross, and so on. I was captured October 14, and it was nearly a month before word got back that I was a prisoner.

They took us first, it turned out, to a hospital at Roulers, a place in Belgium that now is called Roeselare, not far behind the German lines on the Passchendaele front. Next thing I remember is lying in a ward covered with lice. That's when my attitude to getting killed changed. Every half an hour or so Roulers was being hit by shells or bombs. None of them hit the hospital but I was lying there thinking I wouldn't mind being hit. I was in the hospital with maybe three hundred wounded Germans. That made the odds better. I didn't mind going one for three hundred. Just one for one out in the mud wasn't for me.

I was in that hospital for three or four days and then was moved again. Soon we'd get out for little walks once in a while. I thought of trying to grab an airplane on one airstrip I saw, but I wasn't strong enough yet. I didn't know it then, but for the next fourteen months I was going to be moved from one prison camp to another before the war finally ended.

First we were taken to Karlsruhe, which was really a processing place for prisoners. They had an ingenious system. They'd tell prisoners coming in that they were probably lonesome and would like to see some friends. Then they gave you a list of names to pick a few friends from. That way they found out who your friends were and put you in with them. Naturally you'd do a lot of talking. It was later we realized they had listening devices and found out a lot more than we wanted to tell them. It was there, too, that I ran across the worst case of war profiteering. A couple of guys, one from Upper Canada College, had charge of food parcels. They would seize any parcel addressed to a man who had died, or been moved, and would sell them. It was a miserable thing. Some people there were pretty thin, never got any parcels. They should have got the spare parcels free.

My next camp, around Christmas, was Magdeburg, where I wrote a letter the censors didn't like and I was put in solitary for two weeks. Then I was moved to Halle, a camp that was mainly English, with a caste system by which men who had been prisoners the longest got the highest priority in escape attempts. Canadians wouldn't have anything to do with that; they believed in free enterprise, and trying when they could. The one thing we all did agree on was that if an escape was set up for a particular day, nobody would bust in on their routine.

Next move was about the time of my twenty-third birthday, early February, to a camp at Blankenburg, a big building several storeys high, with pretty good rooms and accommodation. I was there when I heard that on November 6, while I was still listed as missing, my friend Wreck Aggett had been killed at Passchendaele, and we would never laugh and kibitz again. But all of us had troubles, and we tried to keep busy. I taught a Belgian officer English and he tried to teach me French. After we'd been doing this for about six weeks he clicked his heels at me (he had a little mustache and a very military air) and said, "Mr. Smitty, the French lessons are finished."

"I didn't know I was that good," I said.

"You are the worst I ever heard," he said. "I cannot listen any more."

At that camp there was a great mixture of nationalities, including Russians. The flying boots I'd been wearing when I was shot down had become useless. One day a white Russian officer named Logvinoff came along and said he had two pair, and handed me the most beautiful boots I'd ever seen, knee-high, of soft, comfortable leather. I didn't know at the time but he had given me his best pair, keeping some old ones for himself. I still have photos with notes on the back that don't identify the prisoners I was with, but just say: "Logvinoff's boots." After the war he came to Toronto and knew only one man in the city, me. He worked as a cleaner and store keeper at Maple Leaf Gardens. My kids used to love him for his tricks, one being to walk on his hands while smoking a cigarette. One winter in the 1950's he died and I flew up from Florida for the funeral.

There were a lot of escape attempts, but again prisoners of long standing had priority. Once there was a huge tunnel that started right in the middle of the camp. A lot got out. The guards sent out dogs to track them. The loudest cheer I heard outside of a Stanley Cup final came when about a thousand of us inside the wire were watching these dogs circle to pick up the scent, everybody yelling, "Spoor, spoor," when all of a sudden one dog squatted down and did his business. We just about rolled around on the ground, cheering and laughing, until even the Germans grinned a little.

All along in the prison camp I was getting Irene's letters and parcels. I hadn't seen her for two years now but our letters went back and forth and I never doubted her for a moment, as she never doubted me. She had a marvellous way of packing a parcel with all the stuff I used to love at home; grape juice, little biscuits. I never suffered for anything.

It was from that camp that I made my only try at escape. My chum there was Seaton Broughall, another flier. We set it up. There were two barbed wire fences around the camp, one a few feet inside the other. We thought we'd try an escape in daylight, on the somewhat flimsy grounds that nobody would be expecting that. Even if we got shot at, the guards by 1918 were oldtimers, we didn't think they could hit us if we moved fast enough. We had our others helping us. Two would run to the first wire and throw our supply packs over, while another two bent over close by the wire. Then Seaty and I would step on their backs and scramble to the top of the first fence, throw a blanket over the top of the second fence, take a jump and roll off the blanket to the ground. We picked a place that was about one hundred yards from the nearest guard. I got over okay. Unfortunately old Seaty was a better flier than he was a tumbler. He didn't do a very good roll, and ripped his pants almost off on the wire. The two of us tore across the field with Seaty's pants flying in the wind and the bullets kicking up just behind us. I'm against using any artificial means of increasing the speed of either horses or men, but I think every Olympic record would be broken any time they wanted to have a race like that. Shooting just behind a man sure makes him run.

At first we thought we'd got away. We did travel a few miles and hid in some bushes beside a river. I'd brought a needle and thread along. Seaton was lying on his belly while I squatted behind him sewing up his pants, when a South African German with a tracking dog came out of the bushes right behind us. He might have thought there was something peculiar in the stance, but he didn't shoot us, for which I'm grateful.

I've been scared before hockey games, scared before horse races, but I wasn't scared right then. Like every other time in war, I never really had the feeling that my time had come.

What they did was take us east to a tougher camp, the former women's workhouse at Schwiednitz, which is in Poland now. I was put in solitary because of the escape attempt, living on bread and water. It wasn't that bad. They used to give us hard buns. I'd bore a hole and fill one with water and then put it on the radiator. It would swell up and become quite tasty.

However, one thing I do remember that wasn't so good. I've always wanted to learn to play the mouth organ. I asked for one and got it. All my life I wanted to learn French and never could get the hang of it. Same with music. I tried to learn to play Home Sweet Home. Played it over and over. One day I saw a rifle come through the bars up above, pointing at me. Whatever the guy said in German I didn't understand, except I knew he was telling me to stop trying to play the mouth organ or he'd blow my head off. I stopped, and never tried again.

We were still at Schwiednitz when the war ended. Early in November the Germans got very tense. They set up machineguns aimed into the camp. I guess they were afraid we'd try to break out because everybody knew the end was near. I don't remember anybody being very disturbed. The poker and bridge games and soccer went on as usual. But after a few days they told us the war was over. From then on they were very good to us. Several weeks later we were taken to a port on the Baltic and shipped back to England. When we landed on Christmas Eve at the god-forsaken place in Yorkshire where we were supposed to go through the usual paper work of repatriation, we found the British had stopped work for the holiday. One western Canadian had worked on the railroad and knew how to get a locomotive engine going. That he did, and took about twenty-five or thirty of us into a nearby city, where we left the locomotive in the yards and caught some regular trains. I had let my aunt and uncle in Manchester know that I was coming. They had a great big welcome-home Christmas dinner ready and didn't touch it until I got there, at midnight Christmas Day. The next day I went back to Yorkshire to be officially checked in.

With so many people wanting to get back to Canada, there were delays but the Red Cross looked after us very well. They offered all kinds of trips to help us put in time before we made it onto a ship. One jaunt I took was to Ireland. We were there having a great time when word came that our boat for Canada was ready.

By that time it was mid-February of 1919. I don't remember the exact date, but it was a nice night when we got home. We pulled into Toronto's main station first. There was no one there. Turned out the big reception was at North Toronto station, where the liquor store is now. We backed up and went there and stepped down into the big crowds of relatives and friends and lovely Canadian girls. Dad was there. So was Irene. I went home with her. God, did she look beautiful to me. I remember her father sticking around for hours as if there might be something going on between us. But we'd waited that long and we weren't going to make any mistakes.

By that time, my father had moved to a house at 22 Glengrove, with Janie and a baby half-sister, Moira, whom I'd never seen. It was several miles north in the city from the home Irene's family now had, on Delaware. I walked the whole way through the soft winter night, singing and thinking what a short distance it really was, and planning. Four years of my life were gone that I would never get back. I was twenty-four and hadn't done a thing yet. But I was going to make up for it, of that I was damn sure.

Chapter Four

The elation I felt that first night home was the beginning of a wonderful springtime. I was twenty-four, Irene not quite twenty-two, and we couldn't get enough of one another after having been apart too long. Today it might have been simple: a leap into bed every once in a while would have taken off some of the strain. But we didn't. We wanted to marry quickly but at the same time were determined to do things the way we both considered to be right. In those days chastity before marriage, as an ideal, had not yet become archaic. It is not difficult to understand why the goal of marriage then was immeasurably more yearned-for than it sometimes is today, when the ache of anticipating the bed part often is long gone.

My own virginity had a certain amount of luck attached. Once on leave in London with Wreck Aggett and two girls we'd met somewhere, I was so innocent that later I asked Wreck what all the grunting and groaning had been about when he and his girl were in an adjoining room for a while. Never having reached that final stage, I really didn't know. He thought I was kidding but when he saw I wasn't, and stopped laughing, he told me, "Well, Connie, it's like this . . ."

Another time I took a girl out and later took her home, which turned out to be away out in the suburbs where she had a room. She asked me up and it was freezing in there, little or no heat. She undertook to inflame me by wrapping herself in a broad yellow ribbon and slowly unwinding it to reveal herself while I watched. But at one point the contrast in colours – the yellow ribbon unwinding from a bare bottom that was blue with the cold – struck me as funny. That ended that. Things were rather strained when, in leaving, I gave her a little gift I'd bought for her earlier and she gave me a necktie that somebody must have left there.

Also, once on a station platform in France I noticed a well-dressed and pretty French girl. I guess I was giving her the eye a bit, because she came up and said, "Voulez-vous coucher avec moi?" I was thunderstruck. I'd believed everything I'd been told, and more, about the dangers of picking up venereal disease from prostitutes, but for some reason I thought all prostitutes dressed in black satin skirts and wore heavy make-up. This one looked like a secretary, or somebody's sister.

"Pas de temps," I stammered.

When she enquired how long before my train left and I told her half an hour, she laughed and said, "Beaucoup de temps!" But I still didn't succumb.

A fourth time, in that visit to Ireland when we were waiting for a boat home, I'm pretty sure an Irish friend urged his sister to go after me while he had a go at the vicar's daughter; but he did, and I didn't, although that time not entirely from lack of trying.

Anyway, Irene and I had our priority; marriage first. There was a toll, however.

Irene had been working then for a steel company on Dupont Street in Toronto. The plant is still there, where Dupont takes a bend a few blocks west of Bathurst. When I'd been back only a few weeks her boss phoned me.

"I want to talk to you about Irene," he said.

"Go ahead," I said.

"For three years," he said accusingly, "we had a very good little girl here who did her job well. Since you got back she hasn't been worth a damn."

"Well, that's too bad!" I said. "I've been away for three years fighting for guys like you – surely to God she's entitled to enjoy me when I come back!"

He still mumbled and grumbled. I told Irene, "Why don't you quit that job? We're going to get married soon, anyway." But she didn't quit her job until just before we did marry, nearly a year later.

One other part of my life right then didn't go as well. When I returned from overseas, I moved back into my father's house in North Toronto, at 22 Glengrove. But I never got along well with his wife, Janie. My resentment of her went deeper than merely surface things. We had little in common. I have always loved a clean house and she was a terrible housekeeper. More important, I always liked to be number one with those closest to me, and I felt that she had taken my father away from me. It was unreasonable, maybe the result of losing my own mother when I was so young, but I didn't attempt to hide my antagonism, then or later. My half-sister Moira was just a baby when I got back, not yet a year old. Naturally she was the focus of the household. I felt like a stranger in my father's house.

Yet I couldn't do much about it, right then. I had higher priorities. I lay awake nights thinking of Irene, when we could marry, and how to go battering into life to get where I wanted to be in the shortest possible time.

I wasn't badly off, financially. All through prison camp, my pay had piled up. The scale for fliers was several dollars more a day than the pay for a lieutenant in the Canadian Army. So I had four-teen months of accumulated pay. Then when I reported in Toronto for demobilization, I met a very understanding officer. He told me that since my re-establishment credit would be based on my last rate of pay, it would be better if I could use the RAF rate. Normally I'd be returned to the Canadian Army for a while and that pay rate would be the basis for my discharge bonus. But he fixed it so that I was discharged from the RAF to the Canadian Army, and de-mobilized, all on the same day, March 10, 1919. Using the RAF scale as my last rate of pay made a difference of about a thousand dollars to me. Two months later there was an auction of lots in Lawrence Park; and I bought one on Dinnick Crescent, which kept going up in value and – with a house built on it – brought me revenue for years.

In the autumn I would start my final year in applied science as a civil engineer, but that was months away, so I looked for a job. My city and CNR experience helped land me one with York Township right away. There I was dealing mostly with costs on construction jobs and got an idea.

It was hard to find people who would do the small jobs. One day a young paving contractor named Frank Angotti, who owned one truck and was about my age, came in with some estimates for concrete work that were figured out wrong.

"You need a partner," I told him.

"Yeah?" he said. "Who?"

"How about me?" I said.

As easily as that, we became partners. I had the small amount of money I needed to go in with him, and when university opened that September – with three-quarters of the graduating class made up of returned men – I was already a fledgling contractor, partners in one truck, a few shovels, and whatever else Angotti had.

It was a full-time job, but I had decided years earlier that an intelligent person could absorb what was going on in a university lecture in about five minutes. I went through my final year studying hard when I had to, but not going to many classes.

I hadn't been back at university long before I figured I needed a car to cut travelling time between the various things I was doing. I bought a 1915 Ford roadster that October. It ran well but had some drawbacks, like hard tires (solid rubber) and a top so rotten that when I got it down and tried to put it back up it fell apart. So Irene and I took the train later that month to Hamilton one Saturday afternoon when, on the cricket field at the Hamilton Amateur Athletic Association grounds, I lined up with a lot of other one-time heroes to receive my Military Cross from Edward, the Prince of Wales. Like a farmer who lives in a shack but has a beautiful barn, I think I had my priorities right. I only paid $260 for the Ford, but a few months later, on January 27, 1920, I ordered for spring delivery a five-ton National truck with a hydraulic hoist and an enclosed cab (you paid extra for an enclosed cab in those days). The price was $7,595. The order also marked another kind of beginning, reading that the truck should be, "Painted blue with white trim, and lettered in white on cab: 'Conn Smythe, Junction 3848' and on the side of body, in white, 'C. Smythe for Sand.' "

That last winter in school, I saw Irene almost every night, and also tried playing a little hockey. In December of 1919, a kind sportswriter covering a game wrote, "Connie Smythe seems to have temporarily lost some of his skating ability in German prison camps." I knew it was more than temporary. I got involved in Varsity hockey in other ways, coaching and managing, whatever needed doing. I knew by then that of all the sports I had tried, hockey was the one that was in my blood, although I had no inkling then, not even a dream, as to where it would lead.

Irene and I had decided that winter that we would be married March 10, the first anniversary of my discharge from the Army. So many men from my university class were coming to the wedding that classes were cancelled for the day. Wreck Aggett would have been my best man, if he had lived. Another old friend from junior hockey days, to say nothing of the Miss Menard horse race, Dago Morton, would have been second choice – but our class book for the 1920 year had his photo in it; Captain Edward B. G. Morton, reported missing in July, 1918, and never heard of again. Art Boyd, my friend from the 40th Battery, was my best man. Irene wore a navy blue suit and fox furs that I had given her. We'd spent the last few weeks before the wedding furnishing an apartment at 16 St. Clair Avenue West, and when we stood up there at the front of the Central Methodist Church it was like a long dream finally coming true. I guess most weddings are lovely, and ours was – my family, her family, and our friends. We didn't have a reception. After we were married we drove to the railroad station to catch the train for Buffalo. For our honeymoon, I had booked a nice suite in the best hotel there, but something had gone wrong. No suite. We took a single room. Maybe it didn't make all that much difference. I was twenty-five and she was nearly twenty-three, and we were both virgins. The odds against that today are extremely high. It never hurt us any, that I noticed.

Around then Angotti and I were always having trouble getting sand and gravel, so I decided I should get my own pit. In the west end of the city where there was plenty of sand and gravel I bought a few acres for what would be peanuts now, $300 an acre or something like that. Sixty years later there is fine housing on that land where the pit was, including the home of my grandson Tommy, son of Stafford and his wife Dorothea. Also, there's a park, Smythe Park, with tennis courts, swimming pool, and a plaque acknowledging my contribution of some land that made it possible. I sometimes stand there and remember. We started right away taking sand and gravel in Angotti's one old truck. You couldn't do that kind of thing today. There'd be protest marches by ratepayers' associations and nineteen levels of government to get permits from. In those days all we had was one mild protest from a woman who lived near the pit.

When exams came, I listened to a friend named Charlie Gage, a great Varsity football player. He told me, "Connie, get all the papers for the last ten years and pick out the questions that have been asked the most often. Get a tutor and study those questions until you're perfect. They can't change the questions much, because the answers don't change."

That made sense. I hired a tutor. Thirty-three and a third per cent was all that was required for a pass. When I sat down to write an exam of, say, ten questions, I would pick out four that I knew by heart, do them, and then get up and go. I always passed. After a while, they had people looking over my shoulder when I wrote exams, thinking I was cheating. They would argue with me that I should finish the whole exam. But I did it my way and it was good enough. I never really learned much at university, I think, but it was enough for my degree.

I've always been amused a little by one thing that happened in that final year. I was terrible at draftsmanship, and everybody knew it. I had some drawings to turn in and I got a really top draftsman, Bob Gouinlock, brother of Roper Gouinlock the architect, to do them for me. He always got an A. I got a bare pass. That is standard, through life. If a guy at the top says something, it's listened to. If the sweeper in his factory says the same thing, nobody pays any attention. I guess when the man marking the drawings saw my name on them, he just automatically started thinking C, or even D.

My partnership with Frank Angotti wasn't going to last long. We worked together on some jobs but apart on others. A few months after I took delivery of my own truck to use in the business, he bought one himself (with no enclosed cab). He was a pretty good guy, but he couldn't stand his second truck, somehow. When he had only the one, we got a lot of paving done. When he got two, he felt he always should know all the time what each of them was doing. If he had had four trucks, it would have driven him crazy. His obsession with keeping track of that second truck hurt our business. Finally I said to him, "We've got to split this partnership."

We talked about how to do it. My idea was something others did at that time: when there were two distinct operations like ours, the paving and the sand pit, one person would set a price and the other would get the choice of which half of the business he'd take. Angotti wouldn't agree to that. We had to go to court. The judge thought my idea was fair enough, but Angotti still resisted. The judge asked him why.

Angotti said, "Well, if I name the price, he might take the paving business, and that's what I want."

The judge said, "All right, let him name the price, and you'll have the choice of what to take."

Angotti said, "Well, he might name a price too high."

The judge sighed, "You can't have it both ways." He ordered me to name the price and let Angotti have his choice. I named a fair price, a few thousand dollars, I forget exactly what. Angotti got his paving business, leaving me with what I wanted, the sand and gravel.

At that time, the Toronto Housing Commission was building a lot of houses on Runnymede, with preference given to returned men. Irene and I applied and were accepted. The price for a three-bedroom house was $4,200 with 10 per cent down. The balance, including taxes, carried for about $80 every 3 months. The house wasn't ready until a year after we were married, but after living in the apartment a few months, I wanted to be closer to the sand pit; so we rented a small house on Colbeck Street, near Jane.

Two things stick in my mind from that period. One was a paving job for Laidlaw Lumber. I think it was the first one I'd bid for on my own. We went into his yard at noon and when we came out that evening with the job done, I'd made a thousand dollars. I phoned Bob Laidlaw and said, "Look, I made more money on this job than I figured I would. I must have charged you too much."

He just laughed. "You gave me a price and I accepted it, Connie," he said. "If you made some extra, count that as a wedding present." I was lucky enough to meet people like that all my life, along with quite a few skunks. And maybe my offer to give him a lower price had some influence on the fact that years later when I was raising money for charities, or crippled children, or even putting together the money to build Maple Leaf Gardens, I could always count on Bob Laidlaw.

One other memory of that time was irritating, though. Harvey Aggett's father came out to have a look at our new house, before it was finished. I overheard him saying to someone else, "Surely Connie could have done better for Irene than this little bandbox." But then he was a plumber, and as everybody knows, plumbers are sometimes a rich and uppity bunch. When we moved into our house, we loved it – and it's still there today, worth more than twenty times what we paid for it. Not a bad bandbox.

Things moved rather rapidly for us after we were married. Irene was soon pregnant and Stafford was born after a winter in which I was out coaching or just watching hockey more than I was home holding Irene's hand. Daytimes, I worked hard at the sand pit. Of course, we lacked all the proper equipment. I would shovel gravel onto an old bed spring to sift it when we were loading our truck. I remember something then that taught me a lesson. There was a man always hanging around looking for a job. I had a thing against him because he had not been in uniform during the war. I kept turning him down. But one day I was standing down in the pit shovelling gravel into this old bed spring and he was standing up on the edge, sort of forlorn, watching me. I was worn out. It was a busy day. Finally I yelled up to him, "Come on down here and grab a shovel. Let's see what you can do!"

Well, he came down and picked out the biggest shovel we had and started to work. He had a job with me from that minute on. His name was Chubb. He lived in Weston. It turned out that he had a lot of things wrong with his insides that got him rejected by the Army, but it sure didn't hamper the way he worked. When he drove the truck he'd be out and back in record time to take out the next full one we'd loaded when he was away. He was the best worker I had. Ever since then I've believed that the way to hire a man is to try him, see how he works out. All the testing and recommendations and work records people use today in hiring aren't as good as just putting a man on the job and seeing what he does. Of course, you have to be able to fire him if it doesn't work out, which is often the problem today.

By then I had a second truck. I looked for one secondhand, found it, and told the man I'd pay him half down and the rest in six months, with no interest.

He said he couldn't do business that way.

"Then keep your truck," I said.

He thought it over and sold me the truck. I paid, as promised, and had it painted blue and white like the other truck – Maple Leaf colours years before there was a team called the Maple Leafs.

I remember sometimes a truck or two used to be parked in front of our place on Runnymede. One day I went out when a couple of kids were reading the sign. One said, "What's that mean, C. Smythe for Sand?"

The other kid said, "Crazy Smythe, for sand." They both broke up laughing, and I did, too.

Those were good days. Long days. The phone might start ringing at 5:00 in the morning, from my foreman at the pit. Irene always answered the phone and took the orders. I'd eat breakfast and get out on the road selling, checking jobs, looking for business. To get around, I still had that 1915 Ford with the solid rubber tires. As everyone knows who's old enough to have ridden on solid tires, they give a really rough ride. As I mentioned, the car's top was rotten and wouldn't go up. The floor boards were in about the same shape. One time I was driving up Church Street with Art Boyd. We were bouncing along over the cobblestones when the floor on Art's side fell out. There's Art with his feet hanging right down on the road.

"What do I do now?" he asked. "Start running?"

One rainy day Irene and I went to a wedding in that Ford. To keep the rain off her hat, Irene sat holding an umbrella.

Irene had to be near the phone and the baby all day, but neither of us minded the hours, or what we were doing. We both knew we were doing it to help make the kind of life we wanted for ourselves and our family. I had a rule all our married life that I'd take her out for dinner at least once a week; once a week also to a movie or the theatre. It's a pretty good way to keep a marriage going, I think, when the woman knows that there are going to be those breaks in the hard work of running a house, raising kids, and – as Irene did then – running to the phone and writing down orders for sand and gravel. We didn't eat at the expensive places, or buy the most expensive theatre seats, but we went out. There was a Stoodleigh restaurant on Bay and another on King. They were middle-priced places. Later, when we were in the money we'd go to the King Edward Hotel on King, which at the time was the best meal in town. Sometimes we would take a trip on a summer evening across the Lake to Niagara and back, on the steamer that used to make that run, with music and dancing. It cost about $1.50 per person, which I could generally afford.

Looking back now and sorting out the first seven years of the 1920's, I can only conclude that I was blessed again with an unerring kind of luck, or fate. My business was growing, I was spending the winters watching hockey, and my home life was perfect. Irene gave me a great deal of love, and the peace of always knowing that she was home doing her job while I was out doing mine. She was a full-time mother and wife, with our new baby, Miriam, to look after as well as Stafford and me. When I got home and young Stafford took a run and jump into my arms to hug me, with Irene right behind him, life just couldn't have been better. I am all for the soft and loving kind of woman. Any man who doesn't have that kind of a wife doesn't know what he is missing. Irene made me feel like a lion.

She had school friends living not far away and kept in touch with her parents. Her mother was one of those quiet typically English wives, a slave to her husband who treated her like a dog.

I worked one way or another every day of the week, but enjoyed it. Some Sunday mornings I played golf. A few years later I joined Summit Golf and Country Club at least partly because among the members were two of my best customers: Willmott Legge, vice-president and general manager of Warren Paving (then called Warren Bituminous Paving Company of Ontario Limited) and Arthur Ridler, vice-president of Constructing and Paving Co. Ltd. I'd play with one of them, sometimes both, every Sunday morning. Every big job they landed, I got the sand and gravel business from them. To handle it, I kept on buying trucks and other equipment until I had quite a fleet operating out of that sand pit – loaders, crushers, and so on. I used to spend a lot of time there myself. So did Frank Selke, who had come to Toronto and was involved with me in hockey, at first part-time and then full-time. One of the first times I really landed on Frank Selke for disloyalty, which became one of his problems as far as I was concerned, was right there. I had bawled hell out of a man for some stupid thing he'd done, and I was in a little sort of a tower above the operation when I heard Selke telling the man that I didn't mean everything I said, my bark was worse than my bite, and so on. You know Selke, the old soft soap. I heard every word. I wish I had a tape of what I said to Selke when I stormed down to straighten him out.

Some things I started then haven't changed, but many have. I banked at Queen and Ossington, the Dominion Bank, and stayed with that branch a long time. I always knew exactly where I stood financially. It was almost all cash in and cash out. A man named Westwater, who'd been a sergeant in the 48th Highlanders, kept my books. He wouldn't take anything for it, at first, said he just wanted to keep his hand in at bookkeeping while he was doing some other kind of job at the Post Office. He'd come two or three times a week and do the books in a room we cleared down in the cellar. I paid cash for wages and pretty well everything else, except gas and oil from Imperial Oil, paid by the month. When I needed it, I found that my credit was good. One time I had to get something printed in a hurry and didn't have the money to pay for it. Nobody in the printing place, Rapid Grip and Batten, knew me. For a while I thought I wasn't going to get the job done. Then one of the partners came out and I mentioned that my father used to do business with them.

"Smythe?" the man asked. "Was that your father, who used to work at one of the papers and run that Theosophist magazine?"

I told him it was.

It turned out that years earlier, the magazine got into difficulties and folded owing the printing firm some money. Eventually they wrote off the debt. Eighteen years later my father came in to pay the bill. They told him thanks, but the debt had been written off, he didn't have to worry about it. Dad insisted on paying anyway. The man who was talking to me, one of the owners, told me this. Then he turned to the other man at the counter and said, "Give Mr. Smythe anything he wants, he'll be good for it." That was because my father had been honest with them. That kind of reputation is the best thing in the world a man can have.

In old pictures of Varsity hockey in those days I'm shown with some pretty good teams – Intercollegiate champions, Allan Cup finalists, the 1927 Allan Cup winner (the Varsity Grads, who also won the 1928 Olympics). Always I am listed as honorary coach. These days when the word honorary is attached to a job, it often means a person who gives mainly moral support. In my case, the word honorary meant that I did not get paid for coaching. Almost every winter night after close of business in the sand pit I was out either coaching or scouting other teams. Hap Day was taking pharmacy then. I wanted him badly to sign with the Varsity team. He played a couple of games with us and was a standout, head and shoulders above some pretty good guys. I went one night to a place on McCaul Street where he was living with about six other fellows from the university, and almost got him to agree, but he needed money badly right then and might have had to leave school if he didn't make some somewhere. Toronto St. Patricks of the NHL made him a good offer which he accepted. Years later when we converted St. Pats into the Maple Leafs he and Ace Bailey were about the only two real hockey players we got in that deal.

Besides the intercollegiate games, sometimes I would take teams to the United States for games with colleges there, especially in the Boston area – with Boston College, Princeton, Harvard. It was that particular experience that eventually took me into pro hockey all the way.

In 1924 Boston Bruins had joined the NHL, the league's first expansion into the States. On our trip there that season, I think in the Christmas break, I managed to start what became nearly a lifelong feud with Art Ross, who was coaching the Bruins for owner Charles Adams. They only won two games in the first half of the thirty-game schedule, and when I arrived with the Varsity team somebody asked me what I thought of the Bruins. I said my Varsity team could handle them anytime, anywhere. I guess if someone did that to me in Toronto I'd be mad, too. Ross was furious. He never really got over it. Our three college games that trip were so good that we packed Boston Garden for the first and second games, winning both, and for the third one they had to call mounted police to handle the crowds outside who couldn't get in on game night. We won that one, too.

A year later when the Boston franchise was pulling good crowds the league added another U.S. team, the New York Americans. The Americans did so well at Madison Square Garden that the Garden decided a second New York team would draw well, too. In March of 1926 the New York Rangers were born, owned by the Garden with Colonel John Hammond in charge. He had the franchise, but no team, and was looking for someone to put one together. Charles Adams of Boston told him, "There's a fellow called Smythe in Toronto who brings in college teams that are just about as good as mine. Why don't you give him a try?"

That spring I'd coached Toronto Varsity to the Intercollegiate championship and a place in the Allan Cup final against Port Arthur. We lost that, largely due to Port Arthur's big beetle-browed goalkeeper, Lorne Chabot. About the same time Hammond's offer to me arrived and I jumped at it. I signed for several years at a salary plus expenses, to go out and find him a team that I then would manage, according to the contract, when the season began. It was the chance to move into bigtime hockey that I had been waiting for.

Also, it had another effect. When Irene first heard about the offer, she wanted to know if that meant we were going to leave

Toronto. I said no, our home and family and business were here. Still, she was doubtful. I knew sometime soon we would need a bigger house. I made up my mind fast, at least partly to reassure Irene. We would start on it now. I've always been pretty good at asking advice of people who know what they're talking about. I asked Home Smith, a big builder and financier of that period. He told me, "Buy location. Houses change, but locations don't."

Within days, Irene and I chose a beautiful deep lot running back from Baby Point Road through big trees into a ravine. Roper Gouinlock said he thought he could bring in the kind of house we wanted for about $15,000. He only missed by $502.94, plus his own architect's fee. An actual start on what was to be our lifelong home was still several months away, but moving as fast as we had was the best way I could tell Irene that no matter where I had to go on business, the Smythe family was in Toronto to stay.

I knew every hockey player in the world right then. I'd been going to Toronto St. Patricks games for years and was familiar with players on the seven teams then in the NHL – Montreal Canadiens, Boston, Montreal Maroons (formed, like Boston, in 1924), Ottawa, Toronto, New York Americans, and Pittsburgh. Also, I had a pretty good line on players in the Western Hockey League, which was very close to NHL calibre – Victoria had beaten Canadiens in the 1925 Stanley Cup, and lost to Maroons in 1926. The Western League was folding. A lot of those players were on the loose. Other teams were after them, too; including the new franchises just granted to Detroit and Chicago. But the real edge I had on other NHL managers was that for years I'd been coaching amateur hockey, watching men on the way up. Some who were playing senior or semi-pro hockey, I knew, were good enough for the NHL. There isn't a man today who could do what I did then. One of the first players I went for was Chabot from Port Arthur, who had convinced me that a big goalie was better than most small ones – and most pro goalies then were small. Then I went to Minneapolis to watch the playoffs in the old semi-pro league there. Two veteran defencemen in that league I really wanted: Ching Johnson, from Winnipeg, twenty-eight (he claimed then – he was really older) and Taffy Abel, twenty-seven, born in Sault Ste. Marie, Michigan.

Both were tough bargainers. I must have reached agreement with Ching Johnson forty times. Each time, when I gave him my pen to sign, he'd say, "I just want to phone my wife." Then there'd be a hitch and he wouldn't sign. In my final meeting with him I said before we started, "Ching, I want you to promise that if we make a deal you will sign, and *then* you'll phone your wife."

He promised. We made a deal. He said, "I've got to phone my wife." I said, "You promised!" He said, "Okay, Connie," and signed.

Abel was even tougher. Finally on the day I was leaving by train I got him to come down for one last talk in my stateroom. He kept holding back. We were still talking when the train made a lurch, starting up. I jumped to the door, locked it, and stood in front of it. "Taffy," I said, "the money's good, you won't do better, and the next stop is two hundred and fifty miles away. If you don't sign, you won't be getting off this train until then." He signed, ran down the corridor, and jumped off the moving train.

They were the toughest ones. On some better-known players, I had a lot of competition. I remember one time having lunch, or something, with James Strachan of the Maroons. We both were after one player, I forget who. "Everything you offer, I'll do better, Connie," Strachan advised me. "You can't win."

He was right that time, but I was determined to get even. Two of the best players anywhere then were Bill and Bun Cook, who'd been with Saskatoon in the Western Canada League. They were on their way east to see Strachan when I intercepted them in Winnipeg and signed them for bonuses totalling $5,000, $3,500 to Bill and the rest to Bun. Bill told me there was a centre named Frank Boucher who'd been playing in Vancouver, had been sold that spring to Boston, and would be a good centre for the Cooks. I wired Colonel Hammond to buy Boucher from Boston, which he did, but I got a shock when I met Boucher a little later at the Ottawa railroad station. He only weighed 135 pounds. I told him Bill Cook must have gone crazy, to recommend him, but to report to Toronto anyway for Rangers' training camp.

Putting that whole team together, mostly of men who'd never played pro hockey before, cost the Rangers only a total of $32,000. I filled out the team with Reg Mackey, a defenceman to spell Johnson and Abel (good defencemen would play forty-five minutes or more, those days), and a second forward line of Murray Murdoch, Paul Thompson, and Billy Boyd. Murdoch never missed a game for Rangers in the next eleven years. Thompson was a star for Chicago after a few years of playing second fiddle to the Boucher-Cook line in New York. Actually, I hired two complete teams, one for the Rangers and one for their farm team at Springfield, which won American League championships for the next two or three years in a row. The only player I failed to get who I really wanted was Mike Goodman, a beautiful skater and scorer from the west, who simply didn't want to play in the NHL, and never did.

Rangers weren't a bad team, I guess. They won their division that first year, third overall in the ten-team league. In their second year they won the Stanley Cup. But by then I was long gone from the Rangers.

If I'd been a politician, I would have stuck with them. But I was no politician. The word was getting around that the Rangers couldn't be much, because so few of them had ever played pro hockey. I wasn't worried. I knew the calibre of the rest. But Colonel Hammond didn't. Babe Dye had been a big scorer with Toronto St. Pats for years. He was offered to me, and I turned him down. Colonel Hammond phoned me and practically ordered me to sign Dye. I refused. "He wouldn't help this team one day," I said. He wasn't my kind of player, too much the individualist, not enough of a team man. That was partly why St. Pats were such a lousy team – even though they also had Ace Bailey and Hap Day playing for them.

Anyway, after enough other big wheels in the NHL kept telling Hammond that he should have picked up Dye when he had the chance (instead of letting him be sold to Chicago), I guess he thought he'd better replace me with someone more likely to do what he was told. By mid-October I had the Rangers working out in Ravina Gardens in west Toronto, all staying at a hotel near the rink, when I got a call to meet Colonel Hammond at the railroad station. When he got off the train and walked down the platform Lester Patrick was with him. I got the message. Hammond offered me $7,500 to settle my contract, and told me Patrick would take over from there. I thought he owed me $10,000, the way the contract read, but I was so downcast I took the $7,500.

To say that I was shattered was putting it mildly, but I didn't stay shattered for long. The Toronto club had been sagging for years and with about a month to go before the season started was still looking around for somebody to run the team. I went to the owners, one of them a man I admired, Jack Bickell. I told him I could run the club the way it should be run. Eventually the directors decided that my lack of pro experience was against me, and hired Mike Rodden, a sportswriter and referee who was a disaster. I think Jack Bickell was on my side but the other owners weren't. He was the best businessman I ever knew in Canada, controlled McIntyre mine and a lot of other big companies, and his liking for my way of doing things was important to me later on.

Even fired by Rangers, and turned down by St. Pats, I was by no means out of hockey. My Varsity Allan Cup finalists of the previous spring had graduated, and had agreed to stay with me and play senior as the Varsity Grads. Also, I was coaching their successors on the Intercollegiate team. I was busy enough around the end of that eventful month, with the firing by New York still giving me some sleepless nights, when one day in the mail I got a letter from the Rangers. It was from Tex Rickard, president of Madison Square Garden then. I'd met him a few months before and I guess something I did had impressed him, not in hockey, but in boxing. He had introduced me to Gene Tunney as the next heavyweight champion of the world. At the time, Tunney had a title fight coming up with Jack Dempsey in Philadelphia, and part of my recruiting for the Rangers had been to take a few players and prospects to Philadelphia at Ranger expense to see the fight. Chatting with Rickard before the fight, I told him I'd taken his advice and bet on Tunney.

"What advice?" he said, looking thunderstruck.

"That he'd be the next heavyweight champion," I said.

"Oh, God!" Rickard said. "Yeah, but not *tonight*!"

Of course, after Tunney upset Dempsey that night I was collecting my bets, and Rickard wasn't collecting anything.

Anyway, now he was inviting Irene and me to Rangers' home opener against the Stanley Cup champion Montreal Maroons, a couple of weeks later. He said a hotel had been arranged for us and there would be a number of other functions, including tickets to see Mary Pickford and other Broadway shows. For the game itself, we were invited to sit in Rickard's own box.

I read the letter, tossed it to Irene, and said, "Well, we're sure not going to that!"

She glanced at it quickly. "Oh, yes, we are!" she flared. "It'll help make up for all the nights I spent alone when you were out with hockey."

She wasn't referring particularly to the few months putting the Rangers together, but to the years before – the winter nights she'd spent alone, looking after Stafford and Miriam – while I was coaching or watching games.

I thought it was over, looking at her and realizing. "Okay," I said. "You win. We go."

It was luck again, and this time she'd made it for me.

I was still a little truculent on the train to New York. By then it was mostly about being chiselled on my contract, $7,500 instead of $10,000. Irene and I walked in and sat down in Tex Rickard's box, while the team I'd put together warmed up at one end of the rink, Maroons at the other. Lester Patrick had added a couple of players, a veteran from Edmonton in goal, Hal Winkler, who later played eight games before he was sold to Boston, and a forward named Oliver Reinikka, who didn't last long.

There was no doubt New York owners and fans were rather in awe of the Maroons, against these unknown Rangers. One newspaper that day had a headline that read: WORLD'S BEST MEETS WORLD'S WORST TONIGHT IN GARDEN.

"Well, Connie," Rickard said to me, "do you think we can hold the score in single digits against these guys?" It was his way of asking, could we hold them to nine goals?

"Hold 'em, nothing!" I said. "You'll beat 'em!"

Indirectly, I think it's true to say that that remark took me eventually into the NHL as a minority shareholder in the Toronto franchise only a few months later. Rangers won the game 1-0, Bill Cook flipping a puck over Clint Benedict after a goalmouth pass from his brother Bun. Maroons, faced with being disgraced by an untried bunch (but what an untried bunch!) got mean and nasty and took a lot of penalties. Even Frank Boucher, later a perennial Lady Byng trophy winner as hockey's gentleman, got into a couple of big fights. The crowd, and Rickard, were delighted. As the game ended, I could see Rickard eyeing me. "Could you come to my office tomorrow morning?" he asked.

I could. When I got there he said, "Anybody as shrewd about this game as you were putting that team together, we need. I want you to be our vice-president, hockey."

"I wouldn't work for you bunch of cheapskates if you gave me the franchise," I said.

He almost fell of his chair. "What?" he said. "What the . . .? What do you mean, cheapskates?"

I told him about Hammond short-changing me $2,500 on my contract. He called in Hammond, who explained that since I hadn't moved my home to New York, my expenses had been lower. He thought the $7,500 was about right.

"Pay this young man what we owe him," Rickard said.

Hammond went back to his office and came back with the cheque. When we started home from the Rangers' opener, we went by way of Montreal where there was a college football game I wanted to see, the eastern intercollegiate semi-final between Varsity and McGill. Varsity had been beaten by Queen's the week before and there was a lot of McGill money around. I bet my new-found $2,500 on Varsity. They won, doubling my money. That same night Rangers were playing in Toronto. Mike Rodden had opined that St. Pats would handle them all right, that Rangers' good opener against Maroons had been just one of those flukes. I didn't think so. I bet Rangers. When they won 5-1, I had built that $2,500 into $10,000 in just three days, from November 17 to November 20. It just about paid for our new house, and all because Irene insisted on those few days in New York.

We weren't long home from that New York-Montreal trip before there was another turnaround. A month earlier, St. Pats hadn't thought I had the right kind of experience to run their team. Now that the story was out about how I'd built the Rangers, who went straight to the top of their division and stayed there, things were a little different. Jack Bickell called me and asked if I'd consider taking over the team. But their attitude wasn't the only factor that had changed. I said I'd only run the team if I could buy it, or part of it. I was only thirty-two, but thinking small was never one of my failings. Incidentally, I held none of this against Jack Bickell, one of the best and straightest men who ever lived – as he was about to prove.

It didn't happen all at once, but in the next six or eight weeks most of St. Pats' owners decided they wanted out. There was an offer from Philadelphia for $200,000 but I argued strenuously with everybody who would listen, including the newspapers, that if Toronto lost its NHL franchise it might be a long time before we got another. Bickell assured me that if I could match the Philadelphia offer, they'd give me the edge. I didn't have more than a fraction of the money myself, but I pounded on doors and lined up some others. I also talked often with Jack Bickell. He listened and finally he said, "I've got about $40,000 in the club. If you can round up the $160,000 to pay off the others, I'll leave my money in on the understanding that you'll take over the team." I agreed. Late in January I put down $10,000 for an option to purchase. On February 14, 1927, a Monday night, the new investors I'd rounded up met with the owners, and we paid another $75,000 and undertook to pay the remaining $75,000 in thirty days.

The next day, February 15, the Globe's headline about the deal carried a subhead: Goodbye, St. Pats!

Howdy, Maple Leafs

Another subhead read that the club had changed hands, names, and colours. I had a feeling that the new Maple Leaf name was right. Our Olympic team in 1924 had worn maple leaf crests on their chests. I had worn it on badges and insignia during the war. I thought it meant something across Canada, while St. Patricks didn't – a name hatched originally merely in an attempt to attract the Irish population in Toronto.

I was named to be Toronto's governor on the NHL board, but also I was busy with the two amateur teams, Varsity and the Grads, both good enough to contend for the Allan Cup. Because of that, we put in Alex Romeril as manager of the Leafs until I was finished with Varsity. The only thing I did right away was tell Romeril to move Hap Day from forward to defence, where he was a star from the start, although the new Leafs lost their first game under the new name and kept right on staggering to the end of the season.

But I had my hands full. My Varsity Grads had won the eastern senior championship, and my college team the intercollegiate. Under the playoff system of the time, they were supposed to play off to see which team represented the east in the Allan Cup. I'd had to beat off a move from people at the university earlier that if I was going to coach the Grads, I couldn't coach the Varsity team. Now I was right up against it. Both my teams were on top, and supposed to play one another. However, it was getting near exam time and some of the college players were worried about taking two weeks off school for the Allan Cup, which was in Vancouver; with a week of games and three-day train rides each way. We talked it over and the college team withdrew after I promised that if we won the Cup, I'd add two from the college team – Dick Richards and Wes Kirkpatrick – to the Grads for the Olympics at St. Moritz the following winter. I give this in some detail, because it was a promise I wasn't allowed to keep.

I thought we'd handle Fort William easily in the Allan Cup. It was supposed to be a three-game series. Dave Trottier had to score in the last minute of overtime (not sudden death) to give us a 2-2 tie in the first game. They won the second. We took the third, so had to play a fourth. That one might have ended in a tie as well, but Ross Taylor scored the winner for us late in the last overtime period on a beautiful pass from Charlie Delahey. When the whistle went, I jumped to the ice and hugged Jack Porter, our captain, and threw my hat high in the air. Incidentally, then and later for a few years with the Leafs, I was a poor coach. I got too emotionally involved to make the kind of calm, quick decisions a good coach should make. My forte as a coach might have been in something else. In the full page coverage the *Toronto Star* ran on the final game of the series, sports editor W. A. Hewitt used my picture with a cutline that said my "uncanny" ability at handling and motivating players had led to the championship.

I guess I should add one footnote. I'd thought it would be a breeze against Fort William and we'd just barely got through, so when the players had a big party I went along with it. I hadn't been a drinking man before, but I got pretty high and then I got sick; just got over to the basin in the hotel room before I let go. I had never felt so rough. I said, if that is what drinking is, it isn't for me. Except for the odd glass of champagne from a Stanley Cup, I stuck to that decision for the rest of my life.

We got home to a huge welcome. The train was held up for three hours near Toronto so that we wouldn't arrive before the victory parade that noon, all the way from the station to the university. But all the glowing speeches didn't mean much a few months later, when I was overruled on my promise that I'd add at least two college players when I took the Grads to the Olympics. In those days Canada just had to show up to win, but I have never forgiven the pressure play put on by a couple of the Grads' players, goalie Joe Sullivan, now a senator, and forward Hugh Plaxton, to have some of their relatives on the team instead of Wes

Kirkpatrick and Dick Richards, the college players I had in mind. "If Wes and Dickie don't go, I don't go," I said.

Some of the other Grads felt the same way, Ross Taylor for one. But I said this was my fight, not theirs, and told them to go, which they did. When I refused, W. A. Hewitt took the team to St. Moritz to win the Olympics the following winter, while I embarked on my first season as manager of the Leafs.

As time went on, I came to see that losing the Ranger job was a blessing. Lester Patrick did a better job in New York than I ever could have. I wouldn't have had Irene and our family with us because when I do a job I want to do it whole-hog, unencumbered, not weighed down by worries of moving a whole family to a new environment. Also, I've seen what happens to other men who go to New York and can't handle all the wine, women, and song. In time I came to see that Colonel Hammond had done me a favour by firing me.

But I wasn't thinking much about that then, trying instead to make something of the Leafs in the season of 1927-28. When I looked at what I had, I wished I hadn't signed all those hotshots from the sticks to Ranger contracts, and had saved a few for myself. Rangers won the Stanley Cup which made it, in effect, my first Stanley Cup. When I was kidded about "my" Rangers coming first and my Leafs last, I vowed publicly that I would put together another Stanley Cup team, this time in Toronto. I said I'd do it within five years, and I just made it.

Chapter Five

When others have written books, magazine articles, and I guess thousands of newspaper columns and stories about my early years with the Leafs, most of the ink usually goes to player deals I made, fights I had with referees and others, and the so-called miracle of building Maple Leaf Gardens in the depths of the Depression with almost all workmen and contractors taking part of their money in Gardens' shares. But that was only part of my life. In hockey, everything I said or did seemed to become headlines. Maybe it was inevitable that my really solid source of income, the one that would have supported my family even if I'd never stepped inside a hockey rink, didn't get much publicity. There were no headlines saying, SMYTHE ADDS FOUR SECONDHAND TRUCKS TO GROWING GRAVEL FLEET; nor, FAMILY HOME ON BABY POINT FULLY PAID FOR, NICE PLACE TO COME HOME TO, SAYS SMYTHE. But I had a private side that few knew about, then or ever.

As our household and family grew, everything got just a little easier, more comfortable. My first new car had been a 1925 Ford roadster to replace the old 1915 flivver. In 1926 I traded the roadster on a Franklin sedan and in the spring of 1929 turned that over to Irene and bought myself a classy Stearns-Knight cabriolet roadster with wire wheels and front fender wells for the two spares, which had shiny chrome covers with mirrors mounted on them. I felt pretty good driving that thing downtown, or to the race track, with Irene beside me. We both hugely enjoyed what we were making happen. We went to a wedding one day and Irene laughed, "Nice that I don't have to sit in front with an umbrella to keep off the rain."

I was on the road a lot in winter, of course. I travelled with the Leafs wherever they went. It was quite a circuit in those days. There was my feud with Art Ross in Boston. Big Bill Dwyer in New York owned the Americans and a lot of racehorses and travelled with a lot of shady-looking people. Benny Leonard in Pittsburgh was always good for a few laughs; a boxer running a hockey team. In Detroit the club, called the Cougars then, was owned by Charlie Hughes. He was in the theatre business and seemed to have a limitless supply of show girls in his suite when he'd ask other NHL governors to dinner – although you had to understand that many of the girls "belonged" to somebody and were friendly but untouchable by anybody else. I was getting my eyes opened to the big world out there, while Irene was left with most of the job of raising the family.

When I got home there was always the catching up to do, both in our love life and in such matters as who needed a new coat or new shoes. We went out with friends or had them to our place, which Irene had decorated in ways both of us liked – polished floors or good rugs, solid and comfortable furniture, pictures of our family around. The house was much bigger than our first, of course. Some of what we had to buy was new, but in the living room fifty years later I could touch a table, and remember us buying it at an auction for $22.

There was always a lot to laugh about in those days, in Irene's stories and mine, but sometimes it was not a laugh. I got home one night and told her about a broadcaster in Chicago, new to hockey, who had ended a rave about the kind of show we were putting on by saying, deadly serious, "Hockey is a game that is never won, until the last man is out!" She laughed, then told me that when I was away one night Stafford ran into the house crying about some big kid down the street who'd beaten him up. Irene said to him quietly, "You have to fight your own battles, Stafford." He ran out of the house with tears streaming down his cheeks and climbed furiously into that guy, who never laid a finger on him again. In fact, that might have been a bad thing; from then on Stafford was the leader on the street and he was rarely good at choosing his friends. If there were two boys, one straight and good at everything and the other a born trouble maker, Stafford would hang out with the trouble maker every time. If somebody in the neighbourhood had a window broken, the chances were Stafford had been in the crowd responsible. But he never backed down from what he had done. He took his medicine. I never had any question about his guts.

Miriam, two years younger, was pretty as a picture. Hughie, born just nine months after we moved into the house on Baby Point (he enjoyed that arithmetic when he worked it out), was the nicest little boy anybody ever had, thoughtful and gentle. Sometimes I'd take Hughie with me in the car to see my father. It was usually just a quick visit, because I couldn't stand Janie's company for long. At Christmas, dad and Janie and Moira would come for dinner, as would Irene's parents. Her father was a heavy drinker. One Christmas he bought as a present a stupid, untrained dog that managed to stink out the house before he'd been there half an hour. At the time we didn't serve anything stronger than soft drinks, so Mr. Sands would get stoked up before he came. I guess I let him go to it for Irene's sake. My own family was sober. Moira says that she was in awe, even scared of me, but that Christmas with us was a happy time with nice presents and great turkey and pies and puddings. I really loved Christmas, joking with the children and kidding dad about everything from his religion to his vegetarianism. Moira says that I bought her her first pair of skates. I don't remember that, but it sounds right. Anything for a kid that dad couldn't buy in a bookstore, he didn't buy. Moira also says that from when she was eleven or twelve, around 1930 or so, I always sent the money so she could go to summer camp. I don't remember that, either, but maybe deep down it had something to do with my own childhood.

My father suffered a financial disaster about that time. A smooth operator named Dr. J. C. Moodie was in Toronto selling stock in an Alberta oil well. Dad put everything he had into it and thought I should invest, as well. I always went by the idea that if I didn't have the money to pay for anything unessential, I couldn't afford it. I didn't have the ready cash so I told Dr. Moodie that I'd take some and pay him at the end of the following month. He said he couldn't do business that way. I told him what he could do with his stock. When the project failed, my dad's savings went down the drain and eventually his house as well. I was told later by a friend at Imperial Oil that there was oil on the Moodie property, all right, but so deep in the ground that the technology of the time couldn't get at it.

Funny thing, though. From when I was a kid dad was always after me about gambling, but he didn't mind taking a flyer on any hole in the ground that somebody who looked respectable called an oil well, or a gold mine. In the early 1930's I gambled a lot. I have some scribbled notes headed, "Wagers, 1931." It was a single sheet of paper and ran from spring to fall. One early win was noted: "Won $2,000 on Caryldon." And others: "Aug. 12, win, Poet's Dream, $4,000." "Sept. 3, Caryldon, $2,000 again." But later I lost at $1,000 and at $440 on Caryldon. I never had anything against gamblers. They are straighter than a lot of people. There used to be a great gambling area in one part of the Gardens, known as the bull ring. I welcomed gamblers there as long as they didn't get in trouble with the law and indirectly bring bad publicity to the Gardens. Once a gambler was arrested at the Gardens. I immediately lifted his season tickets and barred him from the place. The phone rang off the hook from his friends saying I shouldn't do that to such a nice guy, who gave a lot to charity, and so on. So I called him into my office one day.

"They tell me you're a great man for charity," I said. "You bring me receipts for what you've given to charity in the last year or so, and I'll give you your tickets back."

He just looked at me and slunk out. I never heard from him again.

With the big house and the growing family to look after, Irene needed hired help. At first we had a succession of Finnish housekeepers who, it seemed to me, never worked more than a month before they wanted a raise in pay. Either that or they didn't suit Irene. One day in 1931 Irene put an ad in the paper for another housekeeper. A few days later, Jessie Watson, a young woman born on a farm between what is now Queensway and the Lakeshore in West Toronto, came to our back door. That proved to be a good day for the Smythe family. Somebody Jessie knew told her that she probably wouldn't like working for us. That was fifty years ago. Jessie brought neat good looks and a warm personality to our house and it was our luck, and some man's bad luck, that she never married. Our children loved her. When Stafford had the asthma attacks that began when he was small and plagued him all through his too-short life, Jessie would sit with him nights in a small second-floor bedroom fitted with a device to burn a medication whose fumes made his breathing easier. Miriam said not long ago that she can still smell that smoke. But Jessie stayed right in the room with him. Miriam, sometimes difficult to handle as a child, loved Jessie. Hughie would sit in the kitchen and talk to her by the hour and it was a mutual love that lasted. You don't get people like Jessie in your life right at the start. You have to keep trying.

As the years wore on, Jessie and Irene sometimes would do battle for territorial rights in the kitchen. Sometimes I had to act as referee. I mentioned before about loyalty and guts as qualities I cherish. Jessie has 'em both. She spoke her mind, yet was pretty crafty at waiting for the right moment; knowing when to persist in a suggestion and when to let the matter drop and bring it up later, when the chances looked better. I was very lucky with some people in my life; Jessie was one of the absolute best.

Now that Leafs are a national institution, some people tend to forget the way we started: a lousy team, $40,000 in debt, the shareholders giving themselves no better than a 50-50 chance of ever getting their money back, let alone a profit. The years also have tended to obscure the fact that in 1927 I hadn't yet proved anything about my ability as a pro hockey man. There hadn't been anything flukey about putting together the Rangers, but I hadn't actually handled them on the ice. In the spring of 1927, Leafs under Alex Romeril finished last in the five-team Canadian section of the NHL and didn't have five cents to buy better players unless we could sell or deal some of the ones we had. There were only two untouchables, as far as I was concerned, Hap Day and Ace Bailey.

That summer I got Hap Day to work with me at the sand pit. To make sure he'd stay I talked him into buying about 16 per cent of the business, which by then was incorporated as C. Smythe Limited. I wanted him with me summer as well as winter for a long time, which turned out to be one of my best decisions. He was one of the best men I ever met.

Working together that summer of 1927 we sold close to $100,000 worth of sand and gravel, and talked a lot of hockey. I let him in on deals I had in mind. He either backed me up or put in his two cents worth, and by the time we opened camp that October we had nine new guys in Leaf uniforms and even a little money in the bank from deals I'd made, sending players to Detroit, Chicago, and the Rangers. One other part of the new setup didn't work out exactly as I had planned. I insisted on Billy Barker being the Leafs' first president because of the gallant man he had been in wartime – Lt. Col. W. G. Barker, V.C., as he appeared on our first list. I thought that maybe a speech now and again from him in the dressing room would be good. Most of the players had missed the war, but certainly knew its most-decorated heroes. Many of the other directors had been in the war as well, but Barker was by far the most famous. However, he had trouble with alcohol. Trying to stay away from it he carried a case of ginger ale with him wherever he went, and when the impulse came he'd grab a ginger ale. But one night when I'd lined him up to visit the dressing room before an important game, he had to go to Hamilton. On the way he reached down for a ginger ale. There wasn't any. He went into a hotel instead and got plastered, then headed back to Toronto hellbent for Maple Leaf Gardens. On the way up Jarvis Street his car skidded and turned upside down. He showed up on time in the dressing room, clothes torn and covered with blood, and didn't give a bad speech, at all, on the importance of morale. I don't know how much it actually helped morale, but it probably did make a few guys think about the dangers of drinking and driving.

I made one bad deal a few months later, but Hap Day had nothing to do with that. Leafs were floundering and Art Ross acting as if he was making peace between us, convinced me that I needed a big draw, a proven NHL player with colour. He peddled me a real has-been, Jimmy (Sailor) Herberts, for $12,500. It wasn't long before I knew what a mistake I'd made, but getting out without losing Leafs' investment was another matter, rather exciting, besides being an indication of how rotten business sometimes can be.

I had an office downtown at 11 King Street West by that time, running both my contracting business and the Leafs from there. When Herberts first came to see me he brought his wife, a showy woman who wore very short skirts, which got shorter every time she moved around in her chair. Ed Bickle, a director of the Leafs, was in my office at the time. I'm afraid the short skirts sort of kept his mind off the topic at hand, which was that Herberts said he didn't want to play in Toronto because his wife didn't want him to play there. First time he came to the ice for us, he fell coming out of the gate, got mixed up, and lined up with the wrong team. The fans booed and his wife took offence. It wasn't long before I decided we had to get rid of him. Finally we got a nibble from Detroit. They were desperate. Herberts lived in Windsor, and I started to learn a little about selling. I called Charlie Hughes in Detroit and said, "Here's a fellow who will play much better nearer home because his wife doesn't like Toronto. Are you interested?"

"Well," he said, "we'll look at him in a few days when you play here."

Before that happened I spoke to several of my players and told them my plans. It was a question of life or death. If we didn't sell Herberts we might go broke and they wouldn't be paid and I wasn't going to have a job, and everything else, I said. Herberts had to look good. We must have passed the puck to him five hundred times that night and finally he scored two or three goals. Hughes said okay, he'd buy Herberts and send me a cheque the next week, which he did. I think it was for $15,000. But then early one morning in Toronto I got a call from Hughes.

"You get that cheque for Herberts?" he asked.

"Yes," I said. "Why?"

"You'd better get it right down here to the bank today," he said in a low voice. "We're going bust tomorrow."

A drive to Detroit in those days wasn't as easy or quick as it is today, but I got somebody into a car with the cheque, and we got the cheque to the bank and got our money. It was something I could never understand: the cheque was good today, but anybody turning up with a Cougars' cheque the next morning would be told it was no good. I've got no use for fakes. I appreciated what Charlie had done for me and we'd got our money. But I felt sorry for those who wouldn't.

Not all the players we used that year stuck. Some I sold and others went to the minors, but two were going to be around for awhile, Art Duncan and Joe Primeau. Joe only played a couple of games for us at the end of the season, but I liked him. That year, my first full one as an NHL coach, we finished fourth with a fairly respectable eighteen wins, eighteen losses, and eight ties. But I was still looking, and that next summer when Hap Day was limping around the sand pit recovering from a nearly severed Achilles tendon, we could see improvements coming. One of our weak spots was in goal, John Ross Roach. By that time I had fairly firmly in mind a rule about trades that Lester Patrick had told me: you never made a deal unless you got a better player than you were dealing off. He had to be better, argued Lester, because after you got him you had to train him in your system and make him fit in with your team. So it was a bit funny that the best deal I made before the next camp opened was to trade John Ross Roach to Lester for the goalie I'd signed for Rangers myself, and thought was one of the best, Lorne Chabot.

How it happened was that in the spring of 1928 that Ranger team I'd put together made it to the Stanley Cup final, a sensational achievement for a team in its second season. Leafs were out of the playoffs so I went to Montreal for the final, Rangers vs. Maroons. All games were being played in Montreal because Madison Square Garden had booked the circus in around playoff time. It always seemed to me a crazy deal to sell hockey all winter and then rob the fans of the chance to see the most exciting hockey of the season, the playoffs. But the circus was a big draw for weeks and for that reason was allowed to bar Rangers from their home ice at playoff time for many more years.

In the second game in Montreal, Chabot was hit in the left eye by a hard backhand shot from Nels Stewart. Chabot's eye was bleeding so badly that all they did was take off his equipment and send him to the hospital. In those days teams didn't carry spare goalies. Both teams went to their dressing rooms while Rangers tried to rustle up a replacement. Maroons wouldn't agree to let them use Ottawa goalie Alex Connell, who was in the crowd. Frank Boucher said later at one point in the great debate about who would go into goal, I rushed into the Ranger room and said, "Throw the nets on me! I'll play goal!" He said I was so excited that I said "nets" when I meant pads. But eventually Lester Patrick, who had played some goal before, but not much, got into dry underwear and Chabot's wet pads and went out to play goal. Rangers were so afraid that any shot on goal would go in that they checked Maroons right into the ice, won that game, and later two more – with Joe Miller from New York Americans in goal – to win the Stanley Cup.

Chabot didn't play again that season, and rumours began to circulate that Lester Patrick thought his eyesight, or his nerve to play goal, or both, might have been damaged permanently. I made some enquiries and found that Chabot didn't think these rumours were true. It looked like the chance I'd been waiting for. I asked Lester if he was interested in a trade for Chabot, involving our goalie, John Ross Roach. I knew what Chabot could do. He'd beaten my Varsity Intercollegiate champions for the Allan Cup in 1926, before I signed him for the Rangers. And in his second season he'd had ten shutouts before he was hurt. I wanted him badly, but Lester didn't come easily. He would deal only if I'd throw in Butch Keeling, one of the eight players I had left from the original Leafs. I said okay, so we got Chabot, for the 1928-29 season.

Then I dealt $8,000 cash and a player to Pittsburgh for Harold Cotton. I knew Cotton had guts, something we lacked. There's no way you can build a winner if you haven't got a lot of guts. The cash involved was high for that time, but still I might have been taking a little advantage of Benny Leonard, the ex-fighter, who was running the Pittsburgh team. Benny and I got along fine. Being a fighter, he thought all sports were crooked. One day in Pittsburgh we talked all one afternoon about hockey. He kept talking about "my turn." "Now, Mr. Smythe, I know what sport is like," he'd say. "I'm willing to do anything but I want to know when my turn comes." That night they were behind and tied it up with only about thirty seconds to go. He must have thought that I'd let them have that tie, or something, because he looked over at me and then waved up at the clock. The ten minutes overtime we were supposed to play, I don't think lasted much more than thirty seconds and he had his tie. I was glad to get a tie myself, but that's what he figured, that every game was crooked, the same as every fight was crooked. About the short overtime, well, timekeepers sometimes could be influenced in those days.

That autumn also we added Red Horner, up from the Marlboro Juniors, the greatest body checker I ever saw, and picked up Andy Blair, a classy player from Winnipeg. Andy had quite a bad stammer, or stutter. We often used to talk about game strategy in the dressing room. He was one of the most attentive listeners, I thought. One time in Ottawa that season he proved that at least he'd got the drift of what I was talking about. Some crazy referee gave us a string of penalties. That was before the days of the delayed penalty, and eventually we were down to only two players on the ice, Chabot in goal and Blair out front. Before the face-off Blair skated over to the bench and leaned over. I went to see what he wanted. "Ww-w-w-well, C-Conn," he said, "what's the s-s-s-s-strategy n-n-n-now?"

I won't go through all the player changes that we made from then on, but you get the idea. The next season we brought up Charlie Conacher from the juniors, and then Busher Jackson. After a few experiments we put Joe Primeau in as their centre. The famous Kid Line was born. But I must say right here that for all the goals they got and all-star teams they were on, Conacher and Jackson were never half as good players as they were thought to be. They wanted Joe to do all the work, and they'd score the goals, which they were pretty good at. But you have to play hockey in three spaces: your end, the middle, and their end. They didn't do it. I used to play their way myself when I was an amateur, so I knew what was wrong with it. I fought for years to keep Busher Jackson out of the Hall of Fame. I'm a hero worshipper myself and he wasn't a good enough person to earn the hero worship of kids. But they were an exciting line; and we became one of the highest scoring teams in hockey and seemed to be on our way. We still missed the playoffs in the spring of 1930. The real change in the Leafs came a few months later when we got King Clancy in the biggest hockey deal ever made up to that time – and we got him because of a horse race.

I have to go back a little bit to explain this. From when I was a boy going to the track with my father to run his stories back downtown, I'd been interested in the races. I had been interested in other forms of gambling as well, including poker, which some of us started to play in high school. One time in 1915 after I joined the Army I left Irene one night saying I had to get some sleep, had to get up early the next day. Somehow on my way home my need for sleep evaporated and I checked in to a poker game that I knew was going on above a Yonge Street store. The game was operated by a bugler from Dufferin race track, who would take a dollar out of the pot every so often as the house cut. It was worth about $25 a night to him. Among the players that night was a jockey named Watts who had a mount in the King's Plate and said his horse, Tartarean, was going to win it. We were raided a little later by the police and I remember thinking this might be a little difficult to explain to Irene if I was arrested as a found-in, but they let me go, perhaps because I was in uniform. A few weeks later I was in Ottawa, in the Army, when the Plate was run. I laid a bet on Tartarean with a bookie and won. I was so dumb then that I didn't know all jockeys always said their horses were going to win, but that worked out all right and later I'd made a little money from time to time, especially on long shots.

In the late 1920's I owned a horse or two, and thought it was a big deal to have the hockey team's blue and white and maple leaf crest on my racing silks. But I'd never won a race, or even owned a good horse. Then one day at Woodbine there was this horse owner named Mrs. L. A. Livingston, a big woman who always wore big hats and flowing gowns. She came from around Cobourg and in a race that day had entered a horse called The Monkey. In those days they called through the stands when a horse was scratched. I hear away down at one end the cry, "Scratch . . . Mrs. . . . Livingston's . . . MONKEY!" And it comes nearer and nearer, as other criers picked it up. "SCRATCH . . . MRS . . . LIVINGSTON'S . . . MONKEY!" Then I saw her sailing along in her big hat, looking embarrassed as hell, everybody laughing, while the yell goes right down the length of the stands "SCRATCH MRS. LIVINGSTON'S . . . MONKEY!" She never came back. Sold all her horses, and I bought a filly from her called Rare Jewel, for $250.

Just about that time, the Ottawa club in the NHL was in financial trouble, due to lack of support at the box office. They needed money so badly that they decided to sell their best player, King Clancy, then twenty-seven years old. He was not only one of the best defencemen in the league but one of the most colourful, lots of guts. The previous season he'd had seventeen goals and twenty-three assists, almost unheard-of for a defenceman at that time. Ottawa hated to let him go but let it be known he'd be available for the right offer of players and cash. I had the players but we were still playing in the Mutual Street Arena, and even though we filled it about half the time there weren't enough seats to give us much ready cash. With the Depression, the $35,000 Ottawa wanted was, it seemed, the one insuperable drawback. There was another, however. Among all the feuds Clancy had going around the league, helping to fill rinks everywhere but in Ottawa, one of the big ones was with Hap Day. We'd been assured that the last place Clancy wanted to play was Toronto. James Strachan and the Montreal Maroons were said to have the inside track. If we could come up with the cash, I was willing to take a chance that Clancy would play for us, but $20,000 or $25,000 was as high as our directors were prepared to pay. It was going to take a miracle to get the other $10,000. Which brings us back to Rare Jewel, in the autumn of 1930, just a few weeks before the hockey season.

Rare Jewel didn't look like much. She kept on running last. I'd given her to Bill Campbell to train. He had never saddled a winner at Woodbine, and didn't think Rare Jewel was going to change that for him. We sent her to Montreal where the competition wasn't supposed to be as tough. She ran dead last, so we brought her back. Before birth she had been nominated for one of the best two-year-old races, the Coronation Futurity, but Campbell and his partner, a gambling friend of mine named Dave Garrity, didn't want to enter her. I didn't know anything. Like a lot of people who own horses, I was full of blind hope. Dude Foden had been exercising her. After her last blowout that week he came back and told me he thought she was coming around. "It's worth a chance to enter her, Mr. Smythe," he said, and against Campbell's advice I went down and laid down the cash to get her into the race.

What I didn't know then, and they both denied it forever after, was something that happened just before the race. Campbell and Garrity didn't trust one another very much. Garrity waited until Campbell was away from the barn that day and then dashed into her stall and fed her half a flask of brandy. He didn't tell Campbell. But Campbell came back, saw Garrity leaving, and then went into the stall, where he also gave Rare Jewel half a flask of brandy. That was one horse who didn't have to fly on one wing.

Well, all this time I'm over at the grandstand, laying a few bets. I already had bet downtown at the King Edward Hotel a day earlier when I ran into a bookmaker friend. He figured if I was entering Rare Jewel I'd want to bet. I told him I wouldn't bet with him because bookies usually set their own limits on payoffs. "Ah, I'll give you track odds," he said. I guess he thought I was just contributing – making a token donation out of loyalty to my horse. I think it was $40 I bet with him. But as it got near race time I started worrying. R. W. R. Cowie's colt Frothblower was the favourite, carrying about 127 pounds to Rare Jewel's 112. I thought maybe I should put $60 accross the board on Frothblower just to protect myself. I was lined up at the pari mutuel window when Smirle Lawson came along. I'd fired him as Leafs' club doctor the previous spring because he'd told a good game guy with a broken leg that the leg wasn't broken, go out and play. When the guy couldn't skate on it I sent him for an X-ray. It was broken, all right. I told Lawson, "You might be all right as a coroner, Smirle, but for the living you're a dead loss. You're fired." There was still animosity between us as he clapped me on the back at the wicket and said, "Frothblower all the way, eh, Connie?"

I slapped down the money I'd been going to bet on Frothblower and said, "Sixty across on Rare Jewel!" I don't know how much that meant I had bet on her, but she was still the longest shot on the board. I used to watch races from the top of the old grandstand. I was running along the deck there as fast as Rare Jewel was when she came down the stretch. Dude later got fined and suspended three days for rough riding at the top of the stretch, but he got her home in front, though it turned out he'd told his wife, even, to bet $10 on Frothblower.

In those days they put up the numbers of the payoff by hand. In the win column they put up $14.40 and stopped. I thought somebody must have bet a bundle on Rare Jewel just before the windows closed, so that it hadn't showed in the final odds. Then the guy casually put up a 2 in front of the $14.40, making the payoff $214.40 straight, $46.75 place, and $19.95 show! I won between ten and eleven thousand dollars, besides the purse of $3,570. It was quite a day – the first time my colours had ever come down in front anywhere, the first time Bill Campbell had ever saddled a winner at Woodbine, and the longest mutuels price paid in Canada that year. When I went down to the King Edward to see my friend the bookie he could only pay me half of the $4,000 and change he owed me. I had to wait about two or three days before he could gather enough to give me the rest.

But most important of all, when I was telling the Jockey Club to give me a cheque for my bets instead of the cash, I was thinking *now, we can buy Clancy. Now, we are going to win the Stanley Cup.*

A day or so later, Frank Ahearn, one of the Ottawa partners, told me they'd already made a deal with Maroons for Clancy, but they hadn't. I asked Clancy about his prejudice against playing for Toronto. He said, "No, I would love to play in Toronto."

"You've got yourself a deal," I said. "What do you want to be paid?"

"Anything you say," he said. Anything you say! I never had

any trouble with Clancy about money in my life. He was the most *amateur* athlete I ever had. Just loved to play. And that's what Rare Jewel did for me. Somebody once said to me, "But you had the confidence to bet on her." I said, "I had the *ignorance!*" In those days I was like so many horse owners now or anytime; I felt that because I owned a horse, it was going to win.

I didn't have the whole $15,000 or so (the bet and the purse) by the time I made the deal. I gave the whole purse to the trainer and the rider, so more than Conn Smythe and the Toronto Maple Leafs benefited from that fantastic win. But I paid my $10,000 down and five cheques for $5,000 each, post-dated a week apart starting the following week. The price, $35,000 and two players, a young defenceman named Art Smith worth about $10,000 in the hockey market, and a forward named Eric Pettinger worth about $5,000, made it a total of about $50,000 for Clancy, the most paid for a hockey player to that time. Around the league, people wanted to buy tickets to see what kind of a hockey player was worth $50,000. Most people think of 1930 as the first year of the Depression, the year after the stock market crashed, unemployed, hard times. I always think of it as the year Leafs got King Clancy. I must have felt good about it all year, because early in December that year I went to V and S Motors on Sheppard Street, distributors for Stutz and Franklin cars, and ordered a Franklin Transcontinent Sedan to be delivered to our house on Christmas Eve, from me to Irene. Not that I had the money – I had to sign a couple of notes for $500 each due in March and May – but just because I felt so good about the future of the Leafs and of another plan that was to be another major event in my life.

A few months earlier I had started to talk up the idea that we needed a bigger and better arena to play in. I must have been pretty persuasive, at first mainly among people who didn't have any money to put in. We were in Montreal one day for a game with the Maroons. Greg Clark of the *Toronto Star* was in our room at the Mount Royal when I was expounding on what was becoming my pet theme, next to the hockey team itself. With the Mutual Street Arena seating less than 8,000, about half the time we were packing in 9,000 counting standees, but still weren't grossing enough to pay our players what they could have been getting with the richer teams in the U.S. "Also, " I said, "as a place to go all dressed up, we don't compete with the comfort of theatres and other places where people can spend their money. We need a place where people can go in evening clothes, if they want to come there from a party or dinner. We need at least twelve thousand seats, everything new and clean, a place that people can be proud to take their wives or girl friends to."

Clark got so excited that he took up my theme where I left off. He got on the back of a chair, then onto the table, then stood on the bed, telling us we had to do it, we had to get people convinced that we needed a new arena. Somebody else there, I think a car salesman, said we had to come up with a slogan. "That's the way you get things done today – get them saying, 'We have to have a new Arena! We have to have a new Arena!' To anyone who'll listen."

Money was very tight. From my own engineering and construction experience I knew that we were going to need a million, a million and a half, maybe more. But the more I thought about it , the more I was determined to do it. I got a few people together to see what kind of support we had; four Leaf directors, in the King Edward at lunch. My oldtime pal from the racetracks, Larkin Maloney, who was general manager at Canada Building Materials, was completely sold, on my side. But Ed Bickle, partner in a stockbroking firm, was against it, a handicap right from the start. He was supposed to have political connections, as a bagman, but I don't remember him ever helping in anything much. Bill MacBrien, an insurance man, was sort of on the fence. Maloney and I were the only enthusiasts, so we decided to see what we could do.

A big firm of Montreal architects, Ross and MacDonald, had built the Royal York Hotel and other projects in Toronto. Architects in those days seemed to be more powerful among financiers than they are now. Ross and MacDonald had a lot of money at their command because of big jobs they'd done. Maloney and I went to Montreal to see them and tell them what we had in mind; an arena called Maple Leaf Gardens that would handle hockey and a lot of other events, from conventions to wrestling. They listened and proposed the project to Sun Life as a good investment. We were told that Sun Life would back us for about half a million. Then I made a big mistake. I was so excited at the good news that I phoned back to Toronto and told Ed Bickle what we had done. A few days later we were up at Lake Simcoe when someone mentioned to me, wasn't it good news about Bickle arranging the financing from Sun Life!

I said, "Maloney and I did that!"

He said, "Well, Ed Bickle is saying he did it."

After opposing the whole deal! But that was in character for Ed Bickle. Maloney was so angry with me for telling Bickle about it instead of announcing it ourselves that I thought he was going to punch me in the face.

Anyway, by then I was too busy raising money to coach full-time, so I named Art Duncan as co-coach to handle the team when I couldn't. We went to Sir John Aird, president of the Bank of Commerce, to tell him about Sun Life's support, and ask his. He said go ahead. We formed a company, Maple Leaf Gardens Limited, incorporated on February 24, 1931. Our directorate was like an honour roll of successful businessmen. We worked out details of a stock prospectus, 100,000 preference shares at $10 par value, plus 50,000 common shares, no par value. A bonus of one common share would go to anyone who bought five of the preferred. All winter we'd been hunting for a site. The first one we looked at was on the Toronto waterfront, on land owned by the Toronto Harbour Commission. One of the people involved wanted $100,000 on the side to get the sale okayed. I refused to have anything to do with that, which turned out to be lucky. We looked at a site on Spadina just above College, but some of the local landowners were against it. And then we hit on the right one.

The T. Eaton Company owned a lot of land around Carlton and Church. They said they would sell us a property one block north of Carlton, just above Wood Street – not much more than one hundred yards from where I was born. But I thought right on Carlton would be better. There were street cars on Yonge, a block away, another line on Carlton, another on Church. Eaton's not long before had opened their big new store at College and Yonge. I went to see the head man, J. J. Vaughan, and said, "Mr. Vaughan, we are going to draw hundreds of thousands of people to this new Gardens. If we build on Carlton, they'll have to go past your store, or at least see it, on the way to and from games. It would be better for you if we're on Carlton." He thought it over and said okay. We took an option on the corner for $350,000 – and Eaton's also said they'd take some of the stock.

I even sent Frank Selke, whom I'd hired a couple of years earlier

as my assistant, and Ace Bailey, one of our best players, to make a
few calls. Some of the richest men and companies around came in
for an average of around $10,000, with lots of smaller commit-
ments and some bigger ones. One day when the federal government had just made a big addition to the money supply, hundreds
of millions of dollars, Jack Bickell called Alf Rogers, president of
Elias Rogers Co. Ltd. and St. Mary's Cement Co. Ltd., and told
him, "Alf, we've got to have a new arena! We're putting you in for
$25,000."

I could hear Rogers's voice roaring back, "Don't you know
there's a Depression on?"

Bickell argued that there were millions more dollars around that
day than the day before, and that we'd never be able to buy
materials and labour as cheaply again. In the end Rogers came in
for his $25,000.

However, as the Depression deepened, some people who had
committed themselves couldn't come up with the money. When
Sun Life tried to back out, things got a little desperate. I went to
see Sir Edward Beatty, president of Canadian Pacific and a director of Sun Life. I guess he was impressed because he called a few
other Sun Life directors. A group of them told the company that if
it backed out, they'd resign their directorships. Sun Life stayed in.

By then we were levelling the site. We knocked down all the old
buildings, starting with the tobacco store right on the corner.
Everything came down until there was nothing there but a pile of
old bricks. Some people laughed at me for hiring a watchman, but
I had a kid just down from the west who was going to play a year
of amateur hockey with the Senior Marlboros, a good prospect
named Buzz Boll. He needed a job. We got him a little shack, a
stove, and a fifteen cent baseball bat. I can't remember myself
exactly what I had in mind. Maybe that somebody would steal the
corner we were going to build the Gardens on, I don't know.

By then the drawings were finished, a really inspired design that
would allow every customer an unobstructed view of the ice, and
make the Gardens the most up-to-date sports arena in North
America – maybe in the world – if we could just get it built. Contractors had been asked for sealed bids. Sir John Aird, one of the
Maple Leaf Gardens Limited directors, called a meeting in his
office to open the bids. That was one of the worst, and best, days
of my life. We seemed so near to getting the job done. But when

the bids were opened and read, and the amount of money we had in hand or promised or even hoped for, was totalled up, we were – as I recollect – a few hundred thousand dollars short. That wouldn't be much today. Early in 1931 it was a mountain. We had tapped everybody who had any money, not once but two or three times. There was no going back to them and nowhere else to go, either. Sir John and some of the directors thought we should postpone the whole deal until things got better. I left the meeting to take a rest, trying to think what rabbit I could pull out of the hat now. Outside on a bench was Frank Selke.

I told him things didn't look too good. It was a depressing moment, to think that the project was all but being down the drain. Selke had mortgaged his house to buy stock, $4,500 of it. As we talked, an idea began to take shape between us. Suppose we could cut direct labour costs by paying the men partly in stock? Could we convince the unions that it would be to their benefit, keep about 1,300 of their members employed, if they'd agree to take 20 per cent of their pay in Garden's shares?

It happened that day was the weekly meeting of the many unions in the Toronto Labour Council. Selke was a long-time member of the electricians' union. He has said since that he ran all the way to the Labour Temple to make his pitch. The business managers of all the unions listened. At first they were reluctant. If it was such a good deal, why were the rich guys trying to pawn off stock on the workers? Selke mentioned his own mortgage, as evidence of his faith. That helped and in the end, although they said each union membership would have to be approached separately for ratification, the response was favourable enough that Selke ran back down to the Bank of Commerce building to let me know.

The meeting in Sir John's office was still dragging along, going nowhere. I came out to talk to Selke. When I went back in and announced that the men who would build the Gardens seemed willing to take part of their pay in shares, Sir John Aird said quietly, "In that case, our bank will pick up the rest." I have always been given the main credit for building Maple Leaf Gardens in the depths of the Depression. Well, I didn't even know what a Depression was, so I just kept pushing. But to my mind the final decision, the final laying to rest of the feeling among some people that it was a crazy idea, came when the union men came in and Sir John Aird said, for the Bank of Commerce, "We'll pick up the rest."

In the end, the contractors who had submitted the low bid with a price shaved to the bone, Thomson Brothers, lost money on the deal. Allan Thomson and I dealt at the same Dominion Bank branch at Queen and Ossington. Even though they were losing money they were still doing the job. A lot of contractors would have come back to us and tried to renegotiate. I certainly admired Allan Thomson a lot more than one of our Gardens directors right then: Allan Ross, President of Canadian William Wrigley Junior Company Limited, and also a director of the Dominion Bank. He had wanted to be first president of the Maple Leafs. I'd made sure he wasn't. Anyway, when he found that the Thomsons were losing money at the Gardens, he recommended that the Dominion Bank call three of their notes the bank held. To call those notes would have bankrupted the company and Ross knew it. When I heard about it, I was furious. Fortunately, we had money right then. I called the bank the same day I heard about it and said, "We're buying those notes, right now." Then I told Ross what I thought of him.

On June 1, steam shovels moved in to excavate. I don't know how you would build Maple Leaf Gardens today in five months, but partly it was accomplished because the men who built it believed in what they were doing. After all, they were going to be shareholders in it, weren't they? There was just one dissident that I ever heard of, a member of the electrical union that Selke had helped run for so long. The paid business agent, Cecil Shaw, also was connected with amateur hockey around town. Shaw argued with the man and got nowhere. Eventually they continued the argument with their fists. I've always thought maybe it was the best fight ever staged in Maple Leaf Gardens, and at the end Shaw was on his feet while the other guy was on his back looking up at the sky. The Gardens didn't even have a roof at the time.

We hustled stock all that spring and summer. I knew how bad the times were, not just from how tough the stock was to sell. Earlier, on May 1, at my sand pit I had to announce a pay cut for May 15, ranging from 10 to 20 per cent. Hap Day and I, as management, went down to a straight $25 a week. In August the long-time tenant in a house I owned on Willard Avenue wrote to say she couldn't pay the five months' back rent she owed and would I take a chattel mortgage on her furniture for it. All over town people were having mortgages foreclosed, or having to move because they couldn't pay the rent. As a minor footnote, Charlie Conacher came to me in some sort of a personal crisis that summer, needing $500 fast. His IOU dated July 14, 1931, I still hold. I owed money myself, but part of that was because by then I had bought 3,880 shares of Gardens' stock.

I realize now that getting the Gardens up and clean, painted, well-lighted, with ice in and the bands marching out on the ice before a cheering crowd, all done between June 1 and November 12, was amazing. I didn't stop to think about it much that summer. Day and night, practically, I was down there, sometimes with MacDonald, the architectural expediter, sometimes with Allan Thomson, making decisions that would keep things moving. I supplied very little of the building material myself. I didn't want anybody to say I was feathering my own nest that way. Anyway, everything went too slowly to suit me. Because of the design, with no supporting pillars to get in the way of people watching hockey, some of the girders were so huge and heavy that they couldn't be carried in from elsewhere on the equipment of that time, and had to be fabricated on the spot. When Chicago Black Hawks came to town a day before the grand opening, there were still some finishing touches being done. But on the night of November 12, 1931, when the bands of the 48th Highlanders and the Royal Grenadiers marched out on the ice and played "Happy Days Are Here Again," the scene was pretty much as I had imagined it in my rosiest dreams. A lot of the people were in evening dress, including our twenty-two Gardens directors representing presidencies and directorships and sometimes sole ownership of some of the greatest firms in Canada (as well as one of the smaller ones, C. Smythe Ltd.). But up in the capacity crowd of 13,542 among the people who tried to drown out Gardens' president Jack Bickell's speech from centre ice with cries of, "Play hockey!" were hundreds of the men who had built the place, and owned shares in it. Many of them still have those shares, and others who sold, or had to sell, their common stock at $1 a share in the early 1930's kicked themselves over the years. Counting share splits, those original $1 items became worth a hundred times that. But anyway, that night the dream had come true. Something had been built that became famous across Canada. Years later the first place some visitors to

Toronto headed was to Carlton and Church just to stand there and look at the place they imagined around their radios every winter Saturday night after Foster Hewitt had called out his excitement-filled, "Hello Canada!" into the farthest corners of the land, doing more than any other one man to make the Leafs and the Gardens as famous as anything in Canada.

Most of the things we did that summer were right, but some were wrong, and some just didn't work out. The building was right; from that night on, hockey at the Gardens became the hardest ticket in town to get, and just about everybody who was anybody had season tickets. People planning arenas in other cities came to look at ours before they started.

One thing wrong was that, being busy hounding people to get the building finished on time, I hadn't spent the time I should have on our hockey team, which had decided that it was the team of destiny. The previous spring we had finished second to Canadiens in the Canadian division. The Kid Line had scored 58 of the entire 118 goals we'd put in all season, Conacher leading the league with 31. But we had been knocked out in the first round of the playoffs by Chicago without the Kid Line getting a single goal, so there were things to be done – and I knew it. But apparently Art Duncan, whom I'd appointed full coach, didn't. He wasn't a bad player, but he was a bad coach. Conacher and Jackson never did feel very interested in getting in shape. They were too busy driving their new cars and chasing women. The whole team was flabby mentally and physically and Duncan wasn't doing anything about it. Our 2-1 loss to Chicago on the night the Gardens opened was an indication. When we'd managed only two ties in our first five games I asked Duncan what he was going to do about it. He didn't seem to have any ideas except that things would get better, in time, so I fired him. I don't especially like firing people but when it has to be done I don't back off. I'm not the only businessman in the world who knows that when the quickest way out of a bad situation is to fire the man responsible, you fire him; especially if you have somebody in mind who you think can do the job properly.

I had. I'd known Dick Irvin as a great amateur (once he scored nine goals in a playoff game) and then as a pro player in the 1920's – first in the Western League and then, although suffering from an old war wound and well past his prime, for three years in Chicago before he finally packed it in at age thirty-seven. Coaching

Chicago in the Stanley Cup playoffs the previous spring he had knocked us out, knocked Rangers out, and came within a few minutes of beating Canadiens in the final. It was best of five. Chicago won two of the first three games and was leading 2-0 in the fourth in Montreal before the players ran out of gas. They lost that game and also the fifth one. But he had brought the Black Hawks to great heights against a really superior team and when Chicago surprisingly let him go, I went for him.

On November 28 when Irvin checked in we had two points out of a possible ten and were dead last in the league. That night Boston Bruins were in town. Irvin didn't know our players at all, so I said, "Look, I'll run the team on the bench. You sit right behind me and get an idea about these guys, and what we've been doing wrong." We got a lead of about 4-1 and I was feeling like a genius until suddenly Boston was on us, tying it up.

"You take over, Dick," I said. I got out at just the right time. He came through. We won it 6-5.

For years when we shared the stateroom in Leafs' special Pullman, he slept in the top bunk. I know some nights he hardly slept at all because of pain from his war wound, but he was a fine, loyal man.

He was also calm and cool. The first game he coached all by himself was a tie, 2-2 with the Americans. Then in Montreal a few days later Maroons plastered us 8-2 and on the train home everyone was gloomy except Dick. He just said he was beginning to see some things; one being that our players were simply out of shape. That's when he started to give 'em hell. Three days after the 8-2 beating, Leafs blanked Maroons 4-0. I could see how on the ice he could teach, demand, make players do their best. Dick's only flaw, it turned out years later, was that he fell in love with his players, wouldn't fire them or even bench them when they went bad. But in that first year he coached with his head instead of his heart. When he got us all the way from last place to first in the Canadian section of the NHL within his first few weeks I knew I was close to fulfilling the promise I'd made five years before to build a Stanley Cup winner for Toronto.

There is something you can almost smell about the spirit of a team that isn't going to be beaten. Leafs had it that year. Even when we won, they were snarling. On Christmas Eve Harvey Jackson scored in the last second of overtime to beat Canadiens –

and still Harold Cotton, given a minor penalty seconds earlier by referee Cooper Smeaton, challenged the referee to a fight and had to be taken to the dressing room by NHL president Frank Calder.

Lorne Chabot was badly cut in one game, but insisted on going back in. Charlie Conacher got five goals one night in January against the Americans. We scored three overtime goals one night late that month to beat Rangers 6-3. Red Horner broke his collarbone checking Ching Johnson; and a few days later, Charlie Conacher broke a small bone in his hand scuffling with Hec Kilrea in Detroit. Chabot was suspended one game for throwing a punch at a goal judge in Detroit – but Benny Grant was a star in goal a few nights later when, minus Conacher, Horner, and Chabot, we still hammered Maroons 6-0 and both Hap Day and Clancy were fined for their roles in a free-for-all fight that brought nine major penalties.

Then I cooked up something. There was a rule in the league then that if a player got three major penalties, he was suspended automatically for the next game. It occurred to me that both Conacher and Horner, still out with broken bones, had two major penalties each. Next one would mean a suspension. So on February 18 in New York I said to Dick, "Dress Horner and Conacher."

"Why?" he said. "They can't play."

I reminded him of the rule that any player who jumped to the ice when a full team already was out there, would get a major penalty. "If we get a good lead," I said, "send Conacher and Horner out and let them get their third majors." In the last minute or so of the game we were leading 5-3. Out went Conacher and Horner, to earn their third majors and the one game suspension that they could serve in style, because with their broken bones they couldn't play anyway.

Sometimes our tough play backfired, however. One night in Boston Lorne Chabot stuck out his stick and tripped Cooney Weiland behind the net. There was no score at the time. Referee Bill Stewart gave Chabot a penalty, which, in those days, had to be served by the goalie himself. Horner, Clancy, and Alex Levinsky all fanned on saves and Boston got three goals, so that penalty cost us the game. I got into the act, too. Stewart made the mistake of skating too close to our bench and I grabbed him by the sweater. He ordered me out of the game. I refused to leave. Some ushers and cops tried to get me out of there. That brought Baldy Cotton up to challenge everybody in the rink. Finally the Boston president, Charles Adams, came along with a cop and cooled things out. Our injuries hurt us in the last few weeks, but we finished second to Canadiens in the Canadian section and went into the playoffs healthy.

In those days, leaders of each section played off in a five-game series while the second and third-place teams played two-games, total-goals quarter-finals and semi-finals, to see who would meet the winner of the series between the first-place finishers. We got by Chicago, beat Maroons in the semi-final, and came up against the Rangers, who'd had a whole week to rest after polishing off Canadiens.

I couldn't have written a better script myself. The team I'd assembled for the Rangers was still their backbone, five years later. But my Leafs were younger, hungrier, and we had Lorne Chabot in goal, while they had John Ross Roach.

I've always thought that was a great way to do business – if I could manage it – trade away a goalie I didn't want, and then play against him for the Stanley Cup. Rangers were never in it. We scored six goals a game against old Roachy, to win the Cup three straight, 6-2, 6-4, 6-2. Like a tennis match. The first game was in New York, the second in Boston because the circus had taken over Madison Square Garden, and the third was right home in Toronto before almost 15,000 fans who cheered until they could only croak.

When Stafford had finished his stickboy duties that night and he and Irene and I left the Gardens and drove home in the big Stearns-Knight, I felt on top of the world. Leafs were young and on the rise. They were going to get better, not worse. If I'd known that it would be ten years before I would win another Stanley Cup I might have driven into a telephone post.

Chapter Six

In the 1930's I had some good friends in what people now call the media, but I also had to deal with columnists and reporters I didn't like at all. One of the good friends was Foster Hewitt. I had fought for him and he knew it. In the late 1920's there were some Maple Leaf directors who thought we shouldn't broadcast games because it would hurt seat sales. I knew we should broadcast. People who were interested enough to listen to our games on the radio were going to buy tickets sometime, although I didn't realize then that some in later years would travel clear across the country to buy tickets for a team they'd never seen but felt they knew through Foster's broadcasts. By the time we built the Gardens I thought enough of him that I told him to tell the designers exactly where his broadcast gondola should be. He went to a tall building that had windows overlooking the street and walked from floor to floor, looking at the people on the street below until he decided that the fifth floor height, fifty-six feet, was best – and that's the height at which his gondola was built.

Anyway, he and I were good friends without being married to one another. He's a hard man to get to know and, like me, he paddles his own canoe. One time I criticized him for repeating one of the things that made him famous – the line, "He shoots! He scores!" I thought he should learn four or five more words in the English language.

"Aw," he said, "there's no use trying to please you."

"That's rather an unfair statement." I said. "You have been pleasing me."

"But there's no use!" he insisted. "You always want something better than is being done!"

Well, I took that as kind of a compliment. And he isn't the first guy I've liked and admired but still tried to move up a notch or two. Somebody asked me once, "Has there ever been anybody who you didn't feel you had to blast once in a while or give advice to?"

I said, "I've never met them. Have you?"

Too many people who see things being done wrong don't act on them. I remember when Red Horner first worked for me at the sand pit. One day he was digging post holes while sitting down. I said, "If that's the way you're going to play hockey in the NHL, you won't last long." He stood up and the sand really flew from then on.

But I'm not taking anything away from a person when I try to make him do better than he's doing. Foster – nobody could have done as good a job as he did. Nobody has done as good a job since. And nobody is as tough a fighter as Foster. When anybody crossed him, or moved in and tried to take something away from him, brother, you should have seen him fight. He could do it with his fists, too. At university, he licked everybody his own weight as a boxer. He seems mild, but nobody should misjudge him. In his own way, he's as tough a character as you're going to meet anyplace.

Can't say the same for Gordon Sinclair, who is just a cranky old broadcaster now. One time in the 1930's when he was a hotshot writer for the *Star*, they put him on sports for a while. In one column he said my Leafs were yellow. I met him in a hotel lobby that day and handed him the key to my room.

"Yellow, eh?" I said. "Meet me up there and the one who comes out alive wins the argument."

He didn't take me up on it. Said I outweighed him, which must have made him one of the Singer midgets at the time. Anyway, it proved that he had a hell of a lot of nerve to call anybody yellow. Years later I let him back in the Gardens, but at the time he called the Leafs yellow I barred him from the Gardens' press room and he was kept out for many years, much to his surprise.

I guess the other guys I disliked the most in the press were also from the *Star*. I don't even like to mention the name of Lou Marsh, the sports editor, for whom the *Star* later named an annual trophy. I had no use for him. Andy Lytle, who followed Marsh by a few years, wasn't much better, if any. Lytle was a good reporter, a hard worker, but had a mean streak as well as having a lot of trouble with alcohol. As everybody then knew, the *Star*'s owner, Joe Atkinson, was dead against drinking. Andy got in trouble a couple of times and Mr. Atkinson overlooked it, but finally told him, "One more time, and you're gone."

Right away, Andy went on a binge. A doctor who knew about Andy's trouble told me about it and said, "You know, he'll be fired if the paper learns about this. Is there anything you can do?"

I said, "Well, if you can hang on to him and dry him out, I'll get someone else to write his column."

I even tried to do it myself, but couldn't. It taught me that if you don't know anything about the inner workings of a sport, you probably can write six columns a week, easily. If you *do* know, you can't write any. I read the papers every day all my life and rarely saw anything to make me change that opinion. After my own try, I called in Frank Selke and told him, "Look, you get a bunch of back copies of the *Star* and really study Lytle's style. Find phrases that recur, the kind of words he uses a lot – it's got to be authentic Lytle."

So that's what Selke did for three days. By then Lytle was okay again and went back to work. Funny thing, from that day on he never had one good thing to say about the Leafs, Frank Selke, Connie Smythe, or anybody connected with us. I guess he was trying to show us that he was a free man, and didn't owe anybody anything. In 1942, when we were down three games against Detroit in the Stanley Cup final, he wrote a column congratulating Jack Adams of Detroit on winning the Stanley Cup – and that was when we started a four-game sweep to come back and win that championship.

That was one side of sportswriting in those days. Another was that a lot of sportswriters were very low paid and always had their hands out. I knew I could get any story I wanted in the paper for $50 or less; but if they didn't get paid they would either not write hockey at all, or write lies. I didn't believe I should have to buy honest coverage so I did something that I don't think had been done before anywhere I knew. I told the newspaper people, "If you want to see the games, you buy your own tickets. And we're not going to put any ads in your papers, either." They were somewhat surprised. I think they thought we needed them to fill our rink. I thought they needed us more than we needed them, to sell their papers. Anyway, for a few weeks everybody paid to get in, even a guy covering a practice. Finally Mr. Atkinson of the *Star* called me to see him and asked, "What's going on?"

I told him he knew as well as I did.

"Do you want it to go on this way?"

"No," I said. "I'd prefer to have peace."

He thought for a while and then asked what I thought the hockey writers would expect in a year, in cash handouts from the hockey club. "I mean, you're not giving our men money, but if you did what would you expect the total to be?"

I named a figure, I think about $20,000 a year.

He said, "Would you guarantee to spend that money on advertising in our paper if I guarantee that our men will be paid enough, and will conscientiously cover your games?"

I said I would. That's how peace was made with all the newspapers, a deal that each would get a certain sum in advertising from the Gardens each year. And the writers who earlier had their hands out and wouldn't write a line if they weren't paid off had to go back to honest work. More or less honest work. That deal lasted maybe twenty years. I know the best writers are different now, but that is how it was at one time.

Someone once asked me how much of this or other business matters were discussed around our dinner table. The answer is, not much. Hughie has said since that I was a very witty father to have around but maybe that was because I didn't have any competition. It was the era of children being seen and not heard, but it's good to know that Irene and I made use of the floor.

On the day of a game, it was understood that peace would prevail around the house. No young friends of the children were to play there that day. Family disputes, if any, were to be conducted in low voices, or I would come storming out to lay down the law. Usually in the morning I would be at the Gardens for the team meeting and any other business that had to be transacted, but in the afternoons I was to have quiet so that I could think about the game that night. We would have an early dinner – I usually couldn't eat much – and then we'd go to the Gardens. Irene and Miriam always sat in a box right behind Leafs' bench. Even if Miriam had a date on a Saturday night, which became more and more frequent, it would be to pick her up after the game. Stafford and later Hughie were often with me in the seats I had in the greens, up where I could see the pattern of the play. Sometimes they'd run down to the bench with messages: take that man off, put that man on. Once I tried using a phone to keep in touch with Dick Irvin behind the bench, but that didn't work. (He could always not answer.) In some games, I would roam the rink. Ted Reeve once remembered in a column, "that white, white fedora with the ruddy face and flaming blue eyes underneath it, sailing around the Gardens aisles and corridors like the white plume of Navarre, action every step of the way and gathering uproar as it went." That was me. I would be behind the bench, in the dressing room, wherever my feet took me. In those days I knew what every man on the ice was doing, every minute.

Also, I was still learning, sometimes the hard way, that everything I did was not necessarily right. When we were raising money to build the Gardens and I was looking ahead to how it would be run, it was my idea to hire W. A. Hewitt, sports editor of the *Toronto Star*, as general manager of all attractions except hockey. The fact that he was Foster's father, and that Foster's broadcasts were doing a lot to make Leafs into a national institution, had nothing to do with it. W. A. Hewitt was a good newspaperman but like any of that breed that I ever met, didn't know a thing about running anything. They can tell you how to do it, but put them in charge and it's a disaster. That had been Mike Rodden's trouble back with St. Pats. I thought W. A. would be different because he had managed the Ontario Hockey Association. Things went badly enough that after a year we eased him into other jobs and I took over the things like wrestling and boxing, although one thing I learned quickly was to keep the Gardens clear of boxing.

Because of my old experience with Benny Leonard in Pittsburgh, I knew a lot of boxing was crooked. Still, a promoter named Dave Lumiansky from Montreal sold me on the idea of a world championship lightweight bout between a Frenchman named Spider Pladner and the champion, Panama Al Brown. Before the fight Lumiansky was assuring me they would put on a good show when I said, "Look, this fight had better be on the level. Hockey is an honest sport and I don't want anything in this building if it isn't honest."

I should have known what was coming when Lumiansky looked at me sort of surprised and said, "On the level?"

"On the level," I insisted.

"You better be in your seat before the opening bell," he said.

I was. Pladner sent out one left jab, and then Brown hit him with a right. The referee could have counted to fifty and he wouldn't have been able to get up.

My loss of faith in W. A. Hewitt didn't take long, but I really didn't get on to Frank Selke for many years, probably because he was a good hockey man and a hard worker, even if some of his hard work turned out to be against me. When I first hired him before the Gardens was built, I paid him out of what I was getting. I thought that was fair; he was doing some of my work, so there was no reason for the Gardens to pay me for that work, and pay him too. A sportswriter at the *Globe*, Ralph Allen, later nick-named him Little Rollo. I'm not sure exactly what that means but Selke tended to be sanctimonious in his dealings with other people. Years later in an interview in the *New Yorker*, Selke described me as a brilliant but sometimes impossibly egotistical man, which might be true, but to my mind it's better than being the way he was. I like things to be out in the open, seen, and understood. He worked another way. As this is written, it is more than fifty years since I first hired Selke. I think he did well from being my assistant, but when the crunch came it was plain that he had no loyalty to me. Because of his hockey knowledge, hard work, and sobriety he was a good man up to a point, but then he was a minor leaguer, as far as I was concerned.

One of the indirect results of W. A. Hewitt's inability to cope was a good one. When we were hiring people at the Gardens a tall, quiet guy named Henry Bolton came around. He was sent to me by Dave Garrity, my old racetrack companion, who mainly gambled for a living. They were brothers-in-law. I liked Henry Bolton, but when I hired him I said to Dave Garrity, "If Bolton comes in here to work you must never make another bet in the Gardens." I was scared to death of scandal that would tar hockey the way baseball and boxing had been tarred. Garrity promised, and never did make another bet there. Henry Bolton, who later became our attractions manager, was a lovely man; loyal, decent, honourable, and always did the job. He met the public perfectly and had a lot to do with the success of the Gardens, although it was tough going for a while. When we started to lose money in our second year, as the Depression in the country deepened, people in other businesses were taking pay cuts. Bolton was first to suggest that we should cut expenses, starting with everybody taking a pay cut. That's the kind of suggestion that usually comes from a Board of Directors, not one of the employees who's going to take the cut.

But that kind of internal belt-tightening wasn't enough. The people who had invested in the Gardens got worried. One result was that the Bank of Commerce named a trouble shooter, George R. Cottrelle, to join the Board of Directors and protect the bank's interests. Cottrelle didn't come up himself to count the money, or check the books; he sent another man, who I wouldn't talk to. I told him to go back and tell Cottrelle that if he wanted to see me, to come himself. He did, and one of the things he said was that we didn't have a budget, and must have a budget.

I said, "Okay, Cottrelle, you're a hell of a man – how many playoff games are we going to win this year? How many are you going to budget for, both in expenses and income?" I didn't think Cottrelle knew his ass from his elbow, but he knew a little more after he'd gone a few rounds with me. Budgets are a damn joke if you try to impose them on organizations in which no one knows what is going to happen. (Governments have budgets, and look at the shape they're in). The important thing in hockey was to run the business right, pay what you had to pay, take in the most you could. I asked Cottrelle, "How do you know when you might get a chance to buy the best hockey player in the world, someone who would make all the difference to the team? What are you going to do – say, oh, no, it isn't in the budget?"

Cottrelle was around the Gardens for years, eventually as president. At first he really looked down his nose at professional sport. He told me that he was to get absolutely no publicity. Didn't want it. "I'm a banker, not a hockey man," he said. After he'd been on the board for a year or two, I noticed he was getting very cool toward me. I didn't know what was the matter. Then it occurred to me that maybe he had changed his mind about publicity, without really knowing it. I asked him to face off a puck one night. He got his picture in the paper. After that I was the greatest guy who ever lived.

Meanwhile, I couldn't see why Toronto Maple Leafs shouldn't keep on winning Stanley Cups year after year, now that we'd won the first one. And that next year, the 1932-33 season, we would have won at least one more cup if it hadn't been for circumstances that I don't think would be allowed to happen today.

We had pretty well the team that had won the Stanley Cup back in the spring, except that Ottawa, after suspending operations for a year, decided to come back in. That meant that Ottawa players spread around the league had to be returned. We lost Frank Finnigan, but brought up Ken Doraty and Bill Thoms from the farm system I'd been building. Both of them came through well, Doraty especially. He only got five goals during the season, but scored another five in the playoffs, including one that has been a highlight of many a hockey history since.

You could see the effects of the Depression in the arenas that fall: only two thousand for the opener in Detroit; four thousand for our first game at Chicago. We didn't have that kind of trouble at home because we were winning and we were exciting, an unbeatable combination. Over the forty-eight-game season we led the league's Canadian section (Toronto, Maroons, Canadiens, New York Americans, and Ottawa, finishing in that order) while Boston took the American section (Boston, Detroit, Rangers, and Chicago). That meant Leafs would play Boston a best-of-five series while the second and third place teams fought it out to decide who would play the survivor in the final.

As it turned out, Rangers won their elimination rounds easily while Leafs and Boston fought through a very tough series. We split the first four games, three of them in overtime. When we came up to the deciding game in Toronto on Monday, April 3, the winner was supposed to play Rangers in the first game of the final in New York the very next night, April 4.

In the Gardens that Monday night, fourteen thousand, five hundred jammed the place. Joe Primeau had missed the fourth game with an infected foot, but with Bill Thoms at centre on the Kid Line, Conacher had scored twice and Jackson once. Still, we dressed Primeau for the final game, although we didn't use him until we went into overtime, still with no score.

With only fourteen players each, counting Lorne Chabot in our goal, and Tiny Thompson in theirs, it was not exactly a game of blazing speed by the time we got into the sudden-death.

The clock wound on past midnight. We played period after period. King Clancy scored in the fourth overtime period, but the whistle had just gone. In the intermission the players lay on the benches, on the floor, anywhere flat, then went out, and played the fifth overtime. By that time there had been one hundred and sixty minutes of hockey, one period short of three full games. It was 1:30 a.m. Many people had gone home, but others, listening to Foster at home on their radios, came down. I said, "Let 'em free." In a little room down a corridor NHL president Frank Calder called Art Ross and me together to talk about what we should do. There were stories later that Ross and I went to Calder to suggest that we call this game a draw and play again the following night. Or that we decide the winner by the flip of a coin. Neither was true, although both alternatives were discussed. Calder kept saying that something had to happen. If we were going on, the winner had to play in New York less than seventeen hours later and it took almost that long to get there, by train. If we were going to call the game, though, both teams had to agree.

I knew that if I could get an extra five or ten minutes rest for the Leafs, they'd be all right. So I kept the discussion going. I took my time. I did a lot of saying. "On one hand . . ." and, "On the other hand." When I thought the rest had been long enough, I said I would like to consult my players while Ross consulted his. It turned out that Boston players were in favour of calling the game. I wasn't, but I didn't want to go in and announce it. I wanted the decision to come from my players.

So I went in. Baldy Cotton was lying on the floor. To look at him, you'd want to take his pulse and see if he was dead. He could put on a death act better than anyone living; he was dead, dying, pinned to the floor, no life or breath in him, until I said, "Listen, there's talk about calling this game . . ."

Cotton was on his feet in one wild leap, yelling, "No son of a bitch is going to call this game!"

That's what I wanted to hear. The others started to yell, too. They were suddenly goddam mad, in fact. I just about got run down with them going out of there to get on the ice. I went and told Calder and Ross, "My team wants to play."

In the fifth minute of that sixth overtime period, Eddie Shore, tired as he was, tried to clear the puck from a corner in the Boston end. Andy Blair was fresher than most; he hadn't played as much as some, earlier. He jumped in to intercept the puck, passed to Ken Doraty in front of the net, and zip – it was in, the only goal of the game, at 1:50 a.m., 4.46 of the sixth overtime.

Then all we had to do was get to New York to play that night.

We went from the Gardens to Union Station and after 3:00 a.m
boarded our special car to be hitched on to the New York trai
Dick Irvin and I fell into our bunks in the compartment we share
and for once the playboys on the team beat us to sleep,
anything. I might say that with Irvin, myself, and Hap Day, th
captain, all being non-smokers and non-drinkers, it was rathe
hard for anybody to live it up on one of our train rides. For the re
of the night and the next day we rattled across northern New Yor
until we pulled into Grand Central at 4:10 p.m., about four hour
before game time. The rottenest thing was that when I tried t
have the game postponed, the Madison Square people said it ha
to go on because the circus coming in later in the week needed th
time to set up. That was a lie, because now they suggested to m
that we play the second game of the series there, too, meaning tha
there really had been time to get the first one postponed. I tol
them, "You guys told me that because of the circus coming i
there'd be no ice, we couldn't even postpone this first game . . .

They said, "Well, we've changed our minds."

I said, "Well, you can change your minds again! I wouldn't pla
the second game here now if it was the last place in the world!'

When it was announced during the game that the second gam
would be played in Toronto because of the circus, the crowd o
seventeen thousand raised such an uproar that the announce
couldn't go on and ballyhoo the circus. It made us angry, too, bu
we couldn't do anything about it, we were so tired. We lost 5-
The game ended at 10:45 p.m. We went straight to the station t
board a train that left for Toronto at 11:25 p.m. We'd only bee
off the train for seven hours.

But even with a four-day rest before the second game i
Toronto the next Saturday night, we couldn't handle them
Rangers had changed goalies that year, trading John Ross Roach t
Detroit and using Andy Aitkenhead, and he was good. They ha
added Earl Seibert to the defence and he played even better tha
Ching Johnson. We lost the second game 3-1, won the third 3-2
and lost the last one and the Cup, 1-0. The Kid Line was nowhere
shut out for the whole series. Little Ken Doraty scored our sing
goal in the second game and two in the third game.

The next few years were very frustrating, for me. In the year
between 1933 and 1940 we were in the Stanley Cup final ever
year except 1934 and 1937, but never won it. I know now that

should have broken up the Kid Line around 1935 or so. I didn't have the guts. Of course, they were a big gate attraction. I could have found lots of wingers to go with Joe Primeau, but he was the only centre who could make Conacher and Jackson click. Once in the mid-thirties Red Dutton offered me Sweeney Schriner for Busher Jackson. I thought of all the uproar that deal would have caused in the press and the public, so I didn't do it, although I did get Sweeney Schriner later. He was the best left winger I ever saw. That includes everybody – Frank Mahovlich, Busher, Bobby Hull – everybody, good as Mahovlich was. (I never thought much of Hull, because I didn't think he was a team player, but was the kind of star who overbalances a team).

We did change the team, certainly. Teams are always changing, new players coming in and others moving out. Building that first Stanley Cup team I'd got rid of everybody from the old St. Pats, except Ace Bailey, Hap Day, and trainer Tim Daly, come to think of it. Each was good at his job. Bailey was a slick stick-handler and scorer, with lots of guts. Hap Day was the most dependable man on earth. The only thing I didn't like about Day was that he was an inveterate practical joker. Even though I knew that anyone who could keep a team laughing was worth having around, I never really understood what was funny about cutting a teammate's tie in half with a pair of scissors, or bashing in his new hat, or whatever. At the Boston University Club where we stayed there was a fountain. Hap would go around and bet guys $2 each he wasn't afraid to jump into the pool wearing his clothes. He'd bet twenty guys, do it, and make $40. The one thing he did that I laughed at was take a run at big words sometimes that he didn't understand. The best time was a speech he made at his wedding starting, "Now that the marriage has been consummated . . ." After the roar that went up, he learned what consummated meant. But on the ice, I could partner him with anybody and he would complement what the other man had. Some other teams didn't like him being such a heavy lover, on the ice. He'd have those arms around a guy and never let go. He was a "what we have, we hold" man, all the way.

Tim Daly – well – others used to wonder why I put up with so much from him. Once he got drunk in Kitchener and instead of rolling in to the YMCA with the rest at night, wound up somehow in the YWCA. I had to go down and get him out. A player would have gone to the minors, for that. But as a trainer he was perfect. We never lost a stick. When we won the Stanley Cup in 1932 and the players were voting who the prize money should go to, Chabot suggested $10 for Daly. That's when I stepped in and said, "I'll decide where the money goes," and made sure Daly got a proper share, which he deserved.

In the five years after that Stanley Cup win, I made a cleanout again – by the summer of 1937 none of the 1932 players were left with the Leafs except Red Horner, Charlie Conacher, and Busher Jackson. We added good players – Turk Broda, Bob Davidson, Nick Metz, Syl Apps, Gord Drillon, and others, and still weren't good enough. But along the way there were some dramatic moments, to say the least.

One of the worst was the game in Boston December 12, 1933, when Ace Bailey was knocked out of hockey for life. That incident started with a couple of penalties to the Leafs, close together. Dick Irvin sent Clancy and Horner out on defence, with Ace Bailey up front, to kill off the two-man-short situation. Ace was a great stick-handler, one of the smoothest men in hockey. He won the face-off and ragged the puck for a whole minute while the Boston team chased him around the ice. Then there was another face-off. Ace won it again and stick-handled for a while before he shot it into the Boston end. Eddie Shore got it and started up the ice. Clancy met him, knocked him down, and took the puck. As Shore got up, Bailey, still puffing from his previous one-man show, was just in front of him. George Hainsworth in the Toronto goal (I'd traded Chabot to Canadiens for him) had the best view of what happened next – and he said Shore charged Bailey from behind. When Bailey went down his head hit the ice and he lay still. The place was in an uproar, as only Boston Garden could be.

I remember saying right then to Conacher, "Somebody should do something about this, Charlie." As he moved away, gripping his stick and a look of fury on his big, tough face, something happened that made me glance away, and the next thing I heard was a hell of a yell and there was Shore on the ice, bleeding all over!

My God, I thought, Conacher has gone out and killed Shore – and I sent him!

But it wasn't that way at all. Conacher had nothing to do with it. Red Horner told me later that when he skated up toward where Bailey was lying on the ice, Shore was standing there with a little grin on his face.

"I couldn't stand it, boss," Red told me. "I let him have one." It was one punch. Don't ever say a good man who knows how, can't land a good punch while on skates. Shore went down, hit his head on the ice, and started bleeding.

It was like the emergency ward out there. Our guys carried Ace off the ice, and their guys carried Shore off. Odie Cleghorn was refereeing. He gave Shore a major and Horner a match penalty, but that wasn't all that was happening. The crowd came down from the stands when Bailey and Shore were being carried off. I was trying to fight my way through to go with Ace when some fan – I later learned, the hard way, that his name was Leonard Kenworthy – started pointing at Ace and yelling, "Fake! Fake! The bum's acting!" I hit him flush on the nose and broke his glasses. For that I got arrested, taken to jail, and didn't get out and over to where Ace was until about 2:30 in the morning.

Ace was still unconscious. He had a badly fractured skull. In the next ten days two delicate operations saved his life. I stayed in Boston, part of the time at the hospital and part in court, where the judge at least could see my side, explaining to the fan I'd hit, Kenworthy, that whatever I'd done was under great stress and suggesting that we could settle the damages among ourselves and he would dismiss the assault charge. I kept for a long time the legal document that Kenworthy signed, settling for $200, six days after the game. Add the $100 for my lawyer, that punch cost me $300 but was worth it. Red Horner's punch that decked Eddie Shore was a lot more expensive – it got Horner suspended for about three weeks. Shore got off the easiest. He was scared to death, and no doubt sorry, too, because if Ace had died he would have been in court. But when all the circumstances came out in a league enquiry Shore was suspended only sixteen games for putting Bailey out of the game for life.

I didn't think that was enough. No consideration had been given by the league of indemnity for Ace or compensation for the Toronto club because of what it had cost us, in money and in the loss of one of our best players. All that time Art Ross was issuing silly statements about the mental suffering of Eddie Shore. I demanded, and got, a league meeting in Boston late in January to discuss the incident further. Ace was still in hospital there, six weeks after he'd been hurt, but by then was well enough to have a press conference in his hospital room. I demanded that Shore, who had gone to Bermuda so that if he was going to suffer could do it in a warm climate, be suspended for the rest of the season. This, put in the form of a motion, was defeated. The only thing the league did, besides suspending Shore, was arrange that Leafs play against a team of all-stars for an Ace Bailey benefit, all proceeds going to pay his medical expenses and set up a trust fund for him. We played it in Toronto in February. Before the game, Shore and Bailey met at centre ice. The crowd was silent as the two faced one another for the first time since that crushing check. When they hugged one another, there was a huge roar of release from the crowd. Bailey, as fine a gentleman as ever lived, said he knew the result of that check had been an accident. But he never played hockey again.

This brings up, I guess, a time when I should say something about Red Horner. To a lot of people Horner represented best the spirit of the Leafs. The first time I saw Horner he was a Junior trying out for the Marlboros. He came into the Mutual Street rink wheeling a grocery store delivery bicycle with a basket on the front, full of groceries. He asked permission to put the bike in the office, somewhere safe, so the groceries wouldn't be stolen.

I said, "Why didn't you deliver them first?"

He said, "I didn't have time. I would have missed the practice."

The first game he played, he body-checked some real tough bird on the other team and knocked him loose from his senses. All the time he and some of the other good Marlboros were Juniors, I knew when they developed enough that I could get them up with the Leafs, they'd be something. When Red did come up, he led the league in penalties for something like eight years in a row, but I approved of that. He was the first policeman we had and he won many a game for us by other teams ganging up on him and taking more penalties in total than Red would get. You take one season, for instance, when he got 167 minutes in penalties, his highest. I guarantee that if you totalled the penalties that other players got in tangling with him, it would be over three hundred minutes, they were so desperate to kill him off in places like Montreal and Boston. Red was never in the red, you might say, in the number of

penalties he got compared to the ones others got for trying to
bump him off.

I think we lost the Stanley Cup in 1938 because of misjudging
Red's impact on the opposition. It was a brain wave Dick Irvin
had. Just before the final started, Chicago goalie Mike Karakas
broke a toe. The Chicago coach, Bill Stewart, wanted to bring in
Dave Kerr from the Rangers to play goal for the Hawks. I was
damned if I was going to allow that. After all, charity begins at
home. Stewart and I met in a corridor at the Gardens just before
the first game. He called me a son-of-a-bitch for refusing to let
them use Kerr, so the first fist fight of the game took place right
there before a puck even had been dropped. To play goal they had
hauled in Alfie Moore, who had played only eighteen games in
goal for New York Americans two seasons earlier and then had
been out of the NHL altogether, working as a beer waiter. Wouldn't
you know – Alfie goes in there and stonewalls us, and Chicago
wins 3-1. Then the league president ruled Moore ineligible, and
Chicago had to use Paul Goodman from their farm team in the
second game, which we won 5-1. The best-of-five series moved to
Chicago, where Karakas got his toe fixed up with a special boot
and beat us 2-1. That meant they only needed one more win,
which brings us to Dick Irvin's brain wave.

I heard the story later from Doc Romnes, who played for
Chicago then but told it to me the next year, when he was with
Leafs. "In that fourth game we just made up our minds that we
were going to get Horner," he said. "He'd broken my nose in the
second game and I was wearing a football helmet with a face-
guard to protect it. Besides, I'd won the Byng trophy a couple of
years before. So if we were going to do something to Horner, I was
the guy to do it – I'd have the best chance of living to say it was
accidental . . ."

The first chance Romnes had, he shifted in on Horner and
slugged him as hard as he could with his stick. Horner dodged but
was hit a glancing blow and went down. Clarence Campbell, the
referee, signalled a penalty. Horner wasn't badly hurt. Still, he
limped off the ice to the bench. That's when Dick Irvin had his
great idea. He sent Horner to the dressing room. Dick had the idea
that if Horner went off, the whole Leaf team would be so irate that
they'd rise up and demolish Chicago.

It worked exactly the opposite. When the Chicago team saw

Horner go to the dressing room, quitting the game, they felt a great wave of exaltation, ready to fight like demons. Horner was absolutely the victim of a poor bench move; so were Leafs. And to make it worse, Clarence Campbell screwed up his penalty call. Romnes should have got a five-minute penalty for a deliberate attempt to injure. Campbell gave him two minutes, instead.

When I blasted him later, told him he should have given Romnes five, Campbell gave the excuse that he knew Horner wasn't hurt. But hurt or not is not the rule: "attempt to injure" is the rule. We never allowed Campbell to referee again. Owners could do that. Why not? It was our game, our meal ticket. A bad referee can do a lot of damage.

You see, professional hockey is total war. On and off the ice, everywhere you go, it's war. That's what it was that night. They didn't think they could beat us with Horner, so they simply decided to level him. I always admired Horner. By the time he retired in 1940 he had gotten all he could out of himself, and I was instrumental later in getting him into the Hockey Hall of Fame. No more courageous man ever played in the NHL. I was just sorry that in the time he was Leafs' captain – the job I gave him after I sent Hap Day to the Americans in 1937 – we were never able to win him a Stanley Cup. Nineteen thirty-eight should have been the year.

Talk about total war, on and off the ice. My fracases with Art Ross were something like that. He was the most devious man I ever met. I loved to needle him and he was easy to needle. He hated me right from that first time I put the zinger on him the first year Boston was in the league.

One story that isn't often told, maybe for obvious reasons, is related to one that *is* often told – the time I got top hat and tails and wore them to a game in Boston as a joking reply to him saying I had no class. The rest of the story is that about that time Art Ross had had an operation for hemorrhoids. When I was on my way down to the rink in the top hat and tails I saw somebody selling roses, so I bought a big bouquet with the biggest thorns on them you ever saw. We had a doctor with us, Ned Wright, who knew enough Latin to write out a card which said, in Latin," Insert these up your you know where." I got Clancy to skate the bouquet over to Ross's box and bow and present them. Ross was sitting with some people from one of those old Boston families that only speak to each other, or to God. Ross thanked Clancy and then handed the bouquet to one of the women. Trouble was, she could read Latin.

Every place Ross and I met, we fought. He was still coach as well as general manager at Boston. In the Shore-Bailey incident, I think it was Ross whining away about the heartache Eddie Shore was suffering that embarrassed Shore into taking off for Bermuda. But one time I remember best of all was a league governors' meeting in New York, in the late 1930's. Ross was very insulting, he loved to insult anybody. One night he and Red Dutton from the Americans and the senior Jim Norris from Detroit, along with Detroit's Jack Adams and a few others, had an after dinner get-together in a hotel suite. Ross started after Dutton: what a lousy hockey player he'd been; how he figured it was never satisfying to beat Maroons when Dutton was playing for them because winning against Dutton was no credit to anybody; on and on.

Dutton held his temper, but Ross was crowding him and crowding him until finally Jim Norris stepped in between them saying, "Now, let's all be friends." That's the kind of man Jim was. But just as Jim moved in Ross threw a punch. Unfortunately, he didn't hit Red but hit Jim Norris. That was what Red Dutton had been waiting for. He wouldn't have fought if Ross had hit *him*, but when he hit Norris, whom we all greatly respected, Red wouldn't have it. I have never seen a man so completely cleaned in my life, as Ross was. I never saw a man take such a beating and say nothing.

The next day I had a meeting scheduled with Ross, to discuss a deal. I went to his room. His nose was broken, his cheek bone was broken, he'd lost some teeth. He didn't even appear behind the bench to coach Boston's next game. That was a Red Dutton operation if I ever saw one. Couldn't have happened to a more deserving recipient. . . . Yet Ross had unlimited courage, along with his stubborn, insulting, devious way of dealing with people. I was a little sorry about having been on him all the time when his sons came up and joined the RCAF in World War Two, and Ross and I had our picture taken with one of his sons. We weren't so hard on one another after that.

I suppose it goes without saying that a lot of my freedom to go where I wanted, and do what I wanted, could not have been possible if I'd had to deal with a lot of problems around home. That just never happened. Stafford and Miriam and Hughie were growing up, Stafford and Hugh at Upper Canada College, and Miriam at public school and then Branksome Hall until her final year, when she had what she said was the happiest school year of her life at Alma College in St. Thomas. Jessie ruled her side of things with an iron hand, as far as the children were concerned; not only our own, but their friends as well. Irene was not a disciplinarian. Sometimes when I got home from a trip there would be judgments to be made, punishments to be handed out; on rare occasions, a few strokes of a strap. I never took Irene or any of the children on hockey trips; what was going on then needed my full attention, which no man can give if he has family responsibilities with him as well. Also, when I came home the fact that I had been away from my family made home a better place, warmer, I might even say a refuge.

By then we didn't have friends in very much. Irene would have liked to do more entertaining, I think, but I didn't want it. Sometimes Squib Walker, our chief scout, would come to dinner but I guess you couldn't exactly call that entertaining because most of the talk would be hockey; and the children, as I've said, were expected to listen, not talk. Irene had some good friends, one of the closest being Elsie Ridpath, who lived not far away. They curled and golfed and played bridge.

In the off-season I would try to make up to Irene and the family for being so single-minded about hockey each spring until the final whistle blew. From the early 1930's on we had a cottage at Lake Simcoe, not a lavish place at all, where we all used to go for the summer. I always found the swimming, golfing, and family life there relaxing – for a while. Then we'd do something else.

In 1935 Irene and I sailed for Europe and spent a month seeing the sights, the Folies Bergères and everything else that was going. The following year our last child, Patricia, was born and there was never a lack of volunteers to rock her or bounce her on their knees – with Jessie, Miriam, Hughie, and even Stafford lining up to spell off Irene while we went to the races. We'd go to the old half-mile Dufferin and Hillcrest tracks (in the old days Larkin Maloney and I called them Sufferin and Hellcrust) as well as to Thorncliffe (where the shopping centre and apartment buildings are now), Long

When I was 13 dad took me to Belfast. Here we are with Grandpa Smythe in a photo studio in Donegall Square.

For me, organized sports began when I was 10. The St. Alban's Cricket Club needed a scorekeeper and water boy and I got the job. That's me, the smallest. I also sang in the St. Alban's Cathedral School choir and when my mother turned up drunk I lied, and said she was my nanny.

First time I ever had my picture in the paper was with the unbeaten Lower Flat hockey team at Upper Canada College. I stared a lot at the line that read: C. Smythe, capt. That gave me a hold on something. I was poor but on the ice what I said, the others did. I liked that.

One day in front of our first house one kid said to another, "What's that mean on the truck, C. Smythe for Sand?" "Crazy Smythe, for Sand," the other said and they broke up laughing. But every morning at 5:00 the phone would start ringing and Irene would start writing out the orders, sometimes while feeding Stafford, our first child. When I only had one truck I used to sift gravel by shovelling it through an old bedspring. By the mid-twenties I had a fleet of loaders, crushers, and trucks and would have made a good living even if I'd never heard of hockey.

I started World War One as an artilleryman, but in 1917 switched to flying, was shot down at Passchendaele, and wound up in prison camps. Opposite, top left, I'm wearing the boots of a Russian officer named Logvinoff. Mine wore out. He said he had two pairs but I learned later he only kept a beat up pair for himself. On the back of the photo I wrote, "Note Logvinoff's boots." He came to Canada later and worked at the Gardens (opp., lower left). Opposite, right, Irene. This page: "The Maje," my men called me in World War Two. The Army thought I was too old but I did all right until I was hit at Caen and the war ended, for me.

"SEASONS GREETINGS" FROM THE 30TH BATTERY

From the late 1920's to the early 1960's (above) Christmas dinner was at our place, sometimes quite peacefully.

My great grandson Thomas Brent Smythe looks at the old man and, with Stafford and Tom, makes us four generations.

My 62nd birthday: we met in our teens and married eight years later, both still virgins. I never noticed that it hurt our marriage.

The title changed from time to time, but the badge number stayed the same.

As a boy, Hughie (left) was always gentle; where trouble was, you'd find Staff.

Art Ross in Boston always said I had no class. One night I showed him.

Syl Apps (holding cup) and Hap Day typified Leafs, to me: tough but clean.

In the U.S. I'd tell 'em how to sell tickets. "Start winning games," I'd say.

Sid Abel (left) and Gordie Howe, being inducted into Hockey Hall of Fame.

Gardens press room: Alf Jones, Army buddy; King Clancy, Milt Dunnell.

My first horse trainer, Bill Campbell. Together we scored big (see next page).

. . . when Dude Foden rode my Rare Jewel to win at 106-1! That bought Clancy.

(MICHAEL BURNS)

At my first Queen's Plate (Caledon Beau, 1958), with Vincent Massey.

(MICHAEL BURNS)

My stable wasn't big, but only E.P. Taylor won more stakes races.

(MICHAEL BURNS)

Irene named her, John trained her, Fitz rode her: Jammed Lovely, 1967.

Crippled Children's Centre: turning the sod in 1960, with friends.

(MICHAEL BURNS)

Above, with the Queen and crippled kids. Below, with Ruth Atkinson Hindmarsh and Beland Honderich when we finally got the deaf centre opened.

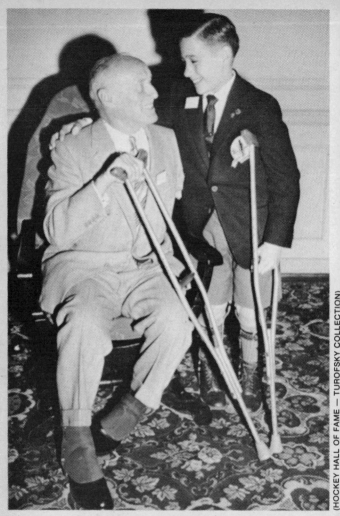

I couldn't always hug them or hold them close, but I could raise money.

Branch, Woodbine, Hamilton, and Windsor. Most years Irene and I went to the Kentucky Derby and every year without fail to Saratoga Springs for the summer meeting. At Saratoga we never stayed in the big hotels. A number of local people with big homes would take guests during the racing season and we liked that better than hotel living. There'd be six or eight paying guests and we'd have our meals together and talk racing, politics, the Lindbergh kidnapping, whatever was going. I've been back there in recent years and Saratoga has changed as much as Toronto has. For one thing, the last time I was there I didn't think Saratoga had as many good-looking women as it used to. Maybe they are all working as topless waitresses or something, instead of going to Saratoga with their sugar daddies.

In those days, the 1930's, I could rent a barn down there for two or three hundred dollars a season, with twelve or fourteen stalls. I had some good runners at that time. One, Skating Fool, set a track record at Keeneland in Kentucky in 1938, six furlongs in 1:06 – and incidentally paid $54.20, which didn't hurt much. At Saratoga when Canadians turned up around the betting ring the cry would go up, "The Brazilians are here!" Meaning, the nuts. That was because of the way we bet.

My Shoeless Joe came in one time at 10-1, which was a good day for the Brazilians, but not so good for the owner, because Shoeless Joe came up with a positive saliva test. I was furious, but it turned out that a man who was rubbing my horses was using a stimulant called coramine that was against the rules, certainly against my rules. I've always believed that all any horse needs is good oats, good hay, and kindness. I was hauled up in front of the racing commission and was so upset that I told them flatly I was going to get out of racing for life, when an owner could be publicly blasted for something a groom did. Jock Whitney, who was on the commission, talked me out of it. "We know you had nothing to do with this," he said. "We know you're interested in the sport. We want you to stay in racing and help keep it in a high place." I had a lot of respect for him and his horses, so I changed my mind about quitting. After the war when I went into racing again I wound up in a lot of arguments with other people, track management, and so on, but we'll get to that later. Everything I've ever done in racing has been to try to make it better, but sometimes that rubs people the wrong way.

I guess it would be about the summer of 1938 or 1939 that I found I was about $30,000 in the hole on my racing operations in the 1930's and Larkin and I decided that to get even, winning bets was faster than winning purses. I had a fast runner named Direct Hit which we took to New York and put him in a cheap race that we figured he could win. Our object was to make $15,000 on the day. But Direct Hit was caught at the wire by a Whitney horse, and we only made $3,000 besides the place money. But we did run him back the next week. He won and Maloney and I picked up better than $15,000.

I remember something else about that second race, too. We had spread out bets around several books. When we went to collect from one of them, a guy named Wolfgang, Wolfgang said he didn't have the money.

"Well," Larkin said, "up in our country when people don't pay their gambling debts we just pour concrete on him."

Wolfgang took a long look at him. Larkin could look pretty mean. "Stand here," the guy said to Larkin. As the bets came in on the next race the guy handed the money to Larkin and paid him off. So we'd made our $15,000. But just before our race in New York started, I got a wire from Dave Garrity in Toronto that a two-year-old I'd left there, Lady Marlboro, had won and paid $67 for $2. So we could have stayed in Toronto and bet $300 and made the same money, with a lot less trouble. It shows you how smart you are when you don't know anything.

From the beginning I wanted Stafford to grow up and follow me in what I was doing. Later, I wondered if in some ways I had made life too easy for him, and in other ways too hard. Miriam – I used to call her Meedee – once summed up one part of her childhood (she, Stafford, and Hugh) by saying, "We never lacked for anything. If we needed a bicycle, we got it. Or money. Or a fur coat."

Partly this indulgence would be an unconscious legacy from my own borrowed bikes, secondhand skates, hand-me-down clothes. For a long time, I never felt that I was too easy on them about money. Just in the last few years, however, something has made me wonder. In his teens, I let Stafford go his own way. He drove a convertible, sometimes with young Patricia standing on the seat with her arms around his neck. If he needed money, he got it, whether or not I was happy with what he was doing with it. But since his death, his widow, Dorothea, has told me that one of the few things she and Stafford argued seriously about was his treatment of Tommy, their son, who is as fine a young man as I've ever met anytime, anywhere. Stafford made Tommy, in his teens, polish cars, cut grass, clean windows, do all kinds of odd jobs. Treated him like a slave, sometimes. Whether Stafford did that because he thought I had brought him up wrong, I don't know. But there is another clue. In Stafford's will, Tommy would not get his share of Stafford's estate until he was thirty-five. Their older daughter received her share much earlier. Tommy has done well as a partner in Doug Laurie Sporting Goods Ltd. He always has had to work for what he has. Stafford must have felt that by the time Tommy was thirty-five he would know how to handle his life, and his money.

Sometimes I think back to the first time Stafford and I talked seriously about his future in my business.

"I'm not going into business with you," he said, flatly.

He was fourteen or fifteen then. I don't suppose there are many people still around who might have seen us walking around Baby Point that night in the middle of 1930's, father and son, stopping now and again in front of a house. I'd say, "All right, so and so lives here – he's in the charcoal business. You want to go to work for him?"

"No."

Walk a little farther. "And here's so and so – with Adams Furniture. That where you want to work?"

"No."

Another stretch along the sidewalk. "This one is with Imperial Oil. How about Imperial Oil, that where you want to work?"

"No."

At the end I said, "All right, tell me, which one of all these do you want to work for?"

He thought it over. After a while he looked at me. I remember the look. In appearance he was something like me, you know. Built like me. I don't remember for sure exactly how he said it, defiantly, resignedly, or what. Maybe I more or less bulldozed him into it.

"I want to work for you, dad," he said. And that was the way he made his decision to join me eventually in the sand and gravel business and in hockey, and take over when I was ready to move over, which wouldn't be for a long while yet.

You might wonder what I had in mind for Hughie. I thought when he was a child that he would be a doctor. He would dissect things to see how they worked. He was gentle, kind, and precise. I thought all Irene and I had to do for Stafford and Hughie was to see that they got the right education to prepare them. That turned out to be true.

Chapter Seven

I don't remember the first time I said it, but the most mis-understood remark I ever made was, "If you can't beat 'em in the alley, you can't beat 'em on ice." Even as wise a man as J. V. McAree, the *Globe and Mail*'s editorial page columnist of the time and the best they ever had, got all outraged about it, so you can imagine how the real career do-gooders reacted. They claimed I was telling my players to go out and bully the opposition. The ex-act opposite is true: I was telling them to refuse to be bullied. If you back up when challenged, somebody is always going to be making you back up. It can be in an alley, across a boardroom table, across your boss's desk, or in an NHL rink. Of course, it is a great line for the stimulation of self-righteousness among people who would have trouble staring down a bunny rabbit, but I never found any trouble explaining the idea to people whose aim in life is to be a winner. I felt pretty good in the spring of 1980, in fact, when I was told that during the Stanley Cup final between New York Islanders and Philadelphia Flyers the Islanders' general manager, Bill Torrey, went to the dressing room and said that a long time ago, up in Canada, a man named Conn Smythe had this idea that no matter how much more skilful you are than another team, you can't win if you allow yourself to be intimidated. Islanders went on to beat Philadelphia Flyers, and Bill Torrey's father wrote me a letter to tell me that I should be proud because my words, and a proper understanding of them, had helped Islanders get into the frame of mind they needed to·beat the Flyers.

When I was adding and subtracting from the Leafs in the 1930's I was looking for brave men, not big bruisers. Of course, we already had Red Horner and a few others who could look after themselves. But Syl Apps was the epitome of the kind of player I wanted. The first time I saw him was in late November of 1934. An Intercollegiate football game between U. of T. and McMaster was a warm-up for the Grey Cup, first game of the doubleheader. Irene and I went early and Apps at halfback for McMaster was running rings around everybody, scoring touchdowns, taking tough tackles, never quitting. I knew he'd been playing senior hockey in Hamilton while going to school. Art Ross had scouted him and come back saying that Apps, who had won a gold at the British Empire Games that year, was going through for the ministry and also was planning to pole vault for Canada in the 1936 Olympics, still two years away, so certainly didn't want to be a pro. Ross said he was damned if he wanted a minister on his team anyway. Well, I still didn't know how good a hockey player Apps was, but he was showing me that he was a great athlete. And Ross had been wrong before, once or twice.

"Smythie," I said to myself, "you've made a lot of boners but this shouldn't be one of them." At half time I jumped to my feet and started to climb across Irene toward the aisle. "Excuse me, Mama," I said.

"Where are you going?"

"I'm going to put that young man on Leafs' list."

"Hockey, even at a football game!" she groaned.

I phoned in Apps's name to the NHL negotiation list. To avoid costly bidding wars, no team could go after a player on another team's list. But the list was limited to a few names. If you couldn't make a deal with a player you'd have to drop him from your list sooner or later. Apps took up a place on our list for almost two years. He was worth it. I talked to him first and then went to Paris, Ontario, and talked to his mother. (Ernie Apps, his father, had died a few years before.) I found her to be a wonderful lady. They weren't rich people. I said that the pro hockey dollar was just as good as any other dollar, and that when Syl had his education at McMaster and had gone to the Olympics he could get a good stake out of hockey and go on to do anything he wanted. She helped me to talk to Syl. Two years later he got back from the Berlin Olympics. Typically, he had made the highest pole vault of his life to come sixth and gain points for Canada. In a few days he signed with Leafs and that season not only won the rookie award but was a close second to Sweeney Schriner for the scoring championship.

He never played a game in the minors. From the start his great skating and clean play made him one of the stars, a man people loved to watch.

We made quite a few changes that year, one of them being that Primeau retired. I briefly tried Apps between Conacher and Jackson, but that didn't work at all. Those two had to have someone like Joe doing all their lifting for them. I wasn't going to sacrifice the Apps talent to work like Primeau had, to make stars out of two other guys. Gord Drillon, a good scorer, came up the same year as Apps. We put them together, first with Buzz Boll, then with Harvey Jackson, and finally with Bob Davidson. That turned out to be ideal. Bob had come up through our minor system, a loyal man. As Primeau had, he got as much kick out of making sure his linemates led the league, as if he had led the league himself. A real Maple Leaf type. Apps was clean but couldn't be intimidated. Once Flash Hollett separated him from a couple of his teeth. I never saw one fellow demolish another as fast as Apps did Hollett.

There was one other player of the late 1930's I should have had years sooner than I did, Bucko McDonald. Jack Adams of Detroit diddled me on that. Adams had been a clean heady player himself, but as a manager he would stop at nothing. Years later, I once saw Toe Blake of Canadiens go down right at the Detroit bench and get kicked around the face by Adams. I don't think it was by mistake. Anyway, the first time I had an interest in Bucko McDonald was around 1933 or 1934. Adams and I were on some kind of a trip together. I thought there was no nicer guy to travel with! He seemed content to take second place all the time to me, which was nice; nobody else trying to hog the limelight. Once on that trip we got talking.

"You got any good players coming up?" he asked me.

"Well," I said to good old Jack, "I've got a couple of young ones coming along and there's another at Buffalo I've got my eye on. He's played mostly lacrosse so far and it will take him a year or two to adapt to hockey, but I think he'll be a good one."

"Who?" he said.

"Bucko McDonald," I said.

When I got back to my office later I said to my secretary. "You'd better get Bucko McDonald onto Leaf's list." She wired his name in to league headquarters and got a reply saying Bucko had just been taken by Detroit. It isn't the kind of thing I would do, taking advantage of something said in confidence. In fact, a few years later I saw Lester Patrick's son, Murray, playing in the minors. I knew he would be a good one, but I called Lester in New York and told him if he didn't get Murray on Rangers' list in twenty-four hours I would put him on mine. He did.

It didn't take me long to get even with Adams. In 1936, the same year Apps turned pro, I was looking for a goalie to replace George Hainsworth, who had followed Chabot in the Toronto nets but was nearly forty-one. I didn't get along with him anyway. I went to a minor league game in Windsor to look at Earl Robertson playing goal for the Windsor Bulldogs against Detroit Olympics, both of them Detroit farms. I liked Robertson, but spent most of my time watching Turk Broda in goal for the Olympics. Later Detroit beat us in the Stanley Cup final, ending it right in our rink with old Jim Norris sitting in front of me. When it was over I leaned over to him and said, "Now that you've won, have a little mercy on me. Sell us that Broda."

He said, "Okay, Connie." I think the price was $8,000, a bargain. Detroit had Normie Smith in goal then, in his prime, Vezina trophy winner the following year, and neither Norris nor Adams could have known that within a couple of years he'd be through. Adams must have ground his teeth every time he saw Broda play for us, after that.

I always believed in Broda. Hainsworth started that season for us, but in Broda's first start he beat Detroit, and I made up my mind. I released Hainsworth outright and said, "Broda is my goalie." He was the best I ever had with the Leafs, although when Johnny Bower came along years later I ranked him with Broda. He was like Broda in some ways. Turk's happy-go-lucky nature fooled some people, but was an asset. When he got beaten 9-0 or something, to him that was just a game. It was over. The next night, it was Turk Broda against the other team again. He knew he could play goal and rise to heights, and the past never worried him, not like some guys who have a bad night and then go all to pieces. He was also as decent and loyal as a man could be, not only in hockey but when he worked for me summers at the sand pit. Decency and loyalty go a long way with me. Not everybody had them. I brought Elmer Lach to Toronto to go to St. Michael's College and he agreed to sign with me, but he deserted – went back out west without a word to me – and played senior a while before going to star in Montreal for many years.

Everything in my life changed in the autumn of 1939 when World War Two began. Right away I tried to get back in the services. This caused all kinds of trouble at home. Irene was really exasperated with me. She couldn't see why, after fighting one war, I had to go and fight another. I felt it was a shame that we had to go back to Europe and win the war again that we thought we'd won for all time back in 1918. But if we had to, I wanted to be there. It was a lot easier to talk that way to reporters in Boston and New York on trips late in 1939 and get headlines about what a fighter I was than it was to talk to Irene. The main thing, I think, was that for years I had been talking to hockey players in military terms – telling them what real soldiers were like, how much they would do for their team, how much they'd give, and how brave they had to be to survive. When war came I had to face that. Had I been talking fiction or fact? Was I a fraud or did I live up to my own principles? I had made myself out to be a warrior and tried to make my players be warriors too. I thought it was up to me to lead, set an example.

Several Gardens' employees and one player, Jack Fox, who had been in our farm system, enlisted immediately. Later, Fox was killed in action. A few were in France before it fell in 1940. I arranged in October, 1939, for Leaf players to take army training with the Toronto Scottish on mornings when the team was in town, and in the summer of 1940 wrote urging every player to join at least the militia. After they had done that, I told them,

1. You might be wanted immediately.
2. They might not need you for a comparatively long time.
3. They might not need you at all, but have outlined a military training scheme which includes you all.

It is my advice, therefore, no matter what your age or your position as a family man, that you sign up immediately with some non-permanent militia unit and get military training in as soon as possible. The advantages are obvious. In case you are honoured with a call to the Canadian forces, you will be ready. If you are not called, you will have complied with the military training regulations and be free to play hockey until called on . . .

I followed up a few weeks later with a questionnaire on what units they had joined, and when. It was a matter of some pride to me that by September, 1940, the club had twenty-five men taking military training – mostly players but also including coach Hap Day (who had made lance-corporal) and Foster Hewitt. Leafs led the league in that respect, by far, although as the years went by I was disappointed with the number of pro hockey players who went active. But those under my control were ready if called, and could not be blamed for a vacillating government that for most of the war refused to put in conscription for overseas service even when lack of it was costing Canadian lives in shorthanded units overseas. As for myself, I have kept a yellowed old clipping on how I was talking then. It is from a Boston paper. I talked about "starting out as a barefoot boy" and about the many people who had helped me along the way to where I had a happy and prosperous family, a successful business, a fine and loyal hockey team, and a group of employees who always had a happy word for me when I came to work. Then according to the reporter, I demanded, "IF I WOULDN'T FIGHT FOR MY COUNTRY, WHO WOULD?" That's the way I felt, in a nutshell.

Saying it and doing it were two different things. I was forty-five. Just telling the country I was available didn't seem to be enough. Nobody was breaking down the doors to get me back into uniform. I, and a lot of other people, thought Canada was dragging its feet. Mackenzie King, the Prime Minister, never said anything straight out if he could possibly dodge it by saying maybe. Right at the time when the Germans were overrunning France, our defence minister, Norman Rogers, was killed in an air crash, which made things worse. Groups of prominent Canadians demanded in full-page advertisements that Major-General Andrew McNaughton, a soldier and scientist who had recently taken the First Canadian Division overseas, and had been on the cover of *Life* magazine as the best general in the Commonwealth Armies, should be brought back to organize our war effort. I made speeches to that effect and wrote letters to newspapers and to Mackenzie King. A lot of others – especially other veterans of the First War – were doing the same. But it was all talk and no action. Eventually I went to my old friend, Bay Arnoldi, who had been in the militia between the wars with the rank of colonel. "How do I get in?" I asked.

He said he could put me to work in the Non-Permanent Active Militia, but first I should take some refresher courses at the university. That I did, writing exams in July, 1940. When I passed with the rank of captain, Colonel Arnoldi put me in charge of "A" troop of "A" company, Canadian Officers Training Corps, University of Toronto, based at the University Armories. We trained on nights and Saturdays. By then the National Resources Mobilization Act had been passed, calling young, single men into compulsory training. They didn't have to serve overseas if they didn't volunteer to do so; another typical Mackenzie King weaseling away from responsibility. At first the call-ups only had to train for thirty days. One camp was at Niagara-on-the-Lake. I spent some time there but was still only part-time and was bugging every senior officer I could find to get me into a unit going overseas. One day my bunch of trainees was to be inspected by Colonel Arnoldi. It looked like rain. Regulations said we had to wear respirators. We put our raincoats on over them. We all bulged in front. When Colonel Arnoldi came along to inspect, an officer with him got off a kind of facetious remark.

"Smythe," this officer chuckled, "you look as if you're pregnant."

I must have been feeling frustrated that day. "Well, why shouldn't I?" I snarled. "I've been screwed by every senior officer in the Canadian Army."

Oddly enough, that remark made a hit. I could get away with it because they knew how hard I'd been trying. I had even taken a refresher in flying, doing all the old loops and rolls and stalls and forced landings to get my pilot's licence restored, although I had hated all flying since being shot down in the First War. Stafford joined the Navy as an ordinary seaman, but I couldn't get into an active unit. I was still running the Gardens and the Leafs, keeping track of my racing stable (I had nine running at Narragansett at one time in 1940), and keeping the sand and gravel business going.

Then one day early in 1941 I had an idea. Why didn't I form a Sportsmen's Battery, like the one I'd served in under Gordon Southam? Some people are reluctant to copy someone else's idea. That's a mistake. If the idea is a good one, it deserves to be copied. I thought if I could go out and form my own Battery, hustle for recruits, and get it organized, they'd *have* to let me take it overseas.

Once again, I went to Bay Arnoldi. He listened. Another Colonel, Richard H. Greer took over from there. He had taken his own Sportsmen's Battalion overseas to fight in the First War. He came to the Gardens and told me he'd help. At the end of June in 1941 I was relieved of my officers' training classes at the university to work on it full-time and on September 5, 1941, the 30th Battery was formed, as part of the 7th Toronto Regiment, Royal Canadian Artillery, Canadian Active Army. How I loved that word, active. I was named the 30th's Officer Commanding, and acting Major, ten days later. The 30th became my challenge. I talked it up. Men with sports backgrounds already in the Army put in for transfers to the 30th. The Mimico Mountaineers had just won the Mann Cup, the Canadian lacrosse championship. They came down in a body and joined up.

Other men with sports connections came in, too – Jim Boeckh, one of the finest golfers in the country, ball players, football and hockey players, even sportswriters. I took in as my batman Scotty McColgan, who'd worked at the sand pit for me from the day he stepped off the train in Toronto and came to say hello to his brother, who worked for me. Scotty had then moved to the Gardens as a security man and was a good mechanic, looking after my cars.

One funny call came from a lady with a broad Scottish accent who said, "Major Smythe, my wee laddie is coming down to join your unit on Monday, and will you please look after him?"

I got a surprise when the wee laddie who showed up was Don (Shanty) McKenzie, who'd been playing for the Argonauts and was more than two hundred pounds. Some wee laddie! He became a first-rate sergeant. He had the size to give orders and make them stick, but he always did it politely.

That was a good time for me, the fall of 1941. I was clearing the decks for what I knew would come eventually: orders to move elsewhere for the kind of training you couldn't do in the old Toronto Armories. Also, I felt I was finally catching up. Jack Bickell had been put in charge of organizing the early stages of Ferry Command, flying bombers to Britain. George Cottrelle was Canada's oil controller. Stafford had been commissioned a sublieutenant and was headed for convoy escort duty on the Atlantic coast. Miriam finished school in the summer of 1941 and immediately joined the women's division of the RCAF, training in Ottawa and Trenton.

Irene and I had only Hugh and young Patricia at home with us by then. Irene would sometimes come down to the armories for parties or a mess dinner. She was also busy with war work and curled a little. I'm pretty sure she was secretly on the side of some higher-ups in the services who didn't feel comfortable with the idea of a forty-six-year-old major going overseas in command of a Battery. I kept hearing how some people in the Army wanted to let me recruit the Battery and then give it to some thirty-two-year-old lieutenant-colonel to take overseas. I was sent to the Maritimes ostensibly to check out the chances of operating a senior hockey team out of an Army camp, recommended otherwise, and then was offered a job as sports officer for the entire army, as lieutenant-colonel, colonel, or something. I told them what they could do with that one. It was the beginning of a long fight to keep my Battery.

Meanwhile, I kept on making my own preparations. Hap would run the gravel pit; I told him to do whatever he wanted when I was away but to have $10,000 cash for me in the bank when I got home. I sold all my horses at sacrifice prices.

I'd been planning the hockey side of the move for more than a year. As far back as early 1940 I had spoken to the Gardens' directors about taking a leave of absence when the time came that I would be shipped out of Toronto. In 1940 Montreal Canadiens had finished last with Pit Lepine coaching. They wanted another coach badly. I called them and suggested Dick Irvin, my coach. That might sound strange. After all, we'd been in the Stanley Cup final more often than not during Dick's years with Leafs. But I didn't think he was tough enough, without me backing him up, to do what needed to be done. I wanted to leave someone in charge who would run the team the way I ran it when I was there. Montreal was delighted at the chance to get Dick, and he took a step up in pay. That gave me the chance to put in Hap Day as coach in the fall of 1940. Hap was everything I wanted. He could do things I couldn't: fire people; bench them; live always on what a man could do today, not what he had done a few years ago.

When the season started in the fall of 1941 the Battery was shaping up well, and I knew I hadn't more than two or three months at the most before we'd be leaving for further training. I have memos from Foster Hewitt and Hap Day, dated September, 1941, in reply to my instructions that they should go out now and buy equipment to last for years – radio and communications stuff for Foster, hockey equipment for the Leafs – because we all knew war shortages would get worse. Both reported that they'd given the orders. And I figured I was leaving Hap with a pretty good hockey team. Lorne Carr and Sweeney Schriner had made a good line with New York Americans, centred by Art Chapman. I'd got Schriner in 1939. In 1941, with the Americans in bad shape financially, they sold me Carr. Little Billy Taylor, between them, made a potent line. Wally Stanowski was a really rousing young all-star defenceman. Another young Winnipegger, Pete Langelle, the one they called the dipsy-doodler because of his dazzling skating, like Stanowski had been called up for playoffs for a couple of years and finally stuck with the Leafs – and also gave all of us a few laughs.

The first time Pete signed with the Leafs, he took the money and bought a new car that I knew must have taken nearly his whole salary. I was concerned, because some hockey players when they first get their hands on real money need a little guidance. I said to him, "Have you arranged to handle your income tax?"

"I don't have any income tax," he said, shrugging it off. "I spent all my money on this car, so I haven't got any money to pay tax on."

I said, "The government isn't going to see it that way."

"How am I going to pay any tax?" he said, baffled. "I'm just breaking even!" He was a hell of a hockey player, and a great income tax man, too.

Also that summer of 1941, I had signed some promising rookies – Bob Goldham, Ernie Dickens, and Johnny McCreedy. So Leafs were pretty well stocked when late in November of 1941, I called a meeting of Gardens' directors and told them I'd be shipping out soon and wanted to start my leave of absence. The idea was that a committee, including Ed Bickle, Bill MacBrien, and Frank Selke, would take over running the Gardens and, with Hap, the team. At that meeting, I was supposed to give some advice as to how I thought things should be done while I was away. But the new committee was in such a hurry! Three or four directors stayed in the room listening to me, while Bickle, MacBrien, and Selke went off into Selke's office. I went by there a few minutes later. Already they were talking about deals they would make!

I asked, "My God, don't you wait until the corpse stops breathing?"

I never saw anybody so anxious to get rid of a man as those three were to get rid of me. It was a strange feeling. I felt I was being taught right that minute that I was finished with Leafs, not only for now, but for ever.

A couple of weeks later, the Japanese attacked Pearl Harbor. Ralph Allen, the *Globe and Mail* sports columnist, red-haired and overweight, came to join the Battery the next day. "Until now," he said, "I wasn't all that interested in getting in the Army. But now I am." He had the right idea. Everything was being speeded up because that was a bad winter in the war, with the Japanese running the Allies right out of mainland Asia and taking control of the Pacific so fast that it was staggering. From various training areas in Ontario, and sometimes back in Toronto on leave, I could keep track of what was going on in the Gardens. Hap Day kept me in touch. He was doing fine with the Leafs. All through the league that season teams were being changed constantly through enlistments and call-ups. In February Boston's entire Kraut Line – Milt Schmidt, Porky Dumart, and Bobby Bauer – wound up in the RCAF. I think close to eighty players were in uniform by mid-winter. We finished second to Rangers but beat them in the playoffs while Detroit qualified to meet us in what would become one of the most famous of all Stanley Cup finals.

I was in Petawawa by then, finishing a course to qualify as a major. I suffered plenty from a distance when that final series started on April 4 in Toronto and we lost 3-2, then 4-2. When the teams moved to Detroit we lost 5-2 and were down three games. Hap told me by phone that he was planning to shake up the team for the fourth game: and he did, benching Drillon and McDonald. We were down 2-0 late in the second period of that one but came alive to win 4-3, swamped them 9-3 in Toronto in the fifth game, and squared the series when Broda shut them out 3-0 back in Detroit. The largest crowd to attend a hockey game in Canada up to that time, 16,218, crowded into the Gardens for the seventh game. And one of them was me, on leave, and being welcomed by Bickle, MacBrien, and Selke the way a skunk is welcomed at a garden party.

It was a weird position for me. No matter who was president in the past, I'd been allowed to run things. Now with president George Cottrelle busy as oil controller for Canada, Ed Bickle as executive vice-president was in charge. We'd never got along. His welcome that night was to bar me from Leafs' dressing room. People always thought that I did exactly what I wanted to, around the Gardens. Some years, that was true. But as a soldier I took orders from my commanding officer and disobeyed only when I knew I was right. Bickle was my superior at the Gardens and how could I be sure he was wrong? Leafs had come back from being three games down. Suppose they lost this final game and people said that my coming back and going into the dressing room cost them the series? Yet I knew and Hap knew what I could do in a dressing room. I was good at touching the raw spots, even with people I trusted. I'd give them as much as I knew they could take, send them out hating me, and they'd go and destroy the enemy, just to show me up.

And Hap came to me, wanted me in.

I said I couldn't, that Bickle had forbade it.

He said he would go and punch Bickle in the face, that the team had put up a tremendous effort but required another, and one little spark might be all the players needed. He said, "When you talk to them, they go out only touching the floor every third step." So I went in. I didn't do much good the first time. But at the end of the second period when we were down 1-0 and going nowhere I went in again, past Hughie, who was stickboy that year, thinking up my speech. I could see that the game had slowed down because both teams were tired. That lessening of the speed made the game exactly right for old Sweeney Schriner and old Lorne Carr and young Billy Taylor. I walked over to the corner where they were and gave it to them hard, one at a time and then all three. I'll never forget Sweeney looking up at me with a grin. "What ya worrying about, boss? We'll get you a couple of goals."

He went out and scored the tying goal. Pete Langelle got the winner. Sweeney put in another as insurance. The final score was 3-1. I went out and got back on the train and returned to Petawawa. Ted Reeve wrote in his *Telegram* column years later, "We didn't see that series, but the Maje got down from Petawawa for the final match and came back feeling so good we got away with only two hours gun drill and the route march was cut down to ten miles."

Incidentally, the only time I ever forged someone else's signature was on a medical for Reeve. There was nothing about his physical condition that was right. He had flat feet, bashed-up knees, arthritis in every joint, dislocated shoulders. You name an athletic injury, and Reeve had it, from lacrosse and football. When we all went through medicals at Petawawa, a doctor there wouldn't sign Reeve's. I guess he was right. But he let me forge his name and I got away with it. Later on, nobody but me could have got him overseas and then to France. Whenever there was a move and everybody had to go through medicals, I would send Reeve ahead with an advance party and they'd miss him. He had missed the First War and wanted to be part of this one. I thought he was the bravest man in our Battery, just to be there.

It was a good thing there were people like him in the country with the idiotic military service law we had. After Mackenzie King foisted on the country what his biographer, R. MacGregor Dawson, called the "incantation" of conscription if necessary, but not necessarily conscription, we were practically forced back into the old days of British Navy press gangs. Call-up training had been extended from thirty days originally to four months and then to indefinite service, but still only for home defence unless a man volunteered to "go active," and serve anywhere. However, the Army needed men overseas, not in Canada, so we got a lot of soldiers to go active by quite nasty ways. I saw it first at elementary training near Brantford. One way was to put together a platoon half of volunteers and half not. They'd train together, sleep in the same hut, get to know one another, always with attempts being made by their officers – speeches, exhortations, extra leaves – to get the reserve men to volunteer for overseas services. Then when training was nearly complete, the C.O. would get up, say on a Monday, and offer the whole unit forty-eight hour passes – *if* everybody had volunteered to go active by, say, Wednesday noon. Then naturally the actives in the unit, wanting the leave, would try to persuade the home defence guys. The persuasion could be verbal, physical, even brutal. I needed ten or twelve men to go active when we were finishing our training. I talked to about fifty non-actives and it was the best speech of my life. I had three fellows stashed in the crowd, to start the rush to the colours. I was really going good, the old pep-talk artist at high form. I would have charged the highest mountain myself after I got through with that speech – and when I finished with a stirring call for men to stand up and volunteer to go with us – my three tame ones stood up and not one other man.

Well, we had to get some, anyway. Some of my bombardiers asked me how many I needed. I said maybe ten or a dozen. They put a bunch of the non-actives under cold showers, some for a couple of hours, until they hollered for help and said they'd go active in the morning. We had a dozen volunteer the next day, as promised. They were good soldiers, as fine a group as you could have got anywhere. Some people looked down on men who wouldn't go active. They should have looked down instead on the prime minister and men in the cabinet who refused to order full conscription, the way favoured in every province except Quebec, as a plebiscite in April 1942 showed. Those fifty soldiers I spoke to in Brantford, I understood completely how they felt about it. I didn't see anything wrong with their view at all. If Canada had put in conscription that night, a sharing of the load fair to all, they would have volunteered happily to go overseas. But they were not going to join up, say twenty of them, and leave the other thirty back home to steal their girls and live off the fat of the land. When there are not enough volunteers to fill an Army, conscription is the only fair way. By Mackenzie King's way, which stunk, fairness went out the window. A couple of Quebec officers I knew at Petawawa used to get very upset if anyone said Quebec wasn't as loyal as the rest of Canada, despite the Quebec attitude toward conscription. I said, well, then, why don't we have conscription in the eight provinces that want it and let Quebec supply the equivalent in volunteers on a pro-rated basis according to population? I thought that would be a simple way of solving the problem. Except that simple ways of solving problems aren't acceptable in politics.

However, other things were more immediate to me. To protect my chances of taking my Battery overseas at my age I felt I had to have the best Battery in the Army. I didn't want to be more than a major – rank didn't matter. In fact, I knew that the only way I could get a promotion would be to take a job away from the Battery, which I wouldn't do. So I had the luck of being able to concentrate on the job I had, unmixed with any ambition to have a bigger one.

I never had any discipline problems that were serious. In fact, people above me probably had more discipline problems with me than I had with my men. They thought so, anyway. In June of 1942, we were moved to Vancouver Island's west coast to defend

against the possibility of Japanese attack. A submarine had shelled
the coast and got everybody's wind up that there'd be an invasion.
The troop train they were going to put us on was made up of those
old colonist cars, the kind they used to take harvesters out west. I
took one look and thought, three or four days on that? I knew a
man pretty well in the CPR, from dealing with them for Leafs over
the years. I talked to him and somehow an on-purpose mistake
was made by the CPR in the tickets they issued. They sent the
whole Battery out there first class, every man with a berth and
meals in the diner. There was a huge Army fuss about it after. The
higher-ups knew somehow that it had been no mistake. But it was
very, very good for morale. The men thought it was a great joke,
which it was, and they gave me the credit, which was a nice
change. A lot of them used to swear at me sometimes. Gunner
Reeve once told me that when I got up at a parade my helmet
would be jumping up and down like the lid on a hot tea-kettle and
at those times the guys in the ranks would mutter, "The Old Man's
really up for it today." But they did like going first class.

So on the coast we manned our guns, and sometimes a big log
would look like a submarine to some trigger happy guy in a gun
pit and we'd give it a few bursts from the Bofors guns. Which
makes me think again of Ralph Allen. He was a sergeant by then,
the most slovenly soldier who ever lived. We had another sergeant
who'd built houses in North Toronto. One day on an inspection
when I came to the other sergeant's gun pit, it looked like a suite at
the Royal York. Then I went along to Allen's. It looked like a
newspaper office – you know, slots all over the place – junk
everywhere. He could see the disappointment in my face.

"Well, what's the matter with it, Major Smythe?" he asked.
"Isn't it all right?"

I said, "Well, Sergeant Allen, it ain't no Taj Mahal."

The Army remembered to send us second class when they
shipped us back across the country in September of 1942 for
embarkation leave before going to England. A few weeks earlier
there was a crisis at home. I was too far away to interfere but, in
time, I stopped being sorry about that. For three or four years
Stafford's steady girl friend had been Dorothea Gaudette, who
was pretty and dark and somebody I liked, all but her religion. She
was Catholic, and her mother didn't like her going out with a Protestant any more than I liked Staff going out with a Catholic.

Even when it was just "going out" there was trouble. Mrs. Gaudette would phone and bawl hell out of me for Stafford keeping Dorothea out late, at a time when her deadline was 11:00 p.m. and his was midnight. When Staff enlisted, they were in love. Being apart while he trained naturally didn't suit them.

In August, 1942, I got a phone call from Irene, badly upset, saying that they were going to be married quietly in a few days by a priest. I had a furlough coming up later in the month and asked, well, maybe demanded, that she get them to wait until I could get home. They wouldn't. Stafford was on leave and was due back in Halifax. In the end they had two services on the same day, one by a priest and the other in a United Church, both quiet, just family, and neither with me present, which probably was just as well. When I did get home later that month letters from both Staff and Dorothea were waiting.

Stafford wrote me from Halifax that he and Dorothea had discussed the religion side years before and had settled that they would be married in a Protestant church and their children brought up as Protestants. Before the marriage he had made this plain to Mrs. Gaudette, "who wouldn't believe that Dot meant that. She just adopted a 'that's impossible' attitude, because Dot is not allowed, etc. So I extracted her promise never to interfere with Dot. However, I fell down in not asking Dot to get the same promise from her mother. I just couldn't on my last night with her. . ."

Dorothea's letter was three handwritten pages, full of qualities in her that I later learned to appreciate.

By the time you get this letter, Staff and I will be married. We felt we owed you an explanation which I am writing, because Staff had done something to hurt you and hated to be the one to tell you. We are being married very quietly on Monday evening by a priest. I know that is against your wishes, but until the end of the war I have to live at home and that is impossible if I get married any other way, as I would be a total disgrace in the eyes of some people. You must believe me that things would have been to your liking if the war was over.

You have been very kind to me, although I guess you never really approved of me going with Staff. We have tried to stop seeing each other more than once because of the difference in our religion, but we just couldn't do it. I promise you that our children will be brought up in a way in which you will be a very proud grandfather . . . I would never have my children go through what I have.

I am sorry that things have to be this way. I would have loved a big wedding, maybe not so big, but with everyone there, and with no hard feelings. Maybe someday a daughter of mine can have the sort of wedding I would have liked. But anyway we will have each other, and the days won't be so long and lonely if we get married now. Our marriage is not starting off very well, but maybe that will make for a happy ending. I guess there is nothing more to say, except that I am very sorry.

Yours sincerely, Dorothea.

Dorothea was a wonderful wife to Staff and in the end, a wonderful friend of mine. At home on leave, I found myself reassuring Irene. On my way to embark for overseas in October I managed to get together with Stafford in Halifax. It was a good reunion. We were proud of each other. His impatience for action -- when in convoys men would die in freezing water or flaming oil -- reminded me of myself nearly thirty years earlier when I'd always been telling other people how to run that war. And back home, soon Irene and Dorothea were going to movies together, becoming friends.

The last communication I had from Maple Leaf Gardens, incidentally, before going overseas, was a telegram from Ed Bickle asking me to resign from the executive committee so they could appoint someone who would be around to attend meetings. I replied that I didn't like the idea but if everyone wanted me off, okay. Apparently it wasn't unanimous so it was dropped. Just another prod from Bickle that, sailing for overseas, I could have done without.

In World War One we came to England to finish off our training; in this one we were trained and nearly ready, although before manning coastal defences we went on a few exercises or schemes. Some of these were fairly rough - must have been - because after a strenuous one in Wales Reeve wrote back to the effect that after the exercise just completed, the general opinion in the Battery was that the next one would be for the Battery to swim the English Channel and back just to see if it could be done. At first we lived in an old barracks in Colchester, but soon were posted along the south coast in three different locations on anti-aircraft duty. My headquarters was in Eastbourne. Occasionally I went up to London on leave and once met Stafford there for dinner. Later that night there was a raid, not a very serious one by that time in the war, but with a lot of guns firing while we walked the blacked-out streets talking and laughing, having a great time.

With my Battery's gun troops scattered, each with an officer in charge, I was often on the move along the south coast, too. That was where it helped to be commanding people who had been involved in sports. Sometimes I could sit for an hour or two in a gun position and talk about old hockey games or old football games with people who had been there or even played in them. Reeve had lived his life in the Balmy Beach area of Toronto. I'd spent time down there, too, paddling for the Balmy Beach juniors, hanging out with Harvey Aggett. We all had things in common. Brigadiers were always turning up who had played football for Reeve when he coached at Queen's or elsewhere. I remember one time marching along with one of them. I saw Reeve and got him to fall in with us. As we marched along I said, "The Brigadier here said he played for you at Queen's."

Reeve craned his neck around me to get a good look at the beaming Brigadier and then said in that gravelly voice he has, "The man's an imposter."

Reeve's knowledge of English literature was considerable. Once in Eastbourne I heard about two authors living there and made arrangements for Reeve and I to call on them, Jeffrey Farnol, a famous writer of swashbuckling adventure stories, and A. S. M. Hutchinson, who wrote the great best-seller of the First War, *When Winter Comes*. While I talked horses with Mrs. Hutchinson I could hear Reeve and Hutchinson talking about Bret Harte and Daniel Defoe. Hutchinson showed Reeve a first edition copy of Sinclair Lewis's famous novel, *Main Street*, autographed on the flyleaf, "To Hutch, from Red."

Gunner Reeve was almost as old as I was, of course. He drank. I didn't. Neither of us chased women to any extent. Sometimes when others would be away on weekend leaves we'd sit around and talk by the hour, often with one other soldier, a good ball player who Reeve and I agreed was a nice quiet man, like us, although often he did ask for a pass from sundown to roll call the next morning. It was some time later that we found he had done a certain amount of free-lance antique collecting in country houses in the area that had been closed up for the war. I've seen the man often since. He might be still in the same business. At Battery reunions, he usually sits near the exit, as if he would like to be able to leave in a hurry if the occasion arose.

As any man who has been away to war knows all too well, times like that are breaks in loneliness. Letters from home were read and re-read, arriving in batches surrounded by long dry spells. Photos and snapshots of my family were the first thing I put up when I moved my quarters: Patricia and Hughie holding up a good-sized fish Hugh had caught, Patricia standing with her thin legs and wide smile between snowbanks on the front walk, Miriam in her Air Force uniform, Irene and Patricia with Hugh in a cadet uniform, a photo of Staff with a scrawl, "From the Navy to the Army."

Irene kept a careful account, I found later, of all her income and expenses when I was away. She was better off than some wives, of course. From my Army pay of $7.75 a day (all but about $100 a month assigned to her) and her $79 a month dependents' allowance, she averaged around $220 a month, but this was augmented by around $400 a month from Maple Leaf Gardens, plus occassional dividends, and $95 a month (plus dividends) from C. Smythe Limited. She saw that my father was sent $100 a month and that all the bills were paid. Dorothea and Stafford were on the west coast by then, Staff hoping for a transfer to the Fleet Air Arm, which he got – and his letters full of the doings of their first daughter.

Among the family letters were others. Ralph Allen left the Battery in April, 1943, after a discharge request from the *Globe and Mail* so he could be their war correspondent. He wrote to me saying he was staying at the Park Lane Hotel, and "to find me just go along Piccadilly and turn left at the third whore – you can't miss it." He also said that his time with the Battery had been "the most profitable if not the most useful sixteen months of my life," which pleased me (I think).

Hap Day's letters kept me up on how we were doing (pretty well) at the sand pit and sometimes let a worry creep through about decisions being made at the Gardens with me gone: "When there are meetings of the executive committee there is no one in there to fight for anything . . .". This bothered me. Selke's voluminous letters – five in one month early in 1944, totalling eleven single-spaced pages with no margins – were full of expressions of loyalty "to you, boss," and news of new players and old, including a mention of the fighting qualities of one rookie, Tommy O'Neill, who Hap Day also commended tersely with two words: Clancy fight. Selke also made a point a couple of times that Montreal was the team least hit by the war because Quebec had the highest percentage of call-up deferments in the country, and some of them were playing for Canadiens.

We were more than twenty months in England. Much of it was a fight to keep my command. On no less than seven occasions, skeptical medical officers ordered me to take special medical boardings (examinations). Each time they rubbed their eyes and marked down another "A," but it was getting on my nerves. Around my forty-ninth birthday in 1944 I stormed into Canadian Military Headquarters in London, intending to have the whole thing out with the highest officer there. He wasn't in. A colonel named Bill Abel from Winnipeg told me I was safe, but I didn't feel fully reassured until a friend of mine from Toronto, then a Brigadier, A. Bruce Matthews, came up from Italy in the spring of 1944 after serving there as artillery commander of the First Division. He was taking over a similar job with the Canadian Second Corps and soon was promoted to Major-General. He had been in action and his outlook was a godsend to me. I explained to him what had been happening, all the medicals, how much I'd gone through to get there, the responsibility I felt to people who had joined my Battery because of me. "I would hate to be sent home and let them think that I got them here, and then walked out without firing a shot," I said.

He said, "Connie, if your unit keeps on the way it is, the best light anti-aircraft Battery in the Army, nobody will ever get you out while I have the power to stop it."

I went out of there feeling as if the weight of the world had just been lifted from my shoulders – and then there was an incident that almost screwed it all up.

Two or three weeks after the invasion of Normandy on June 6, we got our orders. Soon we'd be going, too. Our guns were water-proofed and all our gear lashed down and made ready to be loaded on shipboard. Without equipment there wasn't much to do so we organized a softball house league representing the various gun troops and headquarters, to keep us occupied for the few days before we sailed. Each day we would route march in the morning and break off about noon to play ball on a beautiful estate called Hatch Park, where the massive elms reminded many of us of home.

I played third base for the headquarters' team. Four days before we were to sail a big happy guy from Peterborough, Joe Dwyer, to whom I'd had to assess a few hours of pack drill from time to time, reached second base with none out. The next pitch was hit in a high hopper to me. I faked a throw to first to get Joe running for third, and then blocked him off for the out. There's no way that I expected him to take it easy because I was an officer, and there's no way that he, as buck private, was going to think I expected him to take it easy. Our unit wasn't built that way. So he sailed into me. When I woke up I had four broken ribs. One knee had hit my chest and knocked me back across third base and right through the coaching box. I passed out and swallowed my tongue. Reeve got to me first. He'd been scoring. He used the pencil to pry my tongue out and hold it. I came to just in time to hear someone saying in a scared voice, "We've got to get him to a hospital."

I spat out the pencil. "The hell you say, and that's an order," I said. "Get a civilian doctor." The pain was tremendous and I was thinking, if I'm hurt much at all they'll take the Battery away from me and send it to Normandy under somebody else. Then I passed out again. This is where I have to hand it to Captain Jim Boeckh, my second-in-command. They got a truck. Now, I was very adamant about everybody in the Battery shaving every day. It was part of keeping them aware who was boss. Anyway, when I was being carried off I woke up and my face was against old Sergeant Cox, one of our good ball players, and I said, "God damn it, Cox, you haven't shaved!"

He said, "Oh, Jesus." Then he said, "I kind of wish you'd stayed unconscious."

They put me on a cot and went to town looking for a civilian doctor who would keep his mouth shut. I think the doctor they found had seen a lot of Hollywood movies and thought he was being taken for a ride. Anyway, he counted the broken ribs and taped me up. It wasn't a serious injury, of course, but I could hardly breathe or move my body. Still, I was determined to get away with it. Jim Boeckh got me into a private hospital. I sent for

Reeve and Dwyer so they could tell everybody to keep their mouths shut. They came in, Dwyer still pleading, "It was a mistake, an accident, Jesus, sir." I stretched out to shake his hand. "Well, Joe," I said, "I put you in the bag a few times, but I guess we are now even." Then we all laughed until I had to quit because it hurt too much.

But I guess news like that is too good to keep. The Army heard about it. A colonel came to see me. They had to undress me and then the colonel said, "I'll have to report this, Connie. You can't go overseas like this." My holster was right beside the bed. I reached over and put my hand on the revolver and said, "Now listen, I've been through a tough two and a half years to get here. If I'm not going, you're not going." I don't want to say that the colonel backed out because I threatened him. But I kept talking, telling him that I could run the Battery all right with sore ribs, it wasn't as if I was going to have to charge up a hill and stab somebody with a bayonet. I think he just decided I'd be all right if I got there. He said he'd hold the papers. Jim Boeckh would look after my duties and all I had to do was get mobile. Or at least walk.

I knew that I could get aboard the troop transport all right, but I also knew that across the Channel when we were supposed to climb down ladders into landing craft I'd never make it. My officers and men solved the problem. When we got near the landing area, I would be strapped into a seat in the cab of a gun wagon. Men went in one kind of landing craft, and waded ashore. Vehicles went in bigger craft and drove ashore. My vehicle would be swung out by a crane into a landing craft.

We embarked July 7, waited around for hours, then sailed. It wasn't a bad trip. The ship's captain was rather surly at first, because he had carried some Canadians before who did a lot of drinking on the way across. I told him he didn't have to worry about that with us, and I was right. When he saw that, he put me up in comfort in his sick bay, where I could lie down. On July 9 I was strapped into the seat and had a bird's-eye view of the Normandy coast, swinging out at the end of the landing ship's crane. I remember one other thing about that landing. The landing craft for vehicles had a front that flopped down so that each unit could drive right off into shallow water or the beach. I was second in line, behind a jeep manned by a soldier in full equipment. The landing craft officer, English, didn't speak very plainly. When we got near the beach and the front ramp began to go down, he said, "Stand here." Meaning, wait. But the excited soldier in the jeep thought the officer said, "Land here." When the front went down he drove the jeep out and straight into the water, where it sank without a trace until the driver bobbed to the surface, swimming for dear life, to shore.

I'll never forget the English officer's reaction. I guess in six weeks of landings he'd seen it all. "My word!" he said. "Imagine that man being able to swim in all that equipment!"

The British Navy was shelling from out of sight behind us, when we landed. We were bound for Caen, only a few miles inland to the south, which had been cleared out as far as its southern suburbs a couple of days before. The River Orne crossed those suburbs. A road had been bulldozed through the ruins to the two bridges we were to help defend. My men were gulping and wide-eyed when they saw what war leaves behind. I was being driven by Bob Bridger, the headquarters' clerk, who twenty-six years later came to work for me again at my breeding farm as a security guard and later farm manager. We set up Battery headquarters in a house not far from the bridges. There were still people living in the basement.

Almost as soon as we arrived, we were in action against a day-light raid of Focke-Wulfs and Messerschmitts. The Germans were making a big effort at Caen. In the first few days we had lost eight men, wounded.

Nearly a week later, on Sunday, July 16, we had a visit from Ralph Allen, by then away from the Battery for more than a year, mainly spent in Italy as the *Globe and Mail*'s war correspondent. We had a talk and he went around to see his old friends in the Bat-tery, Reeve and Rookie Taylor and Allen's old nemesis at chess, Scotty McColgan. A few days later Prime Minister Churchill came along to the front with Field Marshal Montgomery, the two of them and a driver in a jeep. I'd told the gun crews to stand smartly by their guns during the visit. But when the jeep arrived, I looked over and there wasn't a soul manning one gun position. They were all over getting their pictures taken with Monty and Churchill.

That visit was a prelude to something big, a major British-Canadian attack to capture a German-held, important height of land a few miles south of us. Huge bomb raids hammered the enemy in advance and then in the morning of July 18, swarms of

British and Canadian infantry and armour crossed our bridges and others along the Orne, heading south into a stubborn defence by the Germans. In two days our troops, with heavy casualties, were four miles down the road.

The next date I remember was July 25.

That morning a doctor took the tape off my ribs, and I could breathe for a change. That night just after dark I went upstairs at headquarters with two other officers and my batman. The rumble of guns and flickering of explosions were all around us, outside the blackout curtains. Then the Luftwaffe came after the bridges.

High flares came first, drifting down by parachute and lighting the whole area. Our guns opened up as we ran for the stairs. I was almost outside when on an impulse that I couldn't explain – it was a warm summer night – I ran back and put on my heavy trench-coat.

When I got outside, attacking planes were coming from every which direction dropping incendiaries as well as anti-personnel bombs that sent out a swath of fragments when they hit the ground. Fires lit up the target area. Our trucks were hit and burning. Some of our gunners had been hit and others had run to take their places. Even in the confusion I was proud of the way my men were standing up. The night was full of gunfire, explosions, shouts, and screams.

I was helping pull a burning tarpaulin off an ammunition truck so we could get the truck out of there when I was hit a terrible blow in my back, either by a bomb fragment or our own exploding ammunition. I came to lying on the ground near the wall of my headquarters' building. A man running by just then stopped and stole my revolver. Here's a fellow, I guess, figured I was through and he needed that revolver so he just helped himself. I tried to move but seemed to be paralyzed from the waist down. With the attack still going on, I felt around to see if anything was missing. The jagged piece of metal that apparently had done all the damage was still sticking quite a way out of my back. Immediately I thought of the heavy trenchcoat, the impulse that had made me go back for it, the tough cloth that must have slowed down the fragment down just enough that although I was badly hit, I was still alive. Lying there waiting for help I thought of all the years that had gone by, how I tried to get into the Army when Irene didn't want me to, tried to get overseas, fought to take my Battery into action.

At that moment a quotation went through my hazy mind, something my father had shown me first and I had memorized because I believed it – and now could see precisely how it applied to me and my plight: "Each man is his own absolute law giver and dispenser of glory or gloom to himself, the maker of his life, his reward, his punishment."

What had happened, I had done myself. But I always thanked some higher power for sending me back to get that trenchcoat.

Quite a few others had been hit, two fatally. Bob Bridger was trying to help a man with a bad nose wound. Staff Sergeant Eric Rule got a truck to take me back to No. 2 Canadian casualty clearing station. Bombs were still coming down. I was in a line-up of wounded outside, lying on my stomach, when I vaguely remember that Scotty McColgan arrived with my kit. He felt the shrapnel in my back. Some other wounded men were being taken in ahead of me. Scotty put up an argument, and got me in.

He says the doctor asked who I was, and then said, "The Connie Smythe from the Leafs?"

"Yes."

"Well," the doctor said, "we don't want to lose him, do we?"

Chapter Eight

I can easily identify the moment when I started to earn my way on to the Canadian government's blacklist and become a candidate for an Army court martial. In that casualty clearing station on the night I was wounded, a major from Les Fusiliers Mont-Royal was on the stretcher next to me. The doctors had given us something to dull the pain but we were wakeful in that dim place full of the groans of others. Talking helped. I knew that his regiment along with the Essex Scottish and the South Saskatchewans had been badly shot up fighting for that ridge Monty wanted, a few miles south of Caen. Some of the South Saskatchewans were on nearby cots. They said Essex Scottish lost three hundred men in two days of fighting. Les Fusiliers Mont-Royal had similar casualties; two companies going in and only a few men straggling back.

I asked the Quebec major how he got hit. He said that after a couple of days of fighting and heavy casualties, he'd had only one experienced non-com left, a corporal. All other NCOs with front-line experience were either wounded or killed. The reinforcements were too green to go into battle without experienced non-coms leading them. But they had to. The major mixed his remaining veteran soldiers in with the new ones to try to steady them, but when the action began they hadn't gone fifty yards before they were shot up and stopped. The major heard wounded men calling and tried to get out to bring some back. That's when he was shot. He spoke bitterly of always being shorthanded and how he hated to send green men into action not properly led.

We were both aware of similar stories being brought back from Italy, where Canadians had been in action for more than a year. The reports were mainly word of mouth, about officers and men wounded two or three times being sent back into the line. Units were so far under strength that men with experience couldn't be given the time to recover fully in body and mind before facing it again. It wasn't fair. A fighting force is like a team, supposed to be at a certain strength, everybody with a job to do. There is a lot of dependence, one man on another. When a unit is badly short-handed it is easier to lose battles and men. It was bitter medicine for Canadians, both alive and well, or wounded as we were, to know that back in Canada were tens of thousands of well-trained soldiers whom the government wouldn't send overseas. Using them might have saved hundreds or even thousands of Canadian lives in Italy and France in 1944. But Prime Minister Mackenzie King and his cabinet said no. The reason was that conscription for overseas service would anger Quebeckers, turn them against the Liberal Party. Mackenzie King and his supporters obviously thought that losing Liberal votes was more important than losing Canadian lives.

As the night wore on, my mind was clear enough to ask the Quebec major for his name and number. It was the beginning of an idea. If I could get enough specific stories of what the government's manpower policy was doing to the Army, I might be able to get something done.

I didn't have many sane conversations that night. I'm hazy about time. But from when I was hit, nothing worked from the waist down. I couldn't pass water or have a bowel movement. It's a fearful feeling to have yourself swelling up with nothing going out, no way to get rid of it. Hours went by. I was in a dim room with a lot of others on stretchers. A doctor was working over in one corner. I called to him to help me, that I thought I was going to blow up. He said I was not as badly off as the ones he was working on. I don't know what time that was in the middle of the night, but a medical officer with a broad Scots accent heard me pleading and said, "Hang on, laddie. I come on at 4:00 and I'll do something for you."

I hung on. I'm told that the Scottish doctor probably tried to insert a tube through my penis but couldn't because the passage was blocked. I don't remember anything except what he did do: he made a quick incision right through the football-sized distension of my abdomen directly to my bladder and shoved in a tube. The pressure shot urine straight to the ceiling. But did it feel good!

We were all either paraplegic or head-injury cases who were taken out of there by ambulance to be loaded into aircraft for England a few hours after daybreak. In the aircraft I can remember seeing only one small nurse and two or three walking wounded in charge of our whole planeload of stretcher cases. When the engines revved up some of the men with brain damage went absolutely wild. I have never seen a stauncher effort than the one that little nurse and the walking wounded put up to control things. They had to knock two or three men out. Blood from the man above me dripped on me steadily all the way. He had a terrible head wound. It was not until we had landed that I found he was one of my own sergeants.

I was among those taken to the Canadian No. 1 neurological hospital at Basingstoke, southwest of London. My inability to urinate had been relieved with the tube and by then I was known as the man with two belly buttons. But two or three days later I still hadn't had a bowel movement. Then a little French Canadian came into my room. The doctor had told me he was an expert on enemas. After he put the enema into me, it was just like one of those old sports stories; a new champion had been born. When he walked out with the seventh panful, there were cheers from everybody. I want to say this to everyone; if the only thing you have in the world is the comfortable use of those two parts that wouldn't work for me, you should quit hollering.

Stafford managed to get leave and came to visit. When he walked into my hospital room and saw me lying there with tubes and needles sticking out all over me, he passed out cold right on the floor. I think if I'd been wounded that way in the First War, I would have gone mouldy and died. Instead, I was getting better fairly fast. About the time I decided I was going to live (even if maybe I'd never be able to empty my bladder or bowels without help), I started feeling that everything I wanted to do had to be done right away. I wrote to Irene to tell her we needed a bigger place at the lake and to get the architects busy; I wanted to see plans when I got home. I told her to buy a new mink coat, spend whatever she wanted on it, and be wearing it when I got home. She got that letter during a late summer heat wave with temperatures in the middle 90's and wrote me back to say that if I came home right away, mink might not be appropriate. She also told me that on the day the telegram arrived about me being wounded, she and Miriam and Dorothea were having morning coffee on the patio at Orchard Beach. They all saw a man arrive, in the uniform telegraph men wore in those days. He opened the gate and started walking slowly toward them; three women each with a husband at some war front, each wondering silently, "Is it for me?"

"Mrs. Conn Smythe?" the man said.

Irene read it, then after a while got decisively to her feet. "Well, I'm not going to sit around here all day," she said. "Who wants to play golf?" She had decided long before that if this happened she was not going to sit and brood. Dorothea couldn't go because her first-born, Victoria, was only a year old, but the others did.

I can't express enough my admiration for the Canadian doctors and nurses who helped me through that time. Doctors would come from the front line for a few days to watch treatment procedures, to see what had happened to cases they'd sent along, and perhaps learn something they could do when they went back. I watched nurses handling men nearly twice their size, rolling them over in bed, lifting them, working like slaves.

Stretched out there pretty well helpless, with the enema the high point of some days, my thoughts were a mixture of present, future, and past.

"Darling sweetie pie," Irene wrote, and I had to smile to think of the disbelief in the faces of friends and enemies alike at the description of me.

A huge basket of fruit arrived, with a message. An RCAF pilot from Quebec, French Canadian, had just been leaving Toronto to fly to Britain when Dave Garrity arrived at Malton. In one hand he had the fruit and in the other a front-page story from the *Star* saying that I had been badly wounded and shipped back to England; was anybody going that way who would take the basket and try to find me? The pilot would and did, and we shared the fruit around the ward.

Patricia, writing (or, rather, printing) from the lake:

Jack made me a rafed and I padled all the way over to Rosses dock. It is ofly hot. We go swiming 4 times a day. Do you think you could play marbles with me when you get home? Love Patricia. XXX OOO.

Amazingly enough (to me) it appeared that others besides my family seemed to feel rather deeply that I should not cash in yet. Jim Boeckh wrote that,

> Every day different men are asking about you and quite a lot of them say how much they miss you. Mackie's cat has disappeared, which will shorten some of Ted Reeve's articles. Our last two convoys have been super – the other night, when you couldn't tell whether your eyes were open or shut, it was so dark, half the Battery disappeared from the middle of the convoy and later turned up in their right place in the column but facing the wrong way, all without passing either the front or back of the rest of the Battery . . .

The rest of the ward wondered why I laughed until my tubes were all rattling.

Someone sent a clipping from Dan Parker's column in the *New York Mirror* to say that Garden hockey fans who loved to boo when I hopped the side boards to take after a referee "are now praying fervently for Smythe's recovery."

A letter from Reeve said that word I'd be all right in the long run had come as a "great relief to me and the rest of the gang," and then hastened to report,

> I was out on Jonesy's gun for a week and had a shot at a Jerry that was brought down during that barrage. Undoubtedly it was one of my well-placed line-of-sights that dealt him the old convincer but I doubt if anyone noticed it. Judging by the clippings and comments in the letters from home your misfortune during the Battery headquarters shelling caused almost as big a sensation as though you had been stabbed in the back by Art Ross or winged in the corridor by Bill Stewart . . . The truth is (even though it may still surprise you) we miss you very, very much. Your faithful gunner, Edward Reeve.

Reeve also mentioned that the "new fellow" was doing okay, and one day I had a letter from him, Major Zouch Palmer. He sounded suitably propagandized, too:

> It's a queer feeling to be writing as commander of the best Battery yet, to the fellow who made it that way – for me it is

just about the proudest moment of my life, and I will do my best to ensure that standard will not be lowered and the 30th will continue to set the pace. They think the world of you, 'The Major' – in spirit the Battery will always be yours . . .

Maybe I am lacking some in modesty, quoting from these letters, but they make me so damn proud. To be somebody's darling sweetie pie and somebody else's irreplaceable "The Major" ain't bad. Anyway, lying there when I put together all I'd had and all I still had, I made up my mind that, well, I'm hurt, but if I can even progress to a wheelchair I'll be all right. If Franklin Roosevelt, crippled, can run the United States, I can run Maple Leaf Gardens.

All the time, my list was growing; names, ranks, numbers, stories of shorthanded units, lack of experienced reinforcements, the whole sorry manpower situation of the Canadian Army. Every time I was moved from one bed to another, or another man came into the bed alongside me, I wrote down who he was and why he was hurt. Some units had gone into action up to 40 per cent under strength. I never met an officer or man unwilling to put it on the record. It was pitiful some things that were happening. The Army was combing all the lesser trades, trying to make infantry reinforcements out of clerks, switchboard operators, people who had been rejected for frontline duty before. One boy who had been working on telephones for two years, and who had talked to me because he was a Leaf fan, was taken that way and wound up paralyzed in the same room with me, only a few weeks later. He had been sent into battle without anything close to proper refresher training as an infantryman.

Early in September I was still a stretcher case when I was put on the hospital ship *Lady Nelson* with five hundred others to go home.

On board ship, I spoke to a couple of padres about the information I was assembling. They helped by bringing down officers from the Italian and French campaigns with stories of what lack of proper reinforcements had done to them. Every one of them gave me his full story, name, and unit, and said that he was willing to stand up in public and state what he had told me, that the Canadian Army was losing lives because units were understrength and reinforcements were inadequate. This was the opposite to the pack of lies being said in Ottawa.

The first Canadian newspaper I saw when the hospital ship arrived in Halifax in mid-September had nothing, absolutely nothing, about the Army being desperate for reinforcements. In fact, you would almost think we'd won the war, and didn't need any more men. A *Globe and Mail* headline read: SMASH SIEGFRIED LINE. Other headlines were: Bewildered Huns Quit Pillboxes in a Daze. New Crossings on Leopold Canal. And so on. There was a sort of euphoria. The Quebec Conference a few days earlier had made us seem big league: Churchill meeting our cabinet; defence minister Ralston and Mackenzie King in there with Roosevelt and Stalin talking and smiling. I thought of the major of Les Fusiliers Mont-Royal with only one experienced corporal, and a hill to take.

We were unloaded from the *Lady Nelson* to a hospital train on Saturday, September 16. Two mornings later I was carried by ambulance from the train to Chorley Park military hospital in Toronto. Irene was with me that same day when George McCullagh, president and publisher of the *Globe and Mail*, came in. He said, "You're a pretty sick guy." I said, "I'm not sick at all. My men are over there, being hard-pressed. The whole Canadian Army is. I have these facts and figures . . ." I told him what I knew and thought. Others had interviewed me in Halifax, but I'd stayed off that subject. Same when sportswriters came to Chorley Park. I still didn't know exactly how to go about what I wanted to do.

McCullagh said, "If you're sure, that should be published. I'll publish every word you say."

I thought it over. In my naivete, thinking myself a good Canadian and nothing but, I thought that the prime minister would, or at least should, welcome the truth for a change, as some people do; that he might stand up in the House and say "Smythe has made allegations. If they're false, we'll crucify him. If they're true, we'll see that no Canadian unit ever goes into battle shorthanded, because the hundreds of thousands of trained troops we now have in Canada will be shipped over there immediately." What a babe in the woods I was.

I dictated a statement, which the *Globe* used on its front page the next day set two columns wide, just under the main headline.

ᴄ Globe an

TORONTO, TUESDAY, SEPTEMBER 19, 1944.

Y, BRITISH L

IADIANS ᴄ CITADEL JULOGNE

Untrained Troops Hazard at Front, Smythe Complains

500,00(OPEN D? SAY NAZ

Major Conn Smythe, M.C., declared in a signed statement last night that "large numbers of unnecessary casualties" have resulted from the fact that "reinforcements received now are green, inexperienced and poorly trained."

Smythe, managing director of Maple Leaf Gardens and commander of the 30th Anti-Aircraft Battery, RCA, in France until he was wounded July 25, dictated his statement as he lay in a bed in Chorley Park Military Hospital. He returned to Toronto yesterday morning aboard a hospital train.

The statement follows:

The need for trained reinforcements in the Canadian Army is urgent.

During my time in France and in the hospitals of France and England, I was able to discuss the reinforcement situation with officers of units representing every section of Canada. I talked to officers from far Eastern Canada, French Canada, Ontario and all the Western Provinces. They agreed that the reinforcements received now are green, inexperienced and poorly trained. Besides this general statement, specific charges are that many have never thrown a grenade.

Practically all have little or no knowledge of the Bren gun and, finally, most of them have never seen a Piat anti-tank gun, let alone fired one. These officers are unanimous in stating that large numbers of unnecessary casualties result from this greenness, both to the rookies and to the older soldiers, who have the added task of trying to look after the newcomers as well as themselves.

I give these true facts of the reinforcement situation in the hope that:

1. Col. Ralston, if he has other information, will know that his facts are out of date or that he has been misinformed;

2. The taxpayer will insist that no more money be spent on well-trained soldiers in this country except to send them to the battle fronts;

3. The people who voted these men should be used overseas when needed should insist on the Government carrying out the will of the people; and

4. The relatives of the lads in the fighting zones should ensure no further casualties are caused to their own flesh and blood by the failure to send overseas reinforcements now available in large numbers in Canada.

London, Sept. 18 (AP means said tonight the war's greatest battles in the forests and lak and Estonia, with th surling more than 500,0 action in an effort to German Baltic armies e of a Soviet salient poin Prussia.

A "deep penetration knowledged northwest the direction of Talli capital, and on the end of an expanded 2 other Red Army units near Baldone, only 1 the Latvian capital o Baltic Sea.

Counter-Attacks Beat

Moscow's nightly merely said the Rus beaten off heavy G west of Jelgava, 25 i of Riga. In this are said they were tryin flank of the Russian at Riga.

A German broadca Warsaw sector had b two days except for across the quarter-m la River between Praga and the Poli one also ignored ssuing one of th muniques since t campaign began J the up reinforcer Vistula opposite said.

A com Underg Polie in

The *Globe* lead editorial that same morning, nearly a full column long, was headed, "Major Smythe's Grave Charges." It extolled me lavishly and at length for this and that, the core of the editorial being:

> The reinforcement situation which he described in his statement will be a severe shock to many people, especially to the parents and families of our fighting men in Italy and France, and those who have relied on Defence Minister Ralston's repeated assurances that the Canadian Army had adequate reserves of trained reinforcements . . . They come at a time when the Canadians are engaged in heavy fighting, casualties for which have not yet been reported. The implications are crystal clear to the least-informed citizen.

The *Toronto Star* immediately started blasting away on the other side – quoting long lists of people as saying I was lying, that the reinforcement situation was fine, and so on. That was what I expected from one of the great Liberal propaganda organs of all time, of course.

The defence department issued a waffling statement to the *Globe* defending training procedures and regarding my claim "that casualties have increased because of insufficiently trained reinforcements," stated: "There is nothing whatever which is known here which would provide the slightest justification for that conclusion." The *Globe* story from Ottawa went on to say that "Army officers of unquestionable political allegiance to the government" – a nice phrase – alleged that I was stirring up a storm for political purposes and would run for the Progressive Conservatives in the next election, which was a total lie. When people's actions are dictated by dishonesty, self-interest, or politics, it seems to make them feel better to claim that others are doing the same.

It's an old, old fight now and there's no use going through all of the furore that followed. There is no official record that I can find stating that I was the one who finally blew the lid off the Army reinforcement scandal, which eventually caused one of our great political crises of all time. I'm sort of the unseen presence. R. MacGregor Dawson, Mackenzie King's official biographer, in his book *The Conscription Crisis of 1944*, mentions that everything seemed rosy at the Quebec Conference but "this feeling of security was shattered in the next few weeks [when] newspapers began to carry stories of poorly trained reinforcements, convalescent soldiers being returned to the front before they had made a complete recovery, and other reports of a disquieting nature." *Broken Promises*, a book by J. L. Granatstein and J. M. Hitsman, says that Ralston didn't really get the truth until he flew to Italy to seek out the facts. That happened a week or so after I made my statement. Bruce Hutchison in his book *The Incredible Canadian* related that when Ralston arrived in Italy that time and asked Eric Haldenby, the brigadier in charge of reinforcements, what the situation was, Haldenby replied, "Do you want the official version or the truth?" Ralston said he wanted the truth, for which all must respect him.

Richard S. Malone's book, *Missing from the Record*, says that Ralston had been receiving reassuring official reports about the manpower situation but by early September was becoming suspicious and "meanwhile, wounded men, invalided back to Canada, started to tell of the growing shortage of infantry reinforcements." I have no way of knowing whether Ralston really was suspicious before I issued my statement, but do know that before the Malone book was published two years later, it was vetted by Charles Vining of Montreal, Ralston's friend and occasional speechwriter, who did suggest some changes that made Ralston look a little better; this might have been one of them. An indication in this respect is that in the National Archives in Ottawa there is the manuscript of a long speech written by Vining for Ralston and headed, Reply to Connie Smythe. This denies every argument I made, but the speech was never given. Why? Because it was written when Ralston was overseas checking for himself. An officer who was on the defence department staff at the time told me years later that when Ralston returned to Ottawa just after mid-October he told his people not to proceed with any court martial against me because I had been right.

What I know firsthand is that I was in bed in Chorley Park a couple of days after my first statement when a staff officer came into my room and said, "You've made some serious charges that, under regulations, cannot be made in public. We are going to court martial you."

I said, "That's the best news I've heard yet." I waved the list I had assembled over the last two months. "You court martial me and I'll publish every one of these names, the regiments they are with, the number of men they were short when they went into battle, and what it cost in casualties."

He just stood looking at me. I told him to get out.

He did, but a few days later he was back and said, "Well, Smythe, what *do* you want?"

I said, "Two things. I got men over there who trusted me – I want to get reinforcements to them. And I want to get the hell out of the Army."

Right from that first statement on, I didn't just allow the issue to die. George McCullagh advised me to leave well enough alone, but I kept at it. I wrote letters to try to counteract the *Toronto Star*'s daily diet of people quoted as supporting the government policy and blasting me as a liar, a political opportunist, and everything else. I told the people in these letters that Canadians were the best assault troops anywhere, couldn't be stopped, but taking a place is one thing and holding it without enough men is another. I wrote,

That's where they take their punishment, having no fresh men to hold the gains they've made. I know it because I've seen it. I'm out of it for keeps, but the South Saskatchewans, they'll have to go back and keep going until we get the reinforcements to them; back and back, and we've no right to lay it on them.

Can't anybody make people see what it's doing? It's the cream of the crop over there. Canada never produced and never will produce anything finer than these young men. If the country loses them she's lost everything, and we don't have to get them killed to lose them – get that straight. We can lose them for keeps by forgetting them, or letting them think we have. And that's what we're doing now, letting them think we've forgotten them while we sit here squabbling like a bunch of lousy politicians over whether it will or won't be good for our unity to send them the help they need. What I want is a fighting chance for those kids and a country they believe in, for them to come back to.

I have always contended that anybody who has to pray for what he wants is going to get a kick in the ass, which he deserves, but I prayed, I actually prayed, that when Ralston returned he would tell the truth. He did. The record shows that he laid it right on the line for the cabinet. But King, to my mind, was the greatest traitor of all time. When Ralston came back he reported that the replacement figures in the thousands he'd been shown earlier really boiled down to a few hundred after he subtracted people in jail, sick, not physically fit, or whatever. The units these few hundred were supposed to support were under strength by thousands. It wasn't good enough. When he insisted that on all the evidence the voluntary system had failed, he was shafted by Mackenzie King and forced out of the cabinet. Then he was replaced by Andrew McNaughton, who should have been ashamed of himself for the rest of his life for turning his back on the Army he had helped to form, and taking out his personal dislike of Ralston by siding with King against the best interests of the Canadian Army. All this politicking caused delays until late November before decisions were taken, but early in January, 1945, the home defence men began to sail for overseas, where they performed well.

It is interesting to read Mackenzie King's diaries on all this.

First he mentions discussing with the Governor General in October "the Connie Smythe-George Drew controversy with Ralston" – blaming it on Ralston!

Later he quotes Ralston as saying that if we run out of reinforcements "McCullagh, Drew and Connie Smythe will have the satisfaction in the end of saying, 'I told you so.' " As if saving face, not lives, was the important thing.

In another passage he tells the Tory House Leader, Gordon Graydon, that "Ralston should have dealt with Connie Smythe at once." Meaning, presumably, by court martial.

A puzzling entry is that in February, 1945, when McNaughton had just lost a by-election partly on this issue, he talked to King about court martialling me; and King wrote that "we were wise . . . in deciding to limit Conn Smythe's court martial to the case of an officer who clearly violated the law." Meaning that they didn't want to argue the reinforcement issue at all, just wanted to get me. The strange thing was that by the time he made that diary entry I had been discharged. I thought the idea of a court martial had been dropped away back in October when Ralston let his staff know that I was right, yet months later the prime minister was still talking to his diary as if a court martial was alive enough that its terms were under discussion. I don't know when he finally dropped the idea. King must have had a brilliant political mind to run this country for so long, but in wartime such politics can be despicable, and he proved that.

But I'm getting a little ahead of myself. My time in Chorley Park was not all spent on military matters. A day or two after I arrived, Irene brought our lovely little daughter, Patricia, who just about caused heart failure among the nurses when she took a run and a jump across the room and flung herself on the bed among all the tubes and things and kissed me and stayed there a minute and then explained to the nurses and others, "I had to kiss my Daddy."

I was still getting a daily enema, as I did every day of my life from then on, but I hadn't given up on the matter of passing water. The hospital joke was that I had a lot of guts, but they were all in the wrong places. The doctors told me that to urinate I would have to use a tube, and a bag strapped to my leg, for the rest of my life. I kept insisting that was not true. But the first time I *knew* it wasn't true came one time when Irene visited me and, without going into details, I was given conclusive proof that *something* was working down there: I passed some semen.

I called in the staff, triumphantly, to have a look at the evidence. They were still doubtful. I didn't have much use of my legs, but could stand at the toilet holding on to support bars, and did that for hours every day, telling the urine to come. One day I was hanging on there, looking out of the bathroom window at the big trees when two squirrels suddenly started a hell of a fight – and the urine came! I let out a blood-curdling yell that brought the nurses charging in. I said, "Look at that! Look at that!" pointing at my penis. One little nurse with a sense of humour said, "Ah, I've seen better than that." That was a memorable day.

Hap Day, Frank Selke, and some Gardens' directors and Leaf players I knew came up to see me at Chorley Park so I kept track of how the team was shaping up for the 1944-45 season. Hap had written me letters when I was overseas. He would never double-cross a living soul and when things were going on that he felt were wrong, he would tell me. No doubt Selke was after my job. I can't say that I blame him for that, but I didn't like the way he was going about it. I considered myself back off leave of absence, managing director again. But when I started trying to do a few things by phone I felt as I had when I took my leave of absence originally in 1942, that this one faction at the Gardens wanted to get rid of me.

NHL president Frank Calder had died early in 1943. Red Dutton took over at the Montreal headquarters on an interim basis but in 1944 my successors at the Gardens saw a chance to get me out of the way by making me league president. They had broached the idea when I was still overseas. The Army would have flown me back to talk about it, but when nobody would guarantee I'd be back with my Battery within a week, I turned it down. At Chorley Park the sportswriters asked if I was going to take the presidency. "I've got a lovely wife, family, and sand and gravel business here in Toronto, plus my work at the Gardens," I said. "I don't owe a penny. I'm free as the air. Damned if I'll give up all that to be president of the NHL." So that settled that.

In late October, I was sent home to the second-floor room at Baby Point, where Irene and Jessie and young Patricia looked after me. Patricia was the most beautiful little girl I'd ever seen. She would run home from school at noon to play checkers, cards, or some other game with me. She used to get angry and run into the kitchen and tell Irene and Jessie, "Daddy cheats, 'cause he always wins." I feel ashamed of that now, but to me, if you're playing a game and you *let* somebody else win, it's a form of cheating. Anyway, I don't think it's a good thing to teach kids that they can win without actually being better, or playing better than the other guy. Life is not like that.

Yet she gave me so much. When I tried a few steps out of my wheelchair and along the room, she'd be with me, holding my hand. The first time I walked the length of the room and back she was as proud as I was. One problem even as the paralysis gradually went away was that because a nerve had been cut one leg shrunk and its toes turned under, which made them hard to walk on. Still, one nice day I walked the length of the outside walk, with Patricia alongside, holding my hand, and I knew I was on my way.

Saturday, December 2, was the first time I showed up at Maple Leaf Gardens. It wasn't to do hockey business. With everything else, I hadn't been able to get in touch with all of the relatives of my men. So I had a note put in the paper that if they'd come down to the Gardens Saturday I'd like to see them. About a hundred showed up – wives, sweethearts, and parents. I had a talk with every one of them, even if for only a few minutes. I really don't want to single out any of them, but one was special – Shirley Rule

– whose husband, Eric, had pulled me into shelter after I was wounded. Eric received the British Empire medal for risking his life to do it. I answered their questions and told them what I could. Some carried babies whose fathers had never seen them. I took all their names and took notes so I could describe how they looked in letters back to the Battery, which was up in the Scheldt estuary by then.

All this time I hadn't seen a hockey game. I listened to Foster Hewitt on the radio, of course, but I wasn't that well and the cold really got to me. For a couple of months before that December 2 gathering, I'd been running the hockey side of the Gardens by telephone from my bedside. But I wasn't ready to watch a game until the night of my fiftieth birthday, February 1, 1945, when Chicago had a game scheduled in Montreal and an NHL governors' meeting would be held the next day. I decided to make that trip to Montreal my big return. Selke had been telling me how terrible the wartime hockey was. I had never seen Rocket Richard before, but I saw a lot of him that night. It was a 1-1 tie and Rocket got the Montreal goal. He went in from the blueline with a big defence-man draped all over him on one side and Johnny Gottselig draped all over him on the other. Still the Rocket walked in, pulled the goalkeeper, and put the puck into the net. I demanded of Selke, "What kind of lies have you been telling me? That's as good a hockey play as I ever saw in my whole life."

I offered Montreal $25,000 for Richard, which they were smart enough to turn down. Some players were coming back from the services now and I tried to buy some even before they were dis-charged – offering $30,000 each for Milt Schmidt from Boston and Neil Colville from the Rangers. Leafs had Wally Stanowski back on the blueline, discharged from the Army, and actually we had a pretty good team that spring, a combination of old guys like Sweeney Schriner, Lorne Carr, Bob Davidson, Nick Metz, and Babe Pratt, and younger ones like Stanowski and a youngster in his teens I could have watched forever, because he worked so hard, Ted Kennedy.

I could feel things turning for the better when I saw the Rocket and knew that hockey was still alive, and then the next night got a great welcome back to my first NHL governors' meeting since 1941, and helped persuade Red Dutton to stay on as league president. A couple of months later we finished the schedule third, twenty-eight points behind Montreal, and fifteen behind Detroit. But we knocked off the Canadians four-two in games, and went on to beat Detroit for the Stanley Cup. It was a pretty good way to come back from the war.

I'd had to go back to Chorley Park for check-ups and some of the doctors thought I was trying to do too much, too soon, but life sure looked beautiful to me in that spring of 1945. If I had been walking better I would have strutted. Still, I knew that a lot of rest and fresh air and sunshine would do me good.

From back in the early 1930's, we'd had the small cottage at Lake Simcoe. A week after I arrived at Chorley Park the previous September, Irene and I started planning a bigger place and Roper Gouinlock drew some rough sketches for us. We picked out a choice lot on the lakefront and soon had builders working. It wasn't far from our smaller place and we really had both places going that 1945 summer, and lots of guests. Patricia was nine, Hughie seventeen. Miriam was around sometimes with her husband, Jack Hoult (they'd met right at the lake when they were kids). Stafford and Dorothea and their baby daughter visited from time to time. We had a putting green at the new place, and a lawn where we could play croquet. I took a lot of kidding, one way or another. The putting green was my pride and joy, because I intended to be playing golf again as soon as I could walk better.

One time my father came up from Hamilton, not long before his last illness. He was eighty-four. He picked up an old piece of stick and sunk every putt he made and then said, "Who's going to waste his time with this?"

That summer also was my introduction to carpentry. Irene and Jessie were saying that they needed a table in a certain area, but thought it would be in the way when it wasn't being used. So I undertook to make one that would fold against the wall. It was the first thing I ever made in my life. I did some swearing. I could never understand what was so funny about the way I went about it, but Jessie and Irene laughed every time I picked up a hammer or saw.

Then there was an early evening in mid-summer that started out fine. Patricia had always been bothered by asthma and other allergies, like Stafford. We never knew when a new one was going to strike her. If she ate a peanut in a chocolate bar by mistake, her eyes would just about pop out of her head. My heart ached for the amount of trouble she had. I could see ahead in life that her health would always be a burden to her, but she was such a happy girl in many ways. One afternoon we played a game of croquet and I won, as usual. She was tired of me winning, and said so. After the game, she decided to stay at the cottage while Irene and I drove to visit Harvey Aggett's mother, not far away, whom I hadn't seen since I came back from overseas. When we got back that night Patricia was lying dead on the veranda. She had had an allergic attack, with no one there to help. I can't describe our shock and grief. Irene and I never really got over it. Yet I always felt that there was some kind of fate involved, that she had been sent to look after me, and get me better, hold my hand on my little walks, and then she was needed more elsewhere. At her funeral some people wondered how I could hold in my sadness. It was because, for some reason, I was not so sad – I was glad that with her health the way it was, she was not going to have to face this world not knowing what the future was, who was going to be her husband, what kind of life she was going to have. I felt that she had gone to a better place. That is the refuge of a lot of people when they lose someone they love. I was finding it out for the first time. Forever after that, I thought of her as a little angel, with us so briefly but never to be forgotten for the happiness she brought.

Yet there was one nagging aftermath. The authorities, probably because they thought it would be kinder not to complicate our grief, never suggested an autopsy; nor did we. The doctor said she had died of natural causes, but we were never told exactly what and there would have been no way of knowing without post mortem examination. Nearly twenty years after, Irene sometimes talked of it wistfully, wondering what could have happened, what precisely did happen. But at the time she was so prostrated with grief that she was ill for months.

Chapter Nine

Frank Selke always said for public consumption that he and I parted company because of a trade he made without my permission, while I was overseas. This is not true but probably sounds better, which is why Selke would say it. The deal in question, Frank Eddolls to Montreal for Ted Kennedy, was made in the spring of 1943. Certainly, I was furious about not even being consulted. Eddolls had joined the Air Force soon after signing with us and I thought trading him was a stinking trick to play on a man who was going overseas. But if that was to be the end of Selke with the Leafs, why did I wait three years before telling him to walk the plank? And why didn't I fire Hap Day, too? Hap had a bigger voice than Selke's in deciding on the trade. Besides, in the end I was glad they did it. Kennedy became one of our great stars; and if I had been consulted at the time I'm pretty sure I would have gone along with it. Eddolls was a good young defenceman with a year in the minors at Hershey behind him. Kennedy at the same time was a sixteen-year-old centre with the Port Colborne Senior team, a kid starring in a men's league, good enough to have been invited to the Montreal training camp in 1942 (they ignored him and he left in a huff). His age made him exempt from military service for a while and Leafs badly needed players while Canadiens, because it was much easier to get war service deferments in Quebec (easiest in the country by far), had a better supply. Anyway, my anger was entirely at not being consulted. It seemed to me that Bickle, having failed to get me off the executive committee, which had to okay deals, had just decided that he and Selke would go ahead anyway as if I no longer had a voice in what was done. I felt that Bickle, with whom I'd never gotten along from the start, was out to downgrade me any way he could. I was sore at everyone involved and wrote to let them know exactly how I felt. However, I didn't come out of the Army gunning for Selke or anyone else.

What did happen between Selke and me, the real story, was that for too long I had been serving under people who didn't know as much as I did about hockey, or running an arena. Bickle's barring me from the dressing room in 1942, the later attempt to boot me upstairs into the league presidency, the resistance I encountered when I tried to get back to work as soon as I could dial a telephone from a hospital bed, led my thoughts in one direction. I had been running this team and this Gardens from when it started. It was time I was president. But when I mentioned this to a couple of other directors, sounding them out, they looked surprised and told me, "MacBrien is vice-president now and it's understood that he'll move up, as usual."

"Maybe we'll have a vote on that when the time comes," I said.

I remember one of them looked at me. "You do that little thing, Connie," he said.

At that time I had in my own name, or owned by Irene and others in the family, only about six thousand shares of Gardens common and four thousand, five hundred shares of preferred. That wasn't enough to make me president, by a long shot. I started buying and looking for support among other shareholders.

Naturally one person I turned to was Selke, who had a few thousand shares. We'd been in this a long time together and his letters to me overseas had been full of vows of eternal loyalty, maybe because he knew I expected that. One night in my office late in 1945 I told him what I had in mind, and that I was counting on him.

"Oh, no," he said, looking very upset. "When you were away I worked very closely with Mr. MacBrien and Mr. Bickle. I don't want to get involved in any fight like this with them."

So Selke's eternal loyalty plus five cents, at that time, would get me a cup of coffee. I was not very surprised, but I warned him. I owed him that. "You're making a big mistake, Frankie," I said. "I am going to be president here inside a year or two and if I get it without your help or votes then it would pretty well prove that I don't need you, wouldn't you say?"

He argued but I told him to get out. He has said that in his last while with Leafs I never had a good word to say about him to the press. That is correct. At first I guess he was pretty sure he was on the right side, and that if I got into a knock-down, drag-out fight and lost, it was quite possible – and maybe Selke had been told this – I would be forced out altogether and Selke would get my job. Ed Bickle and Bill MacBrien would have found him easier to deal with, than me.

But I had other resources. One was Jack Bickell. He said to me, "You want to be president? You'll be president."

That word got around quickly. Perhaps because Selke began to realize the way things were going, perhaps because I was making things tough for him, he resigned in May, 1946, and moved to Montreal Canadiens where he did well, but managed thousands of interviews and a book about his hockey career without making public the real story about why he and I split.

Besides Jack Bickell, my most effective supporter for the presidency was Percy Gardiner. He shared Bickell's view that as I had put the Leafs together, built the Gardens, and everything else, I should keep on doing it until I proved I couldn't. He was a stock broker and in 1947, not long after the Gardens common stock had reached the $80 to $90 bracket and was split four for one, he told me I needed a lot more stock. Even if I became president, it would be a fight every year if someone else had enough stock to overturn me. He had been assembling some. Gardiner thought Peter Campbell, one of the earliest Leaf owners, might buy it. "But I believe Campbell will be supporting you for the presidency," he said.

"I don't think so," I said.

He said in that case he would make the shares available to me at his average cost, about $10 a share. It had been 50 cents in 1935, $4 in 1938, and had stayed strong after the split. But thirty thousand shares at about $10 was $300,000.

I said, "I haven't got that kind of money, or anything like it."

He said, "You pay what you can now. We'll string the rest out over a few years." That's where I got the big block of shares that made my position as head of the Gardens secure as long as I wanted it. I have always thanked Percy Gardiner for quietly and calmly believing in me. He and Jack Bickell were the best friends I had. When I was elected president in November, 1947, the stock was around $20.50, or equal to about $82 pre-split.

I took over a very healthy company. In 1944 $80,000 of the mortgage had been paid off, meaning that in thirteen years the

Gardens had retired $950,000 in original mortgages and contractors' notes. The gate receipts had stood up well and in my first year as president reached a constant sellout position that lasted for decades. Season tickets became so hard to get that some subscribers began providing in their wills who would inherit them. The waiting list for season tickets began to grow and eventually reached close to ten thousand names.

But I continued to go by the axiom that if you win you sell tickets, so the job was to keep on winning. In a hockey way, 1946 was a tough spring. Remember, we had finished a distant third in 1945 when we rose up and won the Stanley Cup, but that was the last hurrah for a lot of our older, veteran players. I could see it, yet as I've said before, my toughness never quite extended to giving the chop to men who had worked hard for me. I talked this over with Schriner and Carr and before the end of the season announced they were going to retire, which I thought was a more honourable way for two great performers to go out, rather than being shipped to the minors. We finished out of the playoffs and I went to Lake Simcoe with Hughie to thresh things out in my mind. Hughie has said since that our weeks there were one long monologue, by me, and rather disjointed, as I worked my way toward deciding to tear the team apart once again and turn it over to younger players.

When Leafs skated out for their first game that October of 1946, I figured they were two or three years away from a Stanley Cup. Twelve players from the 1945 Cup were gone, including one of the most important, Babe Pratt. In January he had been suspended by league president Red Dutton for betting on NHL games and had been reinstated, but I had decided I didn't want him around and sold him to Boston. He soon retired. It was too bad. He was the best all-around defenceman we ever had on the Leafs. Hap had made a deal for him about the same time we got Ted Kennedy. In the middle of the war Rangers were so desperate for players that even Frank Boucher had come back to try to play again, and when Hap offered Hank Goldup along with Red Garrett, a rookie later killed in the war, Lester Patrick traded Babe Pratt for them. That was a deal I whole-heartedly approved. I remember once when Pratt was with Rangers we were tied late in the game when a good forward got hurt and Pratt was moved up to a wing. I thought, "Aha, here's our chance to win." Who got the winning goal? Pratt, playing forward. If he'd looked after himself he could have played until he was fifty. But he was as big a drinker and all-round playboy as he was a hockey player. When Hap got him I said, "Aren't you getting somebody who's pretty rough?"

"I'll handle that," Hap said.

How he did it was, on the road – especially in playoffs – he would room with Pratt. Talk about my campaign a few years later to get Turk Broda to lose weight; I think that after we won the 1945 Stanley Cup with Hap both coaching and rooming all the time with Pratt, Hap had lost so much weight keeping track of Pratt that he could have got into a size twelve shirt.

Anyway, in the autumn of 1946 Leafs' next big team was under-way. We had five new young defencemen to go with Wally Stanowski. Turk Broda was back in goal. Syl Apps, Ted Kennedy, and Nick and Don Metz were the only other holdovers. That November we had 16,318 fans to a game with Canadiens, nearly 4,000 standees. In the spring of 1947 we finished second and were blasted 6-0 by Montreal in the first game of the Stanley Cup final. After that, Montreal's great goalie, Bill Durnan, made one of the few mistakes of his career. He said to a Montreal newspaperman, "How did that club ever get in the playoffs?"

I loved that. I took it into the dressing room with me, and used it as my theme. We won four of the next five games, and the Cup.

But in hockey, the man who stands still slides back. That summer I assessed the team again and found one major weakness. We had two great centres, Apps and Kennedy, but needed one more. We had a wealth of young and popular players but I thought they weren't quite good enough to finish first, and I wanted to finish first.

Early in the season both Montreal and Chicago looked bad, couldn't win. I thought either club might be ripe for a major deal. They were playing one another in Chicago so I went to have a look. I was after either a Canadiens star or a Chicago star and when I saw that game I decided the man we needed was Max Bentley, who was twenty-seven then. I wasted two or three days there trying to make a deal with Bill Tobin, not knowing at the time that he couldn't make a decision without Jim Norris's okay. Every time we got close to a deal Tobin would insist, on Norris's instructions, that it was nothing doing unless I threw in Bob Goldham, which I didn't want to do. I was offering one defenceman, Ernie Dickens, twenty-six, plus an entire forward line, nick-named the Flying Forts because they were all from the Lakehead – Bud Poile, twenty-three, Gus Bodnar, twenty-two, and Gaye Stewart, twenty-four. Finally I gave in on Goldham, who was only twenty-five at the time. I was sure he was going to be good, although I didn't know he'd have as long a run as a TV commentator as he would as a player. Right then he was on our minor-league team at Pittsburgh, so he wasn't exactly indispensable. So I said okay, and although everybody said I was giving up too much in youth and talent, I knew I was right. Max was great: small, slight, shifty, a will-o'-the-wisp skater. The crowds loved him. We did finish first that year, won the Stanley Cup again, and Bentley was a major figure in two more Stanley Cup wins, 1949 and 1951, before I dealt him to the Rangers near the end of his career.

We had a system of sponsored teams at that time, all across the country, junior and senior teams that would supply us players who usually started in the minor pro leagues until they showed they belonged with the Leafs. Through those years, the backbone of the team came up through our own farm system. One attraction we had when going out to sign players of school age was the chance to offer them tuition at St. Michael's College School in Toronto, whose junior teams under Joe Primeau were always powerful. We could go to parents in Winnipeg, Regina, Kirkland Lake, or wherever, and say, "Look, if your boy will come into our system we'll make sure he gets the best schooling he can handle." I've always thought that a boy who excelled in sports as well as school should have the edge on someone who was brilliant in only one phase of life, or one subject. To enter St. Mike's a boy had to be a good student first, although it didn't hurt if he was a good hockey player, too. St. Mike's liked to win. I couldn't name all the great players who went there – from Red Kelly, Frank Mahovlich, Dave Keon, Dick Duff. There was never any question of refusing a boy we sent them because of his religion, although one time that charge was made. One St. Mike's alumnus was very high on a Protestant kid from Cornwall, but the college turned him down. The alumnus came to me and claimed it was because of religion. I went to debate the matter with the priest who was in charge of admissions. He listened to my plea but when I finished he said, "Sorry, Connie, but I've made my decision."

I've had some arguments with priests and usually when they said no, you've had it. So I rose to go. He opened the door for me. Just as I was leaving he added what I guess was the real reason, "You know, Connie, he isn't much of a hockey player."

All this time, a lot of other things were going on in my life. In 1945 dad, at eighty-four, was honoured for his sixty years of service to the Theosophical Society. Editorials and feature stories in Hamilton (where he was living) called him "a rare spirit and an exquisite craftsman" as a poet, and "a journalist of exceptional ability and force." Over the years we had been seeing one another at Christmas and frequent other times when he came to Toronto on Sundays to preach. I visited him in hospital and tried to persuade him to write more. He was a wonderful storyteller. But he would just smile and shrug. I learned the feeling myself, when I became that age, of having only so much energy to spend in a day. When he died on October 25, 1947, it was typical of him that the only will we could find was dated April 20, 1914, leaving his son, Conn, $2,000 "to be paid to him when he is twenty-one" and the rest to Janie, who died several years before dad did. He had his books, a few personal effects, one share of Goodyear Tire and Rubber, and a few hundred other mainly worthless shares. I signed off any claim I had to the estate and got my lawyers to wind things up. Miriam and Stafford took some of the furniture, which they needed in their young marriages. When his thousands of books were gone through, little of monetary value was found. After various small bills were paid a few hundred dollars was left for my half-sister Moira from our father's long life.

Irene's father had been ill all that summer, too, and died a few weeks before dad. I find in my accounts two $388 payments to Miles Funeral Home, a few weeks apart. For months before Mr. Sands' death he stayed under nursing care at our home, sometimes having hallucinations. He had been forbidden alcohol and was desperate for something to drink. Once he claimed that the plate-rail in his room was lined with beer bottles ("Look at them all up there!"), and why wouldn't we give him some?

When I'd come back from the war, in gratitude for the job Hap Day had done I offered him the chance to buy more stock in C. Smythe Limited. He turned it down with a Hap Day smile, saying that with Stafford involved full-time at the sand pit, and me in charge, there wasn't going to be any long-term chance for anyone not named Smythe to be more than a senior employee, so he'd leave his stock position where it was. He liked to run his own show.

Our business was growing and when it became apparent that a lot of returned men were having trouble finding housing, we set up a company called Roseland Homes Limited, with the same directors as C. Smythe Limited – myself, Stafford, Hap, and Art Boyd – and set out to build homes that working men could afford. We sold Roseland 101 housing lots on worked-out sand pit property, at a price less than $1,000 per lot, advanced funds to begin construction, and gave returned men priority in buying. Without going into details, this was not a money-making venture but didn't lose much, either, and of course the sand and gravel company made nearly $100,000 on the sale of land. The first twenty-one houses chalked up an average loss of about $100 per house. But we helped the housing situation for returned men as much as we were able to, and that had been the idea from the beginning.

Around that time, too, I got involved in something that was part of my life from then on. Back in Jarvis Collegiate one of my friends on the football team was Reg Hopper, who had been the first employee of the Ontario Society for Crippled Children back in 1928. I'd had nothing to do with it, except for a few small donations, through the 1930's. When Reg came back from the war, he felt that the society was in the doldrums and needed strengthening and expanding, especially in the line of keeping track of money and soliciting donations. In June of 1946 he and the society's president, Gus Penney of Brantford, came and asked me to be treasurer and chairman of the finance committee. I still wasn't in very good health. I told them I'd think it over. But when I'd been stretched out in that casualty clearing station in France, thinking I was done for, I'd made a promise to myself that if I did ever get back to Canada in one piece, I would try to do something for others. I knew I had neglected that aspect of my life. Reg told me that in the eighteen years since the society was formed, they'd helped maybe three or four thousand children, but that wasn't enough. Sensing that if I went in, it would be for life, I went to seek advice from two men whose opinions I valued – George McCullagh of the *Globe and Mail*, and George Drew, the soldier and gentleman who was Premier of Ontario. McCullagh told me, "Find out exactly what happens to a dollar someone contributes. Follow it through and see where it goes." Drew told me, "Find out what kind of people you'll be associating with."

When I had satisfied myself on those two points, late in the summer, I told Reg I would serve. I was not only ready, I was eager. At the first meeting of the board that I attended with about twelve or so directors from various parts of the province, we had a lunch at the Royal York.

I leaned over to Reg and said, "Who pays for this lunch?"

He said, "The society. We pay out-of-pocket expenses, including travelling, for those who come from other cities – Ottawa, Sault Ste. Marie, and so on."

I said, "Not any more."

He got up right away and announced that from then on, expense accounts were abolished for everyone except society employees, that every volunteer should pay his or her own way. With charities I'm involved in, I have tried to make that a rule ever since. I don't always win but I had the idea that when some little old lady put a worn dollar bill into an envelope and sent it to us with a note saying, "Keep up the good work," we had a responsibility not to spend it buying meals for some director.

One time at a meeting I even got so rough on Reg Hopper that he jumped up and said, "Look, if you want my job for somebody else, it's all right with me." He started for the door. I just got to him before he left, grabbed him by the shoulder and said, "Sit down and shut up. You know when I say some things they don't always come out the way I mean." I've been given a lot of credit for things that the society has done since then, but mainly it was because I had a lot of help. I knew where to go. Years later when we were planning what became a campaign to raise about four and a half million dollars for a new Crippled Children's Centre, I went to J. P. Bickell and asked him if he would be chairman of fundraising. He couldn't, but said, "John David Eaton is the right man for the job." Of course, it was a great idea – you always try to get the top men around to head up a fund-raising campaign, but for some reason people hesitate to go in on a big man like Eaton and put it to them.

When I went to his office he was sitting behind a big desk that had nothing on it, absolutely nothing. I said, "Mr. Eaton, you put in the original money in 1928 to get this society started, but now we need a lot more and we want you to run the campaign for us."

He looked at me for only a few seconds and then laughed. "I'd be delighted," he said. "Now I'll get back at all those people who are always after me for money." Before I left his office, he was on the phone to start putting the arm on people who owed him that kind of favour. I've always been a believer in getting individuals, rather than governments, involved in such matters. Individuals get things done without setting up big expensive departments that go on forever, costing money that would be better spent on whatever the thing is. You can't can the milk of human kindness.

When you're picking the individuals, you have to pick people with guts. Early in my years at Crippled Children one of the society's senior men came to see me with a good proposition, something we should do. To test him out I put up a big argument. He backed right down and agreed with me! I went to Reg Hopper and said we ought to get rid of the guy. "He was right," I said, "but he wouldn't stand up for it." The man was very well qualified but as soon as we could, we replaced him with Ray Auld, a man who had all the qualifications but also that extra one that he'd fight me or anyone else for what he thought was right. He had been with me in the 30th Battery and it was at a Battery dinner I'd suddenly realized he was the man we needed.

A couple of years after I'd first taken on the Crippled Children, I was part of something else that helped to hook me for life to getting out and getting things done for people who couldn't help themselves. The Variety Club was just starting in Toronto. Hunting around for a good long-term project they decided to build a vocational school where handicapped youths could learn trades so they could take regular jobs and be self-supporting. We were going to do the administrative work and they would run it, if we could ever get started.

The main need was land that didn't cost, as one thoughtless joker of the time put it, an arm and a leg. I went to George Drew, told him the plan, and said that there must be a few parcels around the city that were owned by the province. I thought it would be a good thing if he gave us one of them. He got it arranged before he moved into federal politics, transferring to the Crippled Children's Society for $1 a few choice acres at the junction of Kingston Road and the Danforth in Scarborough. The society turned the land over to Variety in return for $1.5 million dollars to be paid over, I think, twenty years. So it benefited both organizations. In the thirty years since then more than three hundred handicapped people have graduated from there to become self-supporting. The big moment for me was in the second week of November, 1949, when the first twenty-four boys, aged sixteen to eighteen, arrived from many parts of Ontario at what by then had been christened Variety Village. They were on crutches and canes or in wheelchairs. We had sent the word through the province to doctors, service clubs, and other organizations asking for the names of boys who had the capacity to become self-supporting. Of ninety-six applicants, we could only take twenty-four, because our dormitories and other facilities could only handle that number. One boy on crutches spoke for them all, I think, when he said that it was good to be with others with handicaps, "getting the one thing in the world we all want – a chance."

Stafford was pulling his weight, wherever he worked. We had twenty-five men at the pit then, and Stafford got two weeks vacation each August like everyone else. I don't remember what I paid him but I had given him stock. As a shareholder and with bonuses, he was getting by. By 1947 our annual sales of sand and gravel were running over $200,000, with the gross profit about one-quarter of that. He wasn't always as respectful as he might have been. One day I was driving over to St. Catharines to the Leafs' training camp when suddenly it struck me that there were twice as many buildings going up, twice as many roads being built, and this meant that there were twice as many cars on the road, which was why I was bumper to bumper all the way. I stopped in Burlington Beach and went into a phone booth and phoned Stafford. "What are we getting a yard?" I asked.

"About a dollar forty."

"Put it up to one seventy-five," I said.

"Have you gone crazy?" he asked.

I told him what I had seen on the highway and had interpreted as signs of a boom. "Well, okay," he said and within a week we had pre-sold most of our next two years' production at the new price. I think his bonus that year went up from $3,000 to $7,000. He was earning it, working from 7:00 a.m to 6:00 p.m. every day, and sometimes I'd have to phone to discuss business after that. In the office he typed company letters himself, and at company meetings acted as secretary. He was learning to run the sand and gravel business (I hoped) just as his early years around the Leafs had grown into heading up our Toronto Marlboro hockey club, with teams in every group there was. That's where he and Harold Ballard became friends. I have a picture taken a few years later at Ravina Gardens at a Toronto Hockey League Atoms league opener. Stafford was wearing the white coat sweater with the Marlboro crest. I was in the same kind of coat sweater with the Leaf crest and Stafford's son, Tommy, between us, just eight years old and with his hair about a quarter-inch long, was dressed in the uniform of the Islington Hornets. Stafford was a first-rate hockey man, and Tommy became one in time. If things had worked out differently, we would have had three generations of Smythes running the Gardens and the Leafs.

Long before then, in 1946, Irene and I had started going to West Palm Beach for two or three months every winter. I couldn't stand the cold or move around as briskly as I once had. Hap would call me after every game to let me know what happened, in detail. My own phone bill ran around $600 a month just from business calls, and sometimes I would fly up for a few days. At practices, I would wear a warm flying suit, the only way I could sit in a cold arena. Running a team by long distance was not ideal, but I hadn't fully come to grips with that yet and anyway, when our time to leave for Florida came just before Christmas in 1948 we had a major worry in our family.

As a child Hugh had seemed frail sometimes, but he managed to take part in sports and win prizes at Upper Canada College for his academic work. When he reached university, his course in medicine gave him a heavy workload. Late in 1948, somewhat run down, he had a positive reaction to a routine test for tuberculosis and wound up in the hospital at Weston. We were at The Breakers in West Palm. I have treasured letters he wrote to us from hospital, although even then his handwriting was deteriorating into the medical scrawl. One was written on New Year's Day, 1949. As well as thanking us for his Christmas presents – "Mother's multitude of very useful and practical gifts, Father's almost overwhelming generosity," – he said he also wished "to thank God for providing me with parents as fine and as loving as you are . . . You parents have given us everything we have ever asked for, and much that we never dared dream of. Yet you have managed to do it, I think, in such a manner that our sensibilities have not become numbed, nor do we (I think) take these things for granted . . ." No warmer words have ever been written or spoken to me.

Hugh was a good raconteur as well about things that he knew would amuse us. Jessie Watson had been in to see him often, keeping him up to date on home, pets, friends, relatives. She had told him a story about her father making friends with our dog Joe, giving him something to eat and putting his coat over him to keep warm; then spending the rest of the evening trying to get his coat back. The dog didn't want to let go. Hugh and I were both devoted readers of the *New Yorker*. He wrote that he thought a James Thurber or Harold Ross would be needed to get Jessie's stories down properly, in which case, he thought they would become great classics of American humour, "if told properly, with Jessie's phraseology." In other letters he told us of visits from Hap Day and Harold Ballard, "with Hap looking so tired and drawn (Leafs were in a slump) that I really felt I should offer him the bed and take a chair for myself." He also told of a newsreel that a friend of his had seen of the opening of Variety Village, "in which the celebrities were identified as including George Drew and Connie *Smith*, causing a big laugh to go up in the theatre."

He was the only correspondent I had, too, who would discuss with me Aldous Huxley, whose books affected him deeply. One such letter, written late in January and mainly about Huxley, ended by enquiring, "What does father want for his birthday? He's got just about everything he needs. At the rate the plumbing and carpentry bills are piled up at 68 (we were re-modelling our home on Baby Point Road), after an expensive Christmas and a trip to The Breakers, perhaps I had better give him a cheque for $1,000.00 and a nice durable suit that will last until the next dividend cheque comes in. Or a loan – I'd probably charge a smaller rate of interest than Stafford would."

He was not yet twenty-two, but already had a sense of family and fun that I valued. Life was not easy for him then, even apart from his illness, which later turned out to be a false alarm, an old lesion. When the scare came, he was engaged to be married. His fiancée apparently could not face the prospect of life with a sick man, but did not have the character to come herself and tell him. She sent his ring back with someone else. A knock at the door. A box handed in – "Give this to Hugh, please."

It was about that time, too, that I bought my first piece of property in Caledon. I wasn't planning immediately to move my sand and gravel operations up there and had no idea of a horse farm, but we were running dry at the pit we'd been using for nearly thirty years. I made an offer to York Township for some property near my pit, a million dollars, but three or four of the do-gooders on the council were afraid that maybe I'd make some money out of it, so they refused and threw away a million dollars the Township could have used. That first Caledon property I bought was from a man named Franceschini who was in trouble with the government and thought that because of my friendship with George Drew I would put in a good word for him. I didn't. His seventy-two acres cost me $10,000. In the next few years I began buying Caledon property in earnest, every farm that came on the market, in an area rich in sand and gravel. Eventually over the next ten years I spent more than $500,000 for about 1,750 acres, worked it profitably, and in 1967 sold a little more than half of it to Armstrong Holdings for $2,490,000. There is no better investment than land, especially land that can be mined and then resold.

At first, I had no idea of running a horse farm at Caledon, as well. We had spent the years from 1944 on planning and then building the new summer place on Lake Simcoe, and enjoyed golfing, swimming, and boating even as the lake was becoming increasingly crowded. Sometimes Irene and I would drive over to Caledon to look around but we never talked seriously about living there, making it our out-of-town place, until one day in 1957 I was swimming at our cottage when I was hit by a motorboat and cut badly around the head. Another inch or two one way or another, and that propeller would have killed me. Irene dove in and pulled me out, battered and nearly unconscious. When I regained my senses, one of the first things I said was, "That's it. We're getting out of here." Soon after that we built our place at Caledon, remodelling and adding to an old farmhouse, and also building a substantial pool house and pool. The furnace to heat the pool house and pool was big enough to run the *Queen Mary* but was still going strong more than twenty-five years later. Because of the chronic pain from my war wounds, I craved warmth the way some people crave liquor, and kept the water in the pool too warm for most people, but just right for me.

Chapter Ten

My office in the Gardens was not elaborate, but I had laid it out the way I wanted. In a comfortable outer office, with chairs for people waiting, sat my secretary, Madeleine MacDonald being the one with the longest tenure. Her initials were at the bottom of blizzards of neat typewritten notes on matters both inside and outside of the Gardens. She dealt with NHL headquarters on all matters of routine, adding and subtracting names from player lists, and so on. Clarence Campbell had succeeded Red Dutton as league president in 1946 and, just as I had predicted, was doing well – because he would do what he was told. Operating on his own, Campbell sometimes made mistakes, but he was the perfect second-in-command – the league governors having designated me, as chairman of the owners, to deal with him on questions of policy he was expected to enforce. The terms of his job were laid out in league minutes: "The president . . . shall discharge all duties imposed on him . . . as may be required by the governors from time to time." Every time I told him what to do and he did it perfectly he was confirming what I had said when I turned down the job; that I was not good for it, because I would not take orders; and Campbell was the right man, because he would. He assured us when he took the job that it would be his career. Once years later a friend of Stafford's, exasperated with something Campbell had done, said, "Why the hell don't you get another guy to run the league?"

Stafford said, "Where would we find another Rhodes scholar, graduate lawyer, decorated war hero, and former prosecutor at the Nuremberg trials, who will do what he's told?"

Beyond the outer office was my private one. When I called

somebody in, a player who maybe needed a little jacking up, a visiting scout, an owner, or whoever, he sat among life-size photos of my team captains, big team portraits of what by the spring of 1950 were my six Stanley Cup winners, and other reminders that this was the home office of the best club in hockey. In my desk drawer I kept very private papers and a few hundred dollars cash, for emergencies. In a briefcase or coat pocket I always had a small flat tin containing rich fruitcake. Irene or Jessie would make sure I had that tin when I left the house in the morning, because sometimes I needed the quick energy it gave. With everything I was involved in, often I skipped lunch. Heading downtown for a meeting – by then I had a chauffeur – I would sit in the back and have a bite, offering it around if anyone was with me. Once a magazine reporter who wanted an interview when I didn't have time wrote later about the oddity of riding down Church Street in a chaffeured Continental munching Christmas cake with, he wrote, "the gimpy ex-soldier who is the most powerful man in hockey today."

There were two other doors in my private office, one leading down back stairs to Church Street, a private exit, the other to a sort of inner sanctum, a thinking and resting place. It was a small room with bookshelves, a refrigerator, a bathroom, and a comfortable couch equipped with heating pad, electric blanket, and other things that helped keep pain at bay. One of the most chronically painful results of my wound was a scrambling and laceration of nerves, including the sciatic nerve. My right leg was a good deal thinner than the left. It hurt like hell, especially when I was tired. When alone sometimes I could get some relief by keeping it moving, so I would jig the leg up and down. Heat helped some. But that leg didn't do my temper any good. Some of my blow-ups, then and later, were because I had been in pain that I could do nothing about. The first person who crossed me got both barrels as a result. They'd go away asking, "What the hell's wrong with that guy?" I did a lot of apologizing, because when I had blown up I would know how wrong I was to take it out on someone else.

I had some frustrations. The great first-place team of 1948, the best Leaf team ever, had Syl Apps, Ted Kennedy, and Max Bentley at centre. Apps, the captain, was thirty-three then and had decided he wanted to get two hundred goals and then retire and take one of several good job offers he'd had. With only a few weeks to go in the spring of 1948 he was eight or nine goals short of the two hundred and I said to him one day, kidding, "I think it's great that you're short that many. It means you'll have to come back for next season."

"Oh," he said, "now, wait, Connie, don't be too sure I won't make the two hundred." I could see the glint in his eye, because there was an awful lot of guts behind that gentlemanly exterior. I would have been smart to bench him for the rest of the season. He went out and scored in almost every game, getting three, a hat trick, in the last game to bring his total to two hundred and one. Then I didn't have a hold on him for next year. He took a big job with the Robert Simpson Company's department stores, but it wasn't long before I think he realized that wasn't exactly his cup of tea. He wasn't a merchandiser. I heard about it and talked to him steadily for a couple of days to persuade him that he had good years in him yet, and should come to the camp in St. Catharines that had just opened. He agreed and said he'd go there on a Sunday night. I went over on Monday and walked into the practice looking around, then said to Hap, "Where's Apps?"

"Didn't show up."

"I can't understand that!" I said. "He never breaks a promise!"

"Well," Hap said, "I don't know, but he called me to say he was coming and I told him I had appointed Kennedy captain and that he'd have to serve under Kennedy. Maybe that was it."

That's the difference between Hap and me. Hap wouldn't stretch a commitment one inch to get out of it. I would have gone to Kennedy and said, "Look, we can get Apps to come back, he was our captain last year, would you mind stepping aside?"

Kennedy would have said, "Yeah, man!" I know it. But that's why we didn't get Appsy back and although we went on that season, too, to win our third Stanley Cup in a row (we had made a deal with Rangers that cost us Wally Stanowski to get Cal Gardner as the other centre) I know in my heart that if Apps had come back and played as long as he could it would have extended Kennedy's time in the league by several years as well. Kennedy had to take up the slack when Apps wasn't there and it meant he was overworked. My old friend Al Nickleson then was working for the *Globe*. Every time Kennedy carried the puck Nickleson would write about how he *laboured* up the ice, etc., etc. Oh, the pity of it all, that kind of crap. Sure he laboured. That was his style. But I never saw anybody catch him when he had the puck, and that's what counts. He should have played years longer than he did.

Anyway, the spring of 1950 was the first time since 1946 that we didn't win the Stanley Cup. In addition, I had to stay home sick for three weeks in a bad flare-up related to my injuries. Once again, as I did every spring, I thought in endless detail about the Leafs. I was not really unhappy about the team. One or two players had been disappointments, but one had been a happy surprise – Bill Juzda, a defenceman we'd got from Rangers as a throw-in on the Gardner deal. We had figured at first he would wind up in the minors, but he just dug in from training camp on and defied us to play without him. He was a big body-checker, along with everything else, guts to burn, gave every ounce, every game. One thing I'd done while I was sick was give him a good bonus and a new contract with a raise.

But the major decision I made during that sick period was that I was not well enough to be the full-time manager any longer. I thought the whole thing through and decided that Hap should be named assistant manager, to do the managing job in consultation with me. He'd earned it; one Stanley Cup as a player back in 1932, and five as a coach in the 1940's. Besides, I figured Joe Primeau was ready to coach the Leafs. He had been a great help to us as coach of St. Michael's Junior teams after the war and later had moved up to coach the Marlboro Seniors. Players responded so well to his quiet, friendly style that he'd won national championships in both categories, the Memorial Cup and the Allan Cup. Adding a Stanley Cup to that would be quite a coaching record. I called a press conference as soon as I could get out of bed and downtown, and said that my health was such that I had to ease up. I would recommend to the Board of Directors Hap to manage, with the title of my assistant, and Primeau to coach. I also talked about players to be brought up and fitted into the Leafs, coaching changes to be made in the farm teams. Covered the waterfront. Hardly a paper could manage it all without taking up a whole page of stories and photos, which was about what I had in mind.

When the season started and the changes had been made, I travelled with the team only when I felt like it. That was the difference that promoting Hap Day brought about. Before, if I was in Toronto, I'd felt obligated to go, ride the trains, fight referees, give interviews. I still threw my weight around a little when I had to. One player who had agreed not to marry before the end of the season got his girlfriend pregnant. In those days it meant he pretty well had to get married. With all that turmoil I figured he couldn't keep his mind on hockey, so I sent him to the minors and then traded him.

When I visited New York now, Irene would come along. We'd take in the current plays and writers like Bill Corum and Dan Parker would come around, another generation of good columnists in the United States following in the footsteps of those I'd met in my earlier days.

In Toronto I had a box just in front of the greens and would be in the thick of things often enough. The night of a famous fight of the time between Rocket Richard and Bob Bailey, a real wild one, I went into the press room after and when a reporter asked me what I thought, I said, "We've got to stamp out that kind of thing, or people are going to keep on buying tickets." You should have heard the editorial writers baying at the moon over that one, which later made the rounds in *Sports Illustrated* and even the *Encyclopedia Britannica*. One night there was practically a riot at the Gardens. Rocket Richard was in that one, too. After he had been sent to the dressing room by the referee I was down in the corridor. Suddenly the door flew open and he charged out again, his eyes blazing the way he sometimes got, in what somebody once called the Rocket's red glare, so mad he was not seeing anything. I stepped in front of him and said, "Rocket! Where are you going! Won't do you any good . . . Get back!"

He seemed to come to. He stared at me. Then without a word, he turned and stomped back into the dressing room. I admired that man tremendously, would have given anything to have him play for me, but that didn't stop me giving it to him when he was the enemy. Once in Montreal I asked for seats where I wouldn't get into trouble and some joker, no doubt Selke, put me right beside the Rocket's mother-in-law. We fought all through the game. Finally we were yelling at each other. When it died down a little I asked her what it was she'd been saying in French. She told me, then said, "That's where I have it on you, Mr. Smitty. I can tell you what I think of you in both languages."

When Leafs won the Stanley Cup again in 1951, knocking out the Canadiens in overtime with Bill Barilko's last goal (he was lost in a flying accident in Northern Ontario a few months later), I had some other decisions to make. Joe Primeau, I thought, had got the most out of the team but I had the conviction he couldn't do it again with the same team. Don't ask me why, it was just one of those feelings. At the same time, Joe was talking about retiring. He had an outside business to look after, and sometimes wasn't well, especially under the tremendous pressure of coaching at that level. But I was determined that he should keep on coaching. Detroit and Montreal had great teams coming up and if Joe quit now some other coach would take the team and NOT win the Stanley Cup with it. Then the fans, being fans, would blame the coach, and say that if Primeau had stayed on they would have won the Cup. Anyway, I felt that Joe should serve another year or two. If he won it again, great. If he didn't, at least the next coach would not have that can of failure tied to him when he didn't deserve it. We had a huge party to celebrate the Cup in 1951. I had it all set up with banners several feet high reading, "May he never retire!" We sang "For He's a Jolly Good Fellow" with that line in it, repeated time and again, "May he never retire, May he never retire . . ." Joe didn't retire, and sure enough in 1952 Leafs were on the way down, as I had suspected would happen, although I didn't know how far they were going to fall.

At that time I knew in a few years I would be out of hockey altogether, turning it over to Stafford; I graduated from the newspapers and radio to become a hot item in the magazine business. There was a close-up in *Life Magazine*, with all the usual stuff about my spats, which I imported from Italy (different colours for different suits), my fedora, my war record. They said I was a dead-end kid dressed up as Little Lord Fauntleroy, the shrewdest hockey owner in the business, and the sort of puritan (the guy wrote with some amazement) who would not allow smoking in the team's special Pullman cars on the grounds that "the President of the United States might stroll through. I don't want anyone to think that pro hockey players are a bunch of bums." Well, it was true: we always had the cleanest and most orderly car in any train we travelled on. Following the *Life Magazine* lead, as sometimes happens in Canada, *Maclean's* published a two-part article on me later in the year, and *Saturday Night* did a long one where the hockey and business side of the Gardens were covered, both being in good shape.

But there was no doubt about it. From 1951 on Leafs were in doldrum years. When Primeau retired in the spring of 1953 after finishing out of the playoffs, and Clancy took over, we made deals here and there but nothing helped. I was spending a lot of energy in other ways too; buying every farm in Caledon that I could get my hands on, and trying to help in one of the greatest threats to hockey that we'd had since the late 1920's. NHL franchises in New York and Chicago were in terrible shape; poor crowds, bad hockey. They had brought it on themselves by bad management, not buying good players when they were available. Bill Tobin in Chicago wouldn't pay ten cents to see the Statute of Liberty take a swan dive into New York harbour. They needed players and a guarantee against going broke. It was as simple as that. Besides making players available to them, from the stronger clubs, I suggested as chairman of the board of owners that we guarantee their income. They figured out what they needed to run a team, $400,000 or whatever it was, and if they didn't get it at the gate, the league would make up the difference. It wasn't charity. We needed them, too, or we wouldn't fill our rinks. It was a good business deal. We kept young Jim Norris in the league that way, when otherwise he might have got out. He became one of the league strengths, later.

Sometimes what we did in Toronto was an example that others followed. By that time we had an attraction in the Gardens something like two hundred and fifty days a year. The rock concerts of the 1970's were still a long way off, but there was nothing that would draw a crowd that we couldn't handle. When a Saturday night hockey game was over, the crew would start getting ready for Sunday night wrestling. Tennis, lacrosse, ice shows, religious revival meetings, and political rallies were easy enough. When we had a chance to bring ballet or the Metropolitan Opera to Toronto, we did it. Some music critics complained later that I had tried to influence them to write more favourably of the Gardens as an opera house. I didn't try to influence them at all. I just called them in to the press room after I read their reviews on the Met's opening night, and told them what I thought of them, which wasn't much. I said they were a worse bunch of crepe-hangers than the sportswriters, which is going some. They finally complained enough over the years that the opera moved out to the O'Keefe Centre, where from some seats you can't hear a thing.

Each year in October, just before the hockey season started, I held a press conference – not a cheer-leading thing for the Leafs, especially. (In those years I would usually pick Detroit to be first, Canadiens second, and Leafs to be back in the pack struggling for a playoff spot, meaning that usually I was right). In October, 1954, I announced that although my health was pretty good, too many other duties were preventing me from giving my job as general manager of the Leafs 100 per cent effort, so I was going to step down on my sixtieth birthday.

What really made up my mind was that my powers as a hockey man were failing. I didn't say so, but it was true. At one time I always knew exactly where every man on the ice was at any given time (such as for a goal, or a bad play). I always knew who to praise or blame. These were not always the men who were praised or blamed by others. I would know if a man had made or missed a check, or made a good or bad pass, that directly caused someone else's good or bad play ten or fifteen seconds later. Now I was no longer sure. Partly this was from missing so much hockey, being away two or three months in the winter. Powers diminish or fail when they are not used, which goes for hockey, sex, running a racing stable, playing the stock market, or anything else. I had new challenges coming up, including helping to raise money for a big new culture centre and hospital for crippled children. I intended to get back into horse racing stronger than I'd ever been, and had spent the summer starting to build my racing stable. Stafford was into his thirties and had an interesting idea about forming a group of young directors into a hockey committee that, with him as chairman, would do some of the managerial things. Hap was only seven years younger than I and after nearly thirty years he deserved to have me off his back, although I did not then discuss with him the idea for transition to younger men running things at the Gardens.

There was some skepticism at my October announcement. Sportswriters gave the impression that they would believe it when they saw it. Maybe some in the family felt the same way, but when we had our annual family dinner at Christmas that year, all our grandchildren and our children and their spouses, I let the adults know that late in January I wanted them to be our guests in Florida. I told Hap the same. So a day or two before my sixtieth birthday they all arrived in West Palm Beach, Stafford and

Dorothea, Miriam and Jack Hoult, Hugh and his wife Bernice, and Hap. We asked some of our Florida friends and for entertainment flew in tenor George Murray and his new bride, singer Shirley Harmer, to lead the singing. Telegrams came from people in hockey, including some I hadn't really expected – from men who had played for me and been traded away. And as of February 1, 1955, I turned over the general managership to Hap, officially giving him the powers he had been exercising anyway.

A few weeks later when I flew to Toronto for a few days and walked in to the Gardens for the first time after giving up the general managership, I must admit that I was overwhelmed by the welcome I got from a lot of men who had been with me all that way. One group of press-room regulars presented me with a silver tray on which all their signatures had been engraved. The players gave me a ten-carat gold replica of the Stanley Cup. I wept unashamedly. I knew I'd been unkind to some of them, sometimes, but I knew myself well enough to know that I always operated explosively and if anybody stood in the way of those explosions, and got hurt, I was sorry. But that was the only way I knew. I think most of them understood; I had their loyalty even when sometimes I didn't deserve it. And I hadn't quite disappeared from the face of the earth. Hap Day emphasized that, telling reporters that in his first day back in his office as full-time general manager, the phone rang and he heard this familiar voice saying, "Is this the manager? Well, this is the president."

Incidentally, at that time Hughie had been one of the club doctors for some years, and Stafford's son Tommy was apprenticing as stickboy. My relations with Stafford were by no means all peaches and cream. He was working hard at hockey and the sand and gravel business, doing a good job for me. After one particularly good year in the middle 1950's I gave him a Cadillac. As soon as he got the car, he wanted the seat I was sitting in. One day when we were arguing some policy matter he said in exasperation, "You're going to have to retire! I should be running this place!"

I said, "I'm not retiring! What the hell have you ever done that I should turn everything over to you?" Two Smythes, much alike in voice, appearance, and other ways, fighting it out.

He stormed out of there and complained to his mother. Maybe she misunderstood what he said, but the way she heard it was, "I've been working all these years for nothing. I think I should get in there and get the money that's coming to me." I think when he said he was working all those years for nothing, he meant that he'd never been his own man, in control. But she took it the other way. When I got home she was very upset. She said I should be treating Stafford better, paying him for what he did. It was one of the few fights we ever had. I said, "You come with me." We walked out of the house at Caledon and drove over to the office on Number 10 highway. I showed her the books, where for years back he never got less than $20,000 a year, sometimes as high as $30,000, pretty good for a young man in those days. Irene went back to the house crying and told Jessie, "Stafford lied to me." But I thought it was more of a misunderstanding.

Anyway, soon after that I had a long talk with Stafford, to encourage that idea of his to get the ownership closer to the players again. His group of young Gardens' directors would figure on making trips with the team, which the older directors now rarely did. We got that going. At first they were just known facetiously as the Glee Club. But the long-term aim shaped up well enough that a year later the board named them the hockey committee, seven men with Stafford as chairman. One function would be to act as a buffer and protect the coach and manager against interference, including from me. Writers were always saying I interfered too much. Interference in hockey is when you tell some employee to do something they don't want to do. When you tell them something that the newspapermen don't like, that is called gross interference.

The idea for the hockey committee was all right. It's a wonder to me that twenty years later Harold Ballard, badly needing new blood around the place, didn't do something like the same thing. Perhaps being one of the originals, he knows the pitfalls. Besides Stafford, only one of them had been a director before; that was John Bassett. I didn't dislike Bassett at that time. He had the *Telegram*, a good newspaper, and he was a sportsman himself, fascinated with sports. Others on the hockey committee, with Stafford, Ballard, and Bassett, were Jack Amell, Bill Hatch, George Mara, and George Gardiner. Good men in many ways. But it just seemed that once the bunch of them got together, a certain amount of good sense went out the window. On the road they drank a lot and hung out together more than they mixed. Not drinking myself, I've never been able to understand people who centre their lives around the party they're going to have. I set up a budget, I think $10,000, to cover their travel and living-it-up expenses. One year they spent $20,000 before the season even opened. The press was quick to scoff, giving them the nickname of the Silver Seven, having something to do with the old hockey team of that name, and something to do with the idea that many had been born with silver spoons in their mouths. But the press is characteristically totally negative. To this day, every Gardens president from 1961 on came out of that group and did a good job.

One area of friction was that you can't put a group of successful young men together and give them nothing to do. Stafford and some of the others had plenty of hockey savvy. His buddy Ballard had been with Stafford for years running the Marlboro hockey club, part of our farm system. They had ideas about running the hockey club, and I often got phone calls in Florida from Stafford generally complaining that everything they wanted to do kept running into a stone wall, Hap Day. They thought his old effective system of defensive hockey wasn't working any more; that two third-place finishes and one fourth under King Clancy's coaching since he succeeded Primeau in 1953 wasn't good enough. Apparently Clancy's own spirit couldn't always be passed on – and it was spirit that he had most of. I remember a time long ago in Chicago when Hawks knocked us out of the Stanley Cup playoffs. I went down to the dressing room to find Clancy dancing around on top of an equipment trunk shouting, "Those sons-of-bitches will never beat us again!" And we weren't even going to be playing them again for six months! But that didn't win games in the spring of 1956, so for the 1956-57 season Clancy became assistant to Hap as manager. Howie Meeker was brought in as coach. All theory and no practice was Meeker's trouble. If he had a team made up of Rocket Richard and four more like him, he couldn't win. So when we finished fifth and out of the playoffs in the spring of 1957, a big crunch was coming. I knew it, and flew up from Florida in March for a press conference in New York that eventually led to Hap Day quitting.

When I held a press conference or made a speech, I prepared very carefully. I could hold audiences, because I worked at it. I never wanted an occasion to arise when people could think, "Oh, well, Conn Smythe is going to talk – he won't have anything new to say." If you want to use the word orchestrated, that was the word for my press conferences, either in person or on television. Even when it seemed right off the cuff, I knew what I wanted to say. Before a television interview, I would have a meeting with the man who would interview me, and tell him exactly what I wanted to talk about, so that he would build his questions to that end, and do research that would complement what I was saying. I would also tell him what I *didn't* want to talk about. A press conference was considerably different, of course, newspaper people being much less controllable than most interviewers on television. Anyway, that time in New York I knew exactly what I wanted to say. I didn't especially like the part that was going to reflect on Hap Day, but I could see no other way out.

To some extent, I blame that break-up with Hap Day on the Silver Seven. The team wasn't going well. Stafford, Ballard, and the others were unhappy about the way players were being used. I had listened and decided that certain things might have to be changed in our system. At the press conference were all the Toronto hockey writers and broadcasters. I said maybe our system was out of date. I took great care not to say that Hap was out of date, but one reporter quoted me as saying something that really riled Hap; that I hadn't lost confidence in Hap Day and, as to the future, Hap would be asked if he was available to carry on.

Day told the papers, "My legs have just been cut out from under me."

Back in Toronto Hap came in and asked if I said what was printed in the paper. I said it was accurate. He said, "It's strange that I should be asked if I was available, after thirty years. But since I have been asked, I don't want the job any more."

I hated to see him go that way, but on the other hand I was turning things over gradually to Stafford, who was chafing under the idea that Day wouldn't change the way he had always done things. If you give a man a job, as I had Stafford, you have to let him do it. As far as I was concerned, nothing changed between me and Hap. I counted him as the best friend I had. He was still part owner and a director of my sand and gravel company, to go with a thriving axe-handle business he had in St. Thomas. We certainly didn't see one another as often as we had, but time healed the breach.

The thing was, we both knew the changes had to come. We had been together a long time, successfully, but I knew that our old give-and-take system wouldn't work when I was gone and Stafford was in charge. I was very happy a few years later when Hap verified my own opinion of the rights and wrongs of what happened. He told Milt Dunnell of the *Star*, "There was no wound when we parted, so there was nothing to heal. If I were living my life over, I would want it to be the same way. As it turned out, I left at the right time. It was the luckiest thing that ever happened to me."

At the time, our mutual respect was strengthened, rather than weakened. We both knew the score. If either had waffled, the other would have been dismayed.

To wipe the slate clean, Howie Meeker was dropped before the next season started. I was happy to hire Billy Reay, a good hockey man who had spent most of his NHL career with Montreal. Clancy stayed as assistant manager, but we did not appoint a successor to Day as manager. I resumed some of that work, Stafford the rest. I wanted to keep my options open to that extent. And that summer I was spending more and more time at the race track again, finding a lot less trouble in dealing with horses than I did with humans.

Chapter Eleven

Three years earlier, when I began buying the land northwest of the city in Caledon Township, I had also started buying cattle. I had them for years, as many as a thousand at times, but my heart wasn't in cattle. What I really wanted was to get back in the horse business. At the time it was a little ticklish. We'd had another brush with the gamblers in hockey a few years earlier. Clarence Campbell suspended Billy Taylor and Don Gallinger for betting on games. There was no element of games being fixed, but the issue was sensitive enough that I hesitated about going into racing, where scandals occurred a lot oftener than in hockey. While I thought it over, I got into it by the back door. Larkin Maloney was already in, with some good horses including Ace Marine, which won the Plate the following year, 1955. We decided to go partners on some purchases in his name. Right off the bat we blew one, going to the United Kingdom and paying £6,000 ($16,592 Canadian at the time) for a horse named Irish Slipper. I learned then that if you wanted to meet real salesmen in the horse business, you went to the United Kingdom. Those Irish and English owners will trade you a rowboat for a battleship any time. It cost another $1,252 to fly Irish Slipper to Canada and he was never worth a damn, except to the veterinarians. I remember the first time I met the vet who was going to be with me from then on, a great country vet, the kind every stable needs. Irish Slipper ran into a fence and smashed some rails, getting a lot of long slivers jammed into his neck close to the jugular vein. We called the nearest vet, Murray Dudgeon of Orangeville, a few miles away. When he was pulling out these slivers he asked a German I had working for me, "How much is this one worth?"

When he heard, he almost fainted. He told me later he'd been used to dealing mostly with horses that were purchased for a few hundred dollars. That's about what we should have paid for Irish Slipper. But at a yearling sale a few weeks later we did better on a dark brown colt by Bunty Lawless out of a mare called Broomflight. We both knew what a great runner Bunty Lawless had been. I told Larkin about the day in Saratoga when he explored all over town for about three hours after getting loose in the morning, and then went out and won a race in the afternoon, just as if he'd needed the warm-up.

"I'm going to buy him," I told Larkin, and did, for $2,500. Our partnership deal, which we soon made public, was that I'd buy and Larkin would put in half. The next month in Kentucky I bought five horses from James D. Norris, old Jim's son, who later became the best friend I had in the United States. But it was Bunty's Flight – the name I gave to the Bunty Lawless-Broomflight yearling – that really set me up in the horse business. He won a couple of stakes as a two-year-old in 1955 and was close in others. We bought eight more horses that year. It was a fairly loose partnership in some ways, close in others. For instance, I didn't own half of Ace Marine when he won the Queen's Plate in 1955, but I acted as an adviser in his training. An old friend from before the war, Johnny Starr, was training both for the partnership and the horses we owned individually. He'd been a jockey's agent when I met him first. In 1936 I'd given him a horse called Exhibition on the cuff – to be paid for out of winnings, $200 a race or something – and he did win a few. From the start, Johnny was wonderfully kind at bringing horses into shape, but sometimes wouldn't work them as hard as I thought he should. I advised Larkin that Ace Marine needed a lot more work, which he got. Then Ace Marine went out and won the Plate.

Incidentally, that was the last Plate run at the east end track that was called Woodbine at the time, later became Old Woodbine, and finally Greenwood. The reason for moving the Plate was that E. P. Taylor and his Jockey Club crowd were building the big new Woodbine track near Malton. Officially back in racing, and a shareholder of the Jockey Club, I took an interest in the plans for New Woodbine. To put it politely, they were a disaster. In February, 1955, I pointed this out in a letter to Taylor.

I hear on every side that this is to be the track to end all tracks, and yet find that the stables are on the opposite side of the race track from the grandstand. . . . This is not good procedure, as can easily be seen at some of the great tracks in the United States, such as Hialeah, which have the stables first, the paddock second, the grandstand third, and the track out in front . . .

I listed the advantages of such plans: the proximity of the stables to the paddock, so that horses could be moved easily between races; the fact that no path had to be made on the track from the stables to the paddock, and so on. The turf course was poorly laid out, too, crossing and re-crossing the dirt track when what needed doing was to build the dirt track big enough to enclose a one-mile turf track. I tried to butter Taylor up by saying that I knew he was a man who wanted the best, and there was still time to change, but I'm afraid you don't change E. P. Taylor without a blowtorch.

As far as I can make out, Woodbine was laid out as it is for only one reason – so that the parking lots could be close to the highway. For that reason, ever since Woodbine was opened in 1956, ginnies have been making the long walk with horses around part of the track from the stables to the paddock, trainers have to waste time dashing back and forth to the stables from the paddock and grandstand during race days, and owners who like to see their horses back at the stables after a race have to drive over instead of having a short, pleasant walk. I pointed out all these flaws in 1955, more than a year before the track opened. Short of building my own track, there was nothing much else I could do after that than keep on beefing about the stupid layout, which I have done.

Larkin and I kept on buying in 1956 and 1957, selling the ones that didn't work out (receiving $5,500 for Irish Slipper, one third of what we'd paid, and considering ourselves lucky) but meanwhile it was understood that if we split up eventually some horses would be mine, some his, and some we'd toss for.

One that became a pillar of my stable was Kitty Girl. We'd bought her half-sister, called Feathered Lady, from Jim Norris in our first batch. A year later I was at his farm in Florida. He pointed to half a dozen nice yearlings and said, "You can have any one you want, Connie."

I bought Kitty Girl because she was the same breeding as

Feathered Lady and a lot bigger; I just liked her looks. She won stakes for me. But I made one other deal on my own in 1955 that some people would consider more important. I got a mare named Seemly from Jim Norris, already in foal to County Delight. She dropped a big, strong colt foal at Caledon. A few hours after he was born, he was frolicking around as though he were a month old. That strong baby we called Caledon Beau.

In 1956, when Caledon Beau was just a frisky yearling, I got another big break. Horatio Luro was in for the Canadian International Championship with Eugenia 2nd, a beautiful chestnut mare. It wasn't as well known then, but Luro is the best trainer in the world at getting a horse ready to go a distance. Jim Norris knew that. He was in Toronto for the race, and we were splitting bets. Every time I looked up he'd be sending down another $50 on Eugenia 2nd. I don't know how much we had on, but Eugenia 2nd came in and paid $55.40. In 1980 that was still a record win price for that race and her time, 2:43 2/5, is still the track record for a mile and five-eighths, which the race was then. When Jim cashed in, he came back with his pockets full of money. We drove up to Caledon for dinner. He spread all the money out on the floor and we counted it, about $7,000, which we split. That was on a Saturday. On the following Monday some broodmare sales were on at Keeneland in Kentucky, and Irene and I attended. When I looked at the catalogue the first thing I saw was that one called Eolia, a full sister to Eugenia 2nd was in the sale. I thought of the way Eugenia 2nd had won that long race. None of those hardboots in the audience had heard about the Canadian International yet, so all Eolia cost me was a little over seven thousand dollars, and her sister had won half of that for me on Saturday. Eolia was in foal to Woodchuck at the time. It was one of those great bargains that you sometimes get if you're lucky enough to be in the right place at the right time with the right information.

You have to keep good records to know what you're doing in the horse business, just as in hockey, so that you know all the pluses and minuses. In my stable each horse had its own ledger sheet, with a running total of expenses and purses, loss or profit. In 1957, the ledger shows that Caledon Beau as a two-year-old was turning out to be my best producer. That year he cost $5,476.20 in everything from training, shipping, blacksmithing, and vet fees, but pulled in $10,380 in purses, the biggest being $3,705 in

September, just before the Leaf camp opened. His profit that year was $4,903.80 and that was just the start.

But soon I was plummeted back into hockey, grappling with a brand-new problem. During the previous season, the first try at an NHL Players Association had reared its troublesome head. I hated the very idea. In a statement to the Board of Directors in the autumn I said that the only question to be answered was whether the Maple Leaf team and its individual players would be better under the direction of the Players Association, or under the management of the Leafs. I didn't want anyone telling us what we had to do. I was especially annoyed that our captain, Jim Thomson, was one of the association vice-presidents. I wanted our captain to be concerned with the Leafs and nothing else. The way I looked at it, the Players Association was causing a good deal of trouble, and had not yet contributed one solitary thing to the betterment of hockey. I traded Thomson to Chicago, bang. Ted Lindsay of Detroit, the association's first president, was traded to Chicago as well. In a sense, we thus isolated the association, and it was nearly ten years before it became effective. Meanwhile, I insisted that George Armstrong, be named captain – I would have made him captain before, but had left it to the hockey committee and Hap, who had chosen Thomson instead.

Stafford was thirty-six then, and his first season with Billy Reay and without Hap was a tough one. The team was just not good enough. While young players who were to become stars later stood up fairly well in the first part of the season, they faded badly at the end, and in the spring of 1958 finished last for the first time in Leafs' history. I put plenty of heat on Stafford to find someone who could turn things around. We talked to Billy Reay about taking another job in the organization, but he wanted another year to prove himself as coach.

Even before the season ended in the spring of 1958, Stafford began checking the records and availability of men in both the major and minor leagues, looking for someone we could hire. In late May he came in to see me about someone called Punch Imlach. I remembered Imlach as a player in the 1930's, on Toronto junior and senior teams. He'd been in the Army, then ran the Quebec Aces, and in 1957 had joined the Boston organization. At the time, Boston had had a one-year deal with Eddie Shore, who owned the Springfield Indians in the American Hockey League. Imlach had been sent to Springfield as general manager but had wound up coaching as well. Under him, Springfield had done well. Stafford said he was worth a look, probably at the 1958 league meetings coming up in Montreal in June.

"Well, talk to him," I said. "But don't offer him anything you can't deliver." I tried to stay out of it, for the moment. I had something else on my mind – Caledon Beau. The Queen's Plate was to be run on June 7, the end of the week when the league meetings were being held. I wasn't happy with the way Caledon Beau was shaping up, and had an idea percolating in my mind. Some athletes needed more work than others. This was a big, strong horse. I couldn't figure out why he wasn't doing better this spring and decided he needed more work. Johnny Starr went along with me, although I think he had some doubts about how much work I had in mind.

We entered Caledon Beau in the Marine Stakes on May 31, a mile race. He finished a badly beaten fourth to M. J. Boylen's Foxy Phil. That was a Saturday. We jogged him on Sunday and on Monday, June 2, put him into one division of the Plate Trial Stakes at a mile and a sixteenth. He came down in front and all the other horsemen were saying I was crazy because if he went in the Plate five days later he'd be running his third distance race in a week. They said that was an impossible task for even the strongest horse. It wasn't. I knew the horse. You can sometimes tell right from the start how strong a horse is. On Plate Day, he was ready. Early in the race, rider Al Coy kept him in a good position. When he made his move it was all over. He won by ten lengths.

That was a wonderful day for me, and not just because of the $26,395 the Plate was worth to the winner that year, or the ceremonial fifty guineas from the Queen. I was happy to be back in racing that big, that fast, and to find that I still knew what made a horse tick. I liked people yelling at me from the stands as I walked across the track, "Hey, Connie! Trust you to come up with an iron horse!" Even so, hockey wasn't far from my thoughts. When I was waving my first Queen's Plate around in the winner's circle I yelled, "I wish it was the Stanley Cup!" As I walked back across the track I could hear one big voice in the crowd boom out, "Okay, Connie, now get yourself some hockey players!"

I didn't know it then, but the hockey Leafs had made the beginning of a big move that week as well. At the hockey meeting Stafford had drafted goalie Johnny Bower from Cleveland, and had talked to Imlach. They didn't get very far, maybe because Stafford wasn't offering what Imlach wanted. I didn't start to pay real attention until a few days later when Boston asked me to stop negotiating with Imlach. They said Lynn Patrick, Boston's general manager, was ill and they might need Imlach badly. Hmmm, I thought. Is he that good? We'd been thinking of him as chief scout, trouble shooter. I told Boston that talks had gone too far to be broken off. A few weeks later, late June or early July, Imlach came to Toronto to talk to Stafford. They were at the sand pit. As far as he was concerned, Imlach said, Leafs had no general manager. That was the job he wanted. They were talking when I walked into the room.

"How are you doing with this fellow, Stafford?" I asked.

Stafford said, "Well, we haven't settled anything."

I said to Imlach, "What's the matter, you want to stay in the minors forever? Are you afraid to take a chance?"

He said he wasn't afraid of anything, but hadn't been offered what he wanted. Later that day Stafford asked him what he'd think of being an assistant general manager, the same title Clancy had. Billy Reay would coach. We told Imlach he would do the general manager's job but I thought a man should prove himself before he got the whole title. Imlach eventually agreed. And that is the way Leafs got the man I eventually considered to be the best coach in hockey, and the worst general manager. People have told me that he is a lot like me in many ways, very demanding, but I don't know. I was never in his class as a coach. However, as a general manager, I never lost a good player because I couldn't get along with him, and Imlach did.

He and I didn't talk much, from the start. Never had occasion to, because Stafford was dealing on that level by then, as chairman of the hockey committee. Early that season we went to last place and stayed there. In November Imlach was called in by the hockey committee to explain what was going wrong. He told them the players were not playing for Reay, that Reay was not tough enough on them, was trusting them too much, and was being let down.

"What would you do?" Stafford asked.

Imlach said he didn't have the power to do anything, being only the assistant general manager.

The committee decided then to give him the full title, if I agreed. When they came to me I said, "All right."

The team kept on going down. Late in November after losing on successive nights, Wednesday and Thursday, Imlach appeared the next morning in my office. He said he knew I'd done some tough things in my life and he was faced with one now. "I'm going to relieve Billy Reay of his duties as coach," he said.

I looked at him hard. He was going to fire the man I thought a lot of and had hired. That took guts. I didn't really like it, but I had known, right back to Hap Day's earliest days, that somewhere in every good hockey club there had to be a man who could make the tough decisions.

"Well, if that's the way it is," is all I said.

He went straight from my office and fired Reay.

I watched him very closely for the next few weeks. He interviewed some other people for the job as coach. Meanwhile, he did the coaching, and the team started to play for him. I sat up in my private box halfway up the stands, which the sportswriters called Berchtesgaden, and for the first time in my life a strange thing was happening. I was there, always with a handy messenger; Clancy or Tommy, Stafford's son, or somebody. I would see a line that wasn't working, a player below par, all the things I had been seeing for years and telling coaches about – except that with Imlach, before I could get the message down to him, he would have done exactly what I wanted him to do. He was the best coach I ever saw. It was as if he were a mind reader.

"Take that man off!" my mind would say, and Imlach would be yanking him off. Not only that, but he got incredible mileage out of players who weren't really that good – he would send a player like Larry Regan off the bench to fill in somewhere, and the guy would play like an all-star.

For a few weeks after he took over, he kept on looking for a coach, and so did the hockey committee, interviewing candidates here and there. Finally I said to Stafford, "You've got your coach. Imlach. Don't look any more." I never changed my opinion of him as a coach, but if I'd been running things I wouldn't have put up with him as general manager as long as Stafford eventually did. Imlach won four Stanley Cups in the 1960's doing the double job, but he should have won six. He wouldn't take orders from anybody. He insisted on doing things his way, and everybody else could go to hell.

But trouble between him and Stafford was still years away. That first year when he pulled Leafs up from last place in the dying weeks of the season and got them into the playoffs on the last night of the season, then into the Stanley Cup final, Leafs were being called the Cinderella team and Imlach in one season had done the job. I stopped worrying about the hockey team and began to take pride in it again.

It was a good time to have the hockey worries removed. By the late 1950's, I'd been working for the Ontario Society for Crippled Children for more than ten years. We had made a lot of progress in that time. We had 257 local organizations in Ontario working for us and 22 nurses (up from 5 in 10 years). We looked after 1,297 campers at our summer camp but had a case load of nearly 12,000 and had a pressing need for a great step forward – a residential treatment centre and hospital for children from areas without such facilities. We also needed a facility for rare and difficult cases to be cared for by surgical and medical specialists available to us in Toronto. It would cost something more than four million dollars to put up what we wanted.

I've mentioned before that John David Eaton agreed to head up our building fund. We had a survey, analysis, and plan drawn up late in 1957. Irene and I were the first donors, promising $50,000 for installation of a treatment pool that would be named in memory of Patricia, our little daughter who had died. I think it was a way of saying thanks to me, as well, that one of the biggest early donations was from the Ontario Sportswriters and Sportscasters Association, pledging $200,000 from proceeds of their annual sports dinner. I went to speak in various Ontario cities, outlining the need to local service clubs and organizations that could help. We never lost a chance for publicity, even the Royal kind. When the Queen and Prince Philip visited Ontario in 1959, one of the biggest spreads of newspaper pictures was from Toronto's Kew Beach, where kids lined up in their wheelchairs one sunny day under a sign that read: The Crippled Children of Toronto WELCOME . . . OUR QUEEN. I had helped that happen and knew it would help our campaign. I accompanied that lovely lady as she toured the lines of kids, stopping to speak to some of them, and Irene followed with Prince Philip. But I was only one of hundreds who worked hard to raise the money, so that in June, 1960, John David Eaton, Conn Smythe, and the Ontario Health Minister, Dr. Matthew Dymond, got together on the same shovel handle to turn the first sod.

The whole campaign was an eye-opener to me in what great humanitarians some people with money are, and what skunks others are. In the humanitarian line I must include Jacques Pigott.

When his construction company's bid for the centre got the go-ahead, I said, "It won't be any more than that, will it?"

He said, "No, and if it's less we'll return it to you." I was astounded later to get more than $100,000 back from Pigott Construction.

The centre, on Bayview in north Toronto, was opened in 1961 and is a model of its kind, written up in many publications, and visited by people all over North America who want to see our place before they go ahead and develop theirs. It would take a book in itself to tell about all the people who have been helped to live better lives through the work done there. I've always been proud of my part in it, doing the thing I could do: pushing Easter Seals, organizing, raising money, and, as a director of the Society for Crippled Children giving hell to anyone not properly supporting the fine doctors and scientists who do the actual work.

I don't know how many dozen horses belonged at one time or another to Maloney and Smythe (or Smythe and Maloney, as the stable appears in my horse ledgers), but according to the Jockey Club's press book, in the six years we were together, ending late in 1960, we won forty-one stakes' races. And that doesn't count the stakes I won or Maloney won with horses that weren't in the partnership; such as a Queen's Plate each, Larkin in 1955 with Ace Marine and me with Caledon Beau in 1958. We made money every year and were also a friend to man in that we made the guys in the press box happy every time they saw us together and could pull out their old line about Lumpy and Grumpy.

It got to be a big operation; too big in the end for two partners with firm ideas. It's nice to have a partner in a small horse operation because you help each other absorb the losses. But when we got that big, well, Maloney had one way around his business and I had another.

When we decided to split, it was precipitated by a difference of opinion; but it was no pitched battle. More of an indicator than a real reason, and it was over our good filly Wonder Where. We had bought her from Frank Selke's Rolling Range Farm as a yearling in 1957. Her sire was Occupy and her dam On The Fly. Larkin named her. One night we were driving along some road where every motel had a No Vacancy sign out.

Larkin muttered, "Everything's occupied. I wonder where people are going to sleep tonight?" And then he thought and I agreed that Wonder Where was a good name for the Occupy filly.

She was big and strong, easy to train, easy to break, and she won a lot for us, including the Canadian Oaks in 1959. The next year, when she was four, she showed signs of tendon trouble late in the season. I thought she should be sent to the farm, but Larkin and the others thought they could get one more race out of her. I never think you should figure on one more race. You should always figure on three more races. If you're only figuring on one more, something's wrong. They took her to Fort Erie and she broke down. We split shortly after and when we were dividing up the horses Wonder Where was transferred to Larkin's name and later had three or four good foals. I look back in the ledgers we kept on each horse and see, in 1960, all the entries dated November 25, recording the Smythe-Maloney split. Some horses went to me, some to him. The ledger entry for Wonder Where is the only one that reads: "To L. Maloney, to race in his name, net profits to be split 50-50. When racing over, goes to Mr. Maloney outright."

After that he did well and I've done well. It's a question of making your own mistakes, and racing is often a game of mistakes, not always the owner's. I'd been second with Major Flight in the Queen's Plate of 1959, running behind to New Providence, but speaking of mistakes, the closest second I ever came was in 1961 with Just Don't Shove. Johnny Longden was in town for that Plate. He was a friend of a friend of mine, or something, and he said, "Sure, I'll ride your horse." He rode perfectly and in the stretch he was on the lead but lost to Colonel K. R. Marshall's Blue Light by the width of a puck, no more than three inches. All the time he had never touched my horse with the whip.

I asked him, "Why didn't you just give that horse one crack?"

He said, "Mr. Smythe, your trainer asked me not to hit him because he might bolt."

"Well," I said, "if he'd bolted, he would have bolted more than three inches and would have won the Plate!"

Even when it cost me the Plate I really marvelled at a man like him, winner of more than five thousand races, still obeying instructions!

All the same, that was one of the best rides I ever had, because he made my horse almost win. I don't like losing but that time, if I couldn't win it myself, I was happy that Colonel Marshall won it. He'd never won the Plate. I figured I'd have lots more chances but he wouldn't. That is, I was happy that he'd won the race until everybody kept coming up to me and saying, "Connie, isn't it wonderful that Colonel Marshall finally won the Plate?" For the first week I agreed emphatically. For the second week I muttered, "Yeah, it's kind of wonderful." But after three weeks of that I began to think, "wouldn't it have been wonderful if Connie Smythe had won that Plate?"

I liked, enjoyed, and felt good with my grandchildren on family occasions, but there was one in particular I figured had inherited the hockey savvy that Stafford and I had: Stafford and Dorothea's son Tom. He would sit with me at hockey games from when he was a little guy of six or seven. Stafford had a photographic memory for hockey plays, as I had, and he started early to develop the same kind of thing in Tom. When Tom was a stickboy for the Leafs, he and Staff would sit down after a game and Staff would say something like: "On the fourth goal, who was on the ice, where were they standing, and who made the mistake?" Tom had the same ability his father and I had to freeze the action after a goal. In many ways Stafford was far tougher on Tom than he was on Tom's sisters; in fact, sometimes I thought he was too tough on the boy, but maybe he was doing that because he felt I hadn't been tough enough on him, I don't know.

Tom worked a little at the old sandpit for me when they lived nearby, and when Stafford and Dorothea moved out of the city to Caledon, nearer the pit there and better for Staff's asthma, Tom worked around the farm for me summers. He was a good rider and would help to break yearlings and school horses out of the gate. We had a rule that no start would be made when there was a big truck going by on Highway 10. One day Tom, on a horse in the gate, was not really sitting properly because a truck was going by and he thought he was safe. I guess the starter couldn't resist this fourteen-year-old leaning on the gate instead of paying attention to his horse, and thought he'd teach him a lesson. Bang, the gate flew open and down went Tom – which the starter hadn't figured on. The horse was loose, which is bad, because any loose horse might hurt itself. I fired Tom. He didn't stay fired long. When I told Irene about it she said quietly, "Look, this is your grandson. If you want to help him be a man, fine, but I can't see that you are helping him by firing him."

As usual in such matters, she was right.

"Why don't you phone him and apologize and ask him to come back to work?" she said.

I did. Often when I got into a row I would talk it over with her. Usually I just wanted to identify the problem so I could deal with it. Half the time she would just say, "Well, it must be you, Daddy."

I patched up a lot of battles because Irene could make me see that I was the one who had blown up, and shouldn't have. I've also heard that her words, "It must be you, Daddy," became sort of a laughing catch phrase through the whole family, stopping many a family fight.

So that was one of the times I fired Tom, besides the once or twice he quit. The last time he quit, he rode his bicycle the several miles from home to the farm on a very hot day, dressed in shorts. He got there just as ninety tons of straw arrived to be unloaded. He wanted to go home for long pants. I told him if he was dumb enough to come to work on a farm in shorts, he could help unload the straw. By the end of the unloading he looked like he'd been through a threshing machine himself. He did the job, and then quit. But there was nothing he did that ever shook my conviction in the late 1950's that first I'd run the Gardens, then Stafford, and then – if he continued to develop as he had – Tom. From when he was a little kid, when I saw him I would stick out my hand and say, "Shake the hand of an honest man," and that's how I always saw him.

It has probably never even been guessed at before, but when I did sell my Gardens stock in November of 1961, concern over

Tom was an issue that I found difficult to handle. It had been understood between Stafford and me for years that eventually he would have the chance to buy me out. Not long after the Crippled Children's Centre opened, and I had that out of the way, I figured the time had come. The young players Imlach had inherited from our system – Carl Brewer, Frank Mahovlich, Bob Pulford, Bob Baun, Dick Duff, Billy Harris, and others – had matured and with the veterans like Olmstead, Bower, Armstrong, Horton, and Stanley were about ready to win it all. A good place for Stafford to move in and me to move out. At the time I had nearly 30,000 Gardens shares registered to C. Smythe Limited, and a little more than 20,000 in my own name. I planned to sell about 45,000 shares, which would give Stafford effective control. In voting power they were backed up by thousands more, including about 2,000 shares Stafford already held, about 7,500 controlled by Harold Ballard, 4,100 by Larkin Maloney, and 6,700 by John Bassett's paper, the *Telegram*.

Stafford and I talked for three days over various aspects of the deal and finally reached an agreement. At the time, I thought I was selling only to him and that down the line, maybe in another twenty years, he'd be doing the same thing, selling to Tommy. He gave me the assurance I wanted that nothing substantial would be changed around the Gardens, that the people who had been so loyal to me were safe for as long as they wanted their jobs, and that the honesty and class I had tried to bring to the place would continue. A few days later when he told me he was selling part of my shares to Ballard and Bassett, I exploded, "That's a lousy deal! That's the worst business mistake you could ever make! You have the whole pot and now you're going to get a third instead, so that every time this place makes a million dollars you're going to give two-thirds of it away!"

Besides, I told Stafford, the partnership would almost certainly ruin the chances that Tommy would take over from him. "Bassett has sons, Ballard has sons. You're selling out Tommy too," I said.

But maybe Stafford didn't have enough confidence to go it alone. I know that for a week I wrestled with cancelling the whole deal. I have thought since, with all the things that happened, The Man Upstairs was trying to nudge me, tell me, "You're doing it wrong, you're doing it wrong . . ."

Even on the last morning, November 23, 1961, when the money was to be handed over, everything signed, and the deal to be announced, I was furious when the first edition of John Bassett's paper arrived and there it was all over the front page. I railed at Stafford, "This is the kind of guy you're taking on as a partner, who can't even keep his word about an announcement deadline!"

But we signed, and I went from my office that day to the press room, which then was right next to the Leafs' dressing room, where we'd called all the Gardens' employees. I had wanted them to hear it first from me, before any newspaper had it.

At a directors meeting that day the new management was made official. I told the directors that it had always been my hope to pass on the company to someone who would maintain it with the prestige, dignity, and character it had enjoyed in the past. I harked back to the organization of the company when we'd been loaded with heavy debt, and compared it to the present when the company not only was free of debt, but owned a sizable portfolio of investments and real estate and had paid out nearly three million dollars in dividends over the years. I paid tribute to Jack Bickell as being the main inspiration for forming the company and as having laid down the principle that sporting interests must come first, and told the directors that Stafford had agreed to buy all my shares and that I had agreed to accept his offer. I therefore tendered my resignation as president and managing director and coupled it with nomination of Stafford to succeed me. Bassett seconded, my resignation was accepted, and after Stafford was elected president and appointed managing director I withdrew.

The minutes then recorded:

Mr. Stafford Smythe stated that it was his desire that his father continue for the rest of his life to hold an esteemed position with the Gardens, and he moved that Mr. Conn Smythe be voted a retiring allowance of $15,000 per annum, and that he be provided with an office, a secretary, a car and driver, seats and other services presently enjoyed, such provision to be reviewed at the end of five years. The motion was seconded by Mr. Bassett.

Mr. Maloney moved that the motion be amended so that the above provisions be provided to Mr. Smythe for his lifetime. The amendment was approved and the motion as amended was unanimously adopted.

Stafford then said that he and his associates, Bassett and Ballard, wished to nominate me to be chairman of the board, with Bill MacBrien as honorary chairman. When that had been passed, I came back into the meeting and took over the chair, to begin arguing right away. Stafford suggested moving the Gardens' business to the Bank of Nova Scotia. I said that was a totally terrible idea; that the Bank of Commerce had supported us in the early days when not many would, and it would be a bad mistake to change the banking arrangements. Stafford said that some of what I said was unknown to him and would be taken into account. As a result, the change was not made. All that was left was for me to say thanks, and walk out.

Game over.

Chapter Twelve

When I look back on my marriage to Irene, I can see that I was the luckiest man in the world. Part of it was that we had started out so young, with so little. When someone in a magazine or newspaper piece referred to me as the hockey millionaire or whatever other tag they felt applicable for their purposes of the moment, back at the bottom of my mind and of hers were pictures of us as kids in our teens, or on early mornings in the kitchen on Runnymede with her taking sand and gravel orders on the phone. What we had, we had built together, and she had an instinctive understanding from our earliest days that we would do some things together and some things apart.

She had a circle of friends she curled with, golfed with, played bridge with, just as I had my racing friends, Army friends, hockey friends, and battles in politics and public affairs. Once after I sold my interest in the Gardens someone asked Irene how she would be able to stand having me around the house all the time. She laughed, "You're joking!" I still needed two offices. If I was at Caledon and a letter arrived at the Gardens that needed immediate attention, it was read to me or sent up right away. Every morning at 9:00 I was either in the office at Caledon involved in sand pit business or horse business, or in the one at the Gardens, which we kiddingly called the Office of Various Affairs. When the races were on, there was scarcely a morning that I wasn't up and at the track by 7:00 with my stopwatch to sit beside my trainer and watch my string go out for works. Afternoons when I had a horse running, we would be back in our box at the track, sometimes taking friends for lunch and the races. She did her own betting, just as she had that long-ago day when she had $10 on the nose of Rare

Jewel at $214.40 for $2. We shared family problems that came up occasionally, golfed, travelled, debated, did everything together that it is possible for a man and his wife to do.

There was only one thing on which we disagreed. As the years wore on through the 1950's, my taxable income from salaries and investments reached a total around $100,000 a year (usually not including anything from racing, where winnings at the track tended to be cancelled out by breeding farm expenses or vice versa). We could have afforded to buy or build a bigger home, and Irene would have liked that.

"What for?" I asked, once. "I don't want to entertain the Queen or Winston Churchill, I just want a comfortable place to live – and we have it." By then we also had our condominium in Florida, our summer place at Lake Simcoe, and the farm at Caledon.

But I understood her reasons, too. Her closest women friends were always moving into bigger places – the Amells, Maloneys, and others. E.P. Taylor had his mansion on Bayview, not far from Bruce Matthews. Jack Kent Cooke, John Bassett, and others we knew had huge places. And we were still in the place we had built for about $15,000 in 1926, with the good-sized living room, dining room, and kitchen on the main floor, and five bedrooms on the second and third. I always figured that was about right. In fact, I always figured the money I saved not drinking, smoking, or moving would have given me enough money to live forever even if I'd never heard of the National Hockey League.

But that argument didn't satisfy Irene. Once, when some friends were moving for about the eleventh time, she said to me, as she often had, "I would like to go and look at some houses."

"Go ahead," I said. I guess she thought she had finally worn me down.

A few days later she said, "There are a couple of really nice houses that I would like you to come and have a look at, with me. See which one you like the best."

"No," I said.

"Why not?"

"I'm staying here," I said. "If you want to buy a house, you go ahead. I'm staying here and Jessie will look after me."

The argument went on, but I had decided that as much as I always wanted to give her the things that would make her happy, this was one place where I dug in my heels, simply because I thought I was right. I would look around the house and think, what more can a man have than this? In many families it is the man who wants to keep moving, while the nesting instinct makes a woman want to stay where she feels secure and comfortable. It was the opposite with us.

But I did try to make it up to her in other ways. At Caledon, for instance, by that time the sand and gravel operations had been in full swing for years. I loved to see and hear the noise because it meant progress and industry to me, not only for us but for the city and the province, even the country. Our house and pool and the vegetable garden, as well as the flowers and shrubs and fruit trees planted on the slope around the pond, were well out of sight and sound of the pit operations. However, the main road in to the house led from the highway past the old farmhouse we had converted into offices and then along the side of the busy pits, weigh scales, rumbling trucks, crushers and everything else.

Every time we drove in Irene, I could see, found it jarring – not the peaceful paddocks and barns to our left, but the chugging machinery on our right. So I had a lane built a few hundred yards south of the office entrance and called it Irene's Drive. On the highway entrance we had to put up a sign saying it was a private road, but when we came there together, or she drove in by herself, she could take Irene's Drive and never see or hear anything noisier than a few yearlings romping in a field, or the stallions standing quietly, mares grazing, horses up from the track getting their strength and condition back on what the horse people call Dr. Grass.

It was either just before or just after Christmas in 1963 that Irene began to have some pain that wouldn't go away or be soothed by normal means. When it was obvious that something was wrong, a series of medical tests brought us the worst verdict that a person can hear. Irene had cancer and it was spreading through the bone marrow. The unvarnished truth was that, barring a miracle, it would get worse and worse, and was terminal.

She was very brave. She kept saying, "Now, Daddy, don't worry about me. It's something we have to put up with. I'm good for years yet." But sometimes at night she would groan with the pain and I felt helpless to help her. I never had the feeling that, busy as our lives had been, I had ever neglected her and I know she didn't think so, either. We had been together all those years, practically from childhood; and from her work and mine we had done what we had set out to do, raise our family. We were still doing what we could to help them and our grandchildren. Hughie and Miriam and Stafford were aware of Irene's condition and took more pains to come and see her, sit with her, and talk with her. The grandchildren came in often as well. I would lie awake some nights and think that it was wrong for God to inflict such pain on her, and remember how much she had brought to my life. Some people might not like me, or approve of me, but there isn't one person in the world who ever met Irene who didn't like her, because that's the kind of woman she was. And that's the kind of girl I had from high school on.

But in a situation like that, it just isn't human, or right, to shut out the rest of the world. She wanted to go on doing what she could, as long as she could, and so did I. We spent more and more time together, and in 1964 as her disease worsened she was still well enough to take a rooting interest in everything I did. That year, as some might recall, was the year of the great flag debate. Lester B. (Mike) Pearson had won the election of 1963 without campaigning on the issue that he planned to give Canada what he described as our own distinctive flag. I and millions of other Canadians were quite happy with the flag we had – the Red Ensign. We had fought under it in Europe during two wars. The Union Jack up in one corner signified the British connection, which in my opinion was the most important single fact of life in Canada.

I started writing to Pearson on the flag issue soon after his election in the spring of 1963. We had known one another then for forty years or so. In the early 1920's I had coached University of Toronto hockey teams to six Intercollegiate junior and senior championships, twice to Allan Cup finals, another time – as the Varsity Grads – to win the Allan Cup. He had succeeded me as coach for a couple of years and the senior team won Intercollegiate championships. So we had old friends, old associations, in common and in my first letter on the subject I was fairly friendly:

> As an old soldier, I worry about the seemingly intense desire of some people to change our national flag, under which so many of your friends were buried in the two great wars. I hope that, intensely patriotic as you are, you will handle this matter with due consideration for the above mentioned.

Within a few months, our correspondence on the matter had escalated to the point where I was telling him, on September 24, 1963, that he "would be doing this country a great disservice" if he changed the flag. He wrote in reply that the Red Ensign was

> very much in the hearts of the Canadian people but I do not think this means that the majority of the citizens of this country consider it satisfactory as the kind of national emblem we should have as a unifying force. Why can't we have a Union Jack as a flag signifying our loyalty to the crown and our membership in the Commonwealth while we have a special national flag which stands for our own country?

Of course, the crux of the matter was Quebec's attitude to the British, which was shown in a number of disrespectful ways, including during Royal visits. I wrote him back again a few days later repeating my earlier arguments and asking for his reasons in wanting to change the flag.

> Do you expect the western wheat to be any harder – the pine trees to be any greener – our snow to be any whiter – the corn to be any sweeter, and all the wonders we have in this country of ours to be improved? Do you honestly expect that you will get one more volunteer from Quebec to fight for our country under a new flag?

I told him I thought a new flag would not unify the country, as he argued, but would divide us more than ever. Although I continued to respect him as a person, everything that he was doing to destroy the character of the country as I understood it I could only lay to politics, to the Liberal dependence on Quebec votes. I bitterly regretted that I had voted for him in 1963. As I wasn't having any impact on him, I switched my support to John Diefenbaker because he was a Red Ensign supporter, too. In 1964 I wrote more than three hundred letters to Members of Parliament, cabinet ministers, anyone I thought might bring influence to bear. When the flag issue was voted on that December it was only after the Liberals had imposed closure on the debate, and I did not think that Pearson allowed his members the free vote that he had promised me once in a letter.

I only had one more shot to fire, however. I tried to prevent

Maple Leaf Gardens from flying the new flag. But on February 20, 1965, the new Maple Leaf flag was flown in the Gardens because, Harold Ballard told the press, letters and phone calls had been more than three to one in favour. I never changed my mind about it, but I had run out of battlefields. I still think I was right: who can say that the new flag, and his other big issue, bilingualism, have made this country more unified than it was before? It is less unified than it had been throughout all of my life. In my files there are still hundreds of stickers I bought and sent out on every letter I wrote for more than a year. The sticker shows the Red Ensign, with the line under it reading: *This IS Canada's flag – Keep it flying!* It goes down in history as a lost cause, of course, but I was happy soon after when Premier John Robarts designated the Red Ensign as Ontario's flag. That was the one that flew from then on anywhere I had the say, and owned the flagpole.

Throughout 1964, I would bring letters home and read them to Irene – letters from Pearson, Diefenbaker, and others. But as the flag issue wound down, officially settled, my deepest grief was not for that lost campaign but for another that Irene was losing faster and faster.

I digress a little here, to that Chilean mare Eolia I bought in 1956 partly with the proceeds of the Eugenia 2nd win in the Canadian International. She was in foal to Woodchuck at the time. The foal she dropped the following year was Willow Strip, a good stakes winner. Then we bred her to Jamie K. and in April of 1958, a spring when a virus caused all our other mares to abort, she dropped a colt foal that became my favourite horse of all time. As our only foal that survived that year, we named him Jammed Lucky.

In his two-year-old year he was already showing a profit of about $7,000 before we came to the big two-year-old races in October, the Cup and Saucer and the Coronation, and he won them both; he earned $58,000 that year, and won seventeen races in all before he was retired to stud. As a stud he became a very knowledgeable horse, but with some idiosyncrasies. Sometimes Irene and I would go up to the paddocks with a little sugar. Some nights he just wouldn't have anything to do with a woman, but would take sugar from me as gentle as anybody living. He was like a watchdog, too. If some yearling or foal fell or was hurt or caught under a fence or something he would stand in the centre of his paddock and trumpet at the top of his lungs. People would come running, knowing there was something wrong by the way he was acting. He would point in the right direction, taking little runs that way, and people would go over and find there was a horse in distress. He was like the father of the tribe.

In 1963 we bred Eolia back to Jamie K. and the next spring Irene and I saw a little filly foal born in Caledon. That year Irene was in the beginning of her cancer. One sunny day she and I were walking around the paddocks and this little filly was lying down and then jumped up and nestled against her mother the way foals do, and Irene said, "Isn't she lovely?" I looked at Irene and thought it could be applied either to my wife or to the filly, and thought, wouldn't that be a good name – Jammed Lovely. And that's how that filly was named.

In the early months of 1965 Irene was bedridden most of the time, and in great pain. We were sleeping in separate rooms so that when she slept I would not disturb her, but were just across the hall from one another. Sometimes I would go in and sit with her, or she would come in to my room in her dressing gown, restless and in pain. We had nurses but in the early part of the year they were not in attendance twenty-four hours a day, as they were later. It was heartbreaking to see what the pain was doing to her. Medication helped some, but had terrible side effects in loss of coordination. Once I saw her take something in her hand and try to put it in her mouth, but she couldn't – her hand went to her ear, instead. One night when I was reading she came in and sat on a couch at the end of the bed.

"How is it?" I said.

She groaned, "I don't think I can take it."

I was in mental agony myself. I didn't think it was right for anyone to have to endure such pain. I reached out to tap the table at my side and said something that tore the heart from me. "You know, in this night table I have my old Army revolver. If you can't take the pain any more, and want to end it, you tell me. I will stop your suffering myself."

I meant that, and not because I did not think out the consequences. I thought about what our children would think, and then I thought, well, if my children want to see someone keep on suffering the way Irene is, I don't care what they think of me. It was in that period that I came to realize that I was in favour of mercy killing – not mercy killing with a revolver, but that, too, if it was the only way. I can't imagine a good God asking a lovely person like my wife to suffer that much when a doctor could give her something that would end it, forever.

Soon after that (in early May, I think, of 1965, a nice spring evening outside and the leaves beginning to show) she came in to my room again, suffering badly.

She sat again at the foot of the bed and looked at me. "Daddy," she said, "do you still have that revolver handy?"

"Yes, I have," I said. I took a deep breath and said, "I'm ready to use it if you say you can't stand it any longer."

She looked at me for a long time, then said, "Well, Daddy, it's bad but I think that is a coward's way out."

At the time it didn't seem wrong to me and today it seems more right then ever. I was proud of her for showing that courage, but not proud of myself that she had to demonstrate to me what real bravery was, that she could take it and never ask for relief. The next morning, I talked to Hughie. He said that he would give her something, a heavier painkiller. I said that was not for him to do, but I phoned her doctor and told him flat about the scene the night before, and how much in pain she was and how brave she was, and I said to him, "If you don't increase that dosage so that she ends her pain, I'll end your God damn pain." And I would have. To permit a person to suffer like that is beyond all humanity.

The weeks wore on until early June. One day when Irene was lying weakly in bed, Jessie sitting with her, Irene said, "After I'm gone, you tell my husband that he usually has been right, and that one of the things he was most right on was in keeping this house, so that when I die I can be here in my own room where I have lived most of my life."

She died peacefully in her sleep in the first hours of a Sunday morning, June 20, 1965. Our night nurse at the time was Margaret Grose, a young woman who had grown to love and respect our family in the months that she had been there. I was asleep when Margaret came into my room and told me that Irene had died. I went in to Irene's room and lay down beside her and took her in my arms and held her. It was an extraordinary thing. I thought she would be cold, in death, but she was as warm as she always was, when she was alive. It was just a little more than forty-nine years after we had become engaged, a little over forty-five years since we had married. I lay beside her thinking jumbled thoughts, grieving that she was gone, but happy that the one I loved so much would not have to endure any more pain.

I did not want her to be taken from her home until the funeral, so after the necessary things had been done she lay there at rest for the next two days. I asked publicly that no flowers be sent, because I wanted to look after them myself. I had St. Paul's Anglican Church decorated with her own favourite pink flowers in a way I thought she would have liked. I also passed on to others one of her last wishes, that her funeral should not be sombre and that people attending should wear cheerful colours. So when about two thousand people came out on the soft June afternoon, the kind she had loved for golfing or swimming, the women were in light-coloured dresses and the men in summer suits. A Red Ensign draped her coffin. The only flower arrangement in the church that was not pink was a maple leaf in white and blue chrysanthemums on the chancel steps. The service began with "Abide With Me" and ended with "Now The Day Is Over," two of Irene's favourite hymns. Then we bore her out to the west part of the city to Park Lawn Cemetery to lie beside Patricia in the family plot where I would be buried, too, when my time came.

When I think back to Irene's death, I can see certain patterns that ended and others that began. What can a man do when he has lost the one person who meant most to him in the world? One of the things I did seems to have been a recognition of my own limited time on earth; or maybe a token of how lucky I knew Irene and I had been together. I made gifts of a thousand dollars or more to a lot of people I loved and my more official donations that year totalled $66,605, including $25,400 to the Crippled Children and $25,000 to the University of Toronto to set up a foundation in Irene's name to do research on pain. Then as winter came I travelled to Florida as usual, played golf, swam, spent more time pondering breeding match-ups, but still could not fill the hole in my life that ached when I was alone.

Some people then and later thought I might marry again, but the truth was, I was married still, if only to a memory. Not that I didn't like the company of women (some of whom liked my company, too) but I never seriously then or later considered placing another woman where Irene had been in my life. It would not have been fair. There are a lot of skeptics in the world, but as I've said, I feel there is another world and that there is some kind of communication between that world and this. The feeling persisted that Irene was still with me, somehow. In 1967 when Jammed Lovely was eligible for all the big three-year-old stakes, I had that feeling of communication very strongly.

Others around our stable felt it, too. Jim Fitzsimmons was riding most of our horses at that time but he'd been offered a ride on the favourite, Betemight. A few days before the Plate I told him he was free to choose his mount, leaving it entirely up to him. It was the choice between our fairly long shot and the favourite, maybe the difference between a straight ride fee and a much larger percentage of the winner's purse, but he didn't hesitate.

"I got to stay with you," he said, looking up at me. (Up at me! No wonder I like jockeys!) "I got to stay with your whole outfit."

He didn't spell out why he "got to" stay with us, but maybe he had a feeling of his own. Even when Jammed Lovely ran second in the Oaks a week before the Plate – it was run in the slop – I told reporters, "This filly is going to win the Plate." Meanwhile, Ron Turcotte, then well on his way to becoming one of the great riders in North America, came in to take the mount on Betemight and Avelino Gomez was riding the second favourite, Pine Point.

I still had such confidence that I offered every owner in the race a bet – my horse against his – the winner to send $5,000 to the Crippled Children's Society. I couldn't get anybody to bet, even though my horse was eleven or twelve to one. Finally just before the race J.-Louis Lévesque of Montreal, a fine man, owner of Courant d'Air, said he wouldn't take my horse to horse bet but would donate $10,000 to the Crippled Children if he won. In a moment of exuberance I said I'd do the same if I won. That cost me $10,000.

It was some horse race. Fitzie kept Jammed Lovely in striking distance all the way but coming into the stretch he was running fourth on the rail and was boxed in behind one tiring horse, Ette Rule, and inside the two-horse Windfields Farm entry, Battling and Blenheim Park. Just as I was thinking I didn't know how he was going to get out, he showed me. He came out from the rail to go around Ette Rule, then cut back to the rail where there was enough room for him to pound into the lead. As they came down the stretch his big challenge came from Gomez on Pine Point, but when Pine Point got up to his boot Fitzie let Jammed Lovely out another notch and won by a neck. After the race he sounded very brave. "If we'd gone another time around the track, we still would have won," he said, but I was happy to take it the way it came. (She paid $24.90. I had bet quite a lot.) I even had the group all planned to honour not only the filly, but my dear little wife who had named her. I took three of my grand-daughters across the track with me; Mary, the daughter of Stafford and Dorothea; Anne, daughter of Hugh and Bernice; and Debbie, daughter of Miriam and Jack Hoult; three pretty fillies with Irene's blood in them, and their grandfather happy in a grey topper. A nice thing, too, was that every time I turned around that afternoon there were cheers and clapping. I tipped my hat happily walking back across the track and then took my crowd to the Directors' Lounge and ordered champagne all around. In a few minutes I was heading for the elevator when somebody called to me to come back.

"Anybody who wants to see me can come down to the stables," I yelled. Mike Walsh, my driver, took me over to the backstretch. Don't think we didn't have it all planned, right to the Red Ensign draped over the rail in front of Jammed Lovely's stall, while Johnny Starr and his assistant, Donnie Walker, and all the grooms, exercise boys, hot walkers, helpers, newspapermen, and friends celebrated something that had started three years before, another sunny day up in Caledon when Irene had looked at the little filly, saying, "Isn't she lovely?"

Chapter Thirteen

Sometimes I wonder how long the memory of a government is, and whether that memory somehow can be translated into vindictiveness. Is there a blacklist in men's minds so that anger and contempt for Conn Smythe in Mackenzie King's diary, for instance, becomes part of a shake of the head twenty years later when powerful men among King's successors are passing on their wisdom to the next generation of our rulers, usually the Liberals? I called Mackenzie King a traitor over the conscription issue and felt that Mike Pearson broke his word on the flag issue and bowed down to Quebec in other matters that have done Canadians no good that I know of. I said so publicly and privately. I have never tried to disguise my pride in the British tradition of Canada or my contempt for anyone who allows any one part of this country to act as a law unto itself. I feel I have earned some rights to speak out in a land whose freedom I helped to defend, and to speak – as long as it doesn't slander someone – without retaliation. But somehow, somewhere, did I make an enemy of someone large or small in the government who decided not long after Irene's death that here was a guy, Smythe, who maybe should be gone over with a fine-tooth comb?.

I think it is possible.

I have no evidence, except that after a long life of thinking I was a pretty good Canadian, suddenly, everywhere I turned (except at the racetrack), I was in trouble. The tax department suddenly was on my tail. Maybe you have to think everybody is a crook even to work successfully in that department. Anyway, I was glad to come out of it with my flags still flying, and only wish that my son Stafford had been able to do the same, and had not been so harshly treated at least partly because he, too, was a Smythe.

It is true that Stafford and I often disagreed, starting with me thinking he was crazy to let Ballard and Bassett into what could have been his alone, the Gardens. I didn't like some of the changes they made; selling advertising space everywhere but on the players' bare backsides; cutting out things I had valued, such as the live military bands playing at Leafs' home games. Stafford did look after our Gardens' oldtimers with every bit as much concern as I had done, but the partnership itself guaranteed there would be things done that I would not like. Stafford ran the hockey end pretty well but after a few years, as I often told him, he should have taken over as general manager and paid Imlach whatever was needed to keep him forever as the best coach in the NHL.

Ballard ran everything except the hockey. I'll say this about Harold; he's a real old-fashioned buccaneer. If there's gold on that ship, it doesn't matter what flag you fly. Harold is going aboard and get that gold. He might do a lot of good things with that gold, but that doesn't make it right. I've known him most of his life as a good giver, a good friend, but I would not give him a job at ten cents a week. His way of doing things is not mine. When I didn't like things Harold did, I tended to take it out on Stafford because he was my son, my heir, and the president.

Early in March, 1966, when I was in Florida, I finally came to the end of the line with the Gardens over a Ballard deal – he booked Cassius Clay (Muhammad Ali) into the Gardens to fight Ernie Terrell. I called John Bassett, chairman of the board, and resigned as a director. "This fight has been kicked out of every place in the U.S. because Clay is a draft dodger and a disgrace to his country," I told him. "The Gardens was founded by men – sportsmen – who fought for their country. It is no place for those who want to evade conscription in their own country. The Gardens was built for many things, but not for picking up things that no one else wants."

Bassett refused to accept my resignation quietly, or indeed at all, but insisted that it be put to the whole board. Meanwhile, when our scrap hit the front pages – "Gardens' founder resigns over Clay fight" – I told the reporters that I was resigning because the Gardens' directors were putting cash ahead of class. The fact that the Gardens were making more money than ever under that kind of management did not matter a bit to me.

I resigned, and continued to take shots where I could. When I was honoured guest at the Canadian National Exhibition's sports day and induction of Clarence Campbell and nine players into the Hockey Hall of Fame, I told the audience that I'd been traded by the Gardens for a black Muslim minister and a lot of cash. I mentioned that seats at the Gardens had been rebuilt to get more people in, so narrow that only a young man could sit in them and only a fat old rich man could afford them. Also, the NHL was going for expansion the next year, a money grab. Each of six new teams would pay $2 million to enter, and each of six old teams would benefit by that amount – but the real price, I claimed, would be inferior hockey for years. Which happened.

I was still consulted on hockey matters, but not by the Gardens. A government-sponsored committee was doing yet another study of hockey. They came to see me and I told them that the idea of a national team was a failure and always would be. It just happened that my opinion of Father David Bauer, founder and organizer of the national teams, was not as high as his own opinion of himself. My view was that setting up a third-rate team that the taxpayers had to pay for, to go over and get beaten in Europe, was a waste of money; that we should send professionals, the best, and never should treat Canada as a third-rate country, especially in hockey. A few years later, we did start sending the pros.

For the first few years of the 1960's I hadn't seen as much as usual of Stafford's son, Tom. He took his father's side on most things, including Clay. But then, of his own accord, he began to sit with me at games. We'd get along fine until I would get out the needle against his father. Then Tom would just get up and say, "Look, grandpa, if you're going to fight about father that's not fair and I'm not going to stay," and he would leave. Eventually I stopped blasting off to him. For a while Stafford and I weren't speaking. We were both too big to swallow our pride. But at the same time, I know, Tom was working on his father the same way he did on me, that we should forget about Cassius, the important thing was our family. Finally we buried all the hatchets forever. Some time after Irene died, after the Clay incident, Stafford had a whole new office suite at the Gardens built and furnished for me. I could see the care and thought that had gone into it and knew that whatever we had said and done to one another, it was past.

In the last directors' meeting, in fact, that I attended, I moved that the salaries of both Stafford and Ballard be doubled. They had earned it. I wished later they had taken the raises and used the extra money to pay for things that, it turned out, had been charged to the Gardens by contractors instead of to them personally. But at the time I moved the salary increases, they just laughed and said their salaries were high enough.

Stafford and I had good times together after that, many laughs, as in a more relaxed way we often talked about how our family life had been when he was a kid. One time I remember, in Florida, he and Tommy and I were sitting around after dinner talking about cars. At one time when he was in his teens I'd had a Buick that I really liked. "But the second one I got was no good at all," I said. "A real gasburner. Never gave me more than about eight miles to the gallon."

He laughed. Stafford had a lovely laugh. His face would get so merry. It turned out that when I'd had that second Buick was about the time Stafford either had his first car, or used to borrow Irene's. Anyway, when he had no money to buy gas to drive past Dorothea's house, he would siphon it out of the Buick. No wonder my mileage was low. It made me remember my own lifting loose change from my father's pockets long ago in that room on Bond Street. I heard of other things he'd done, too, like coming down the drainpipe from his room at Baby Point when Irene and I were away so that he and his pals could go out at night when Jessie thought he was asleep. I learned a lot about his boyhood, late in life. It was fun to remember. And from sitting with Tom at hockey games, I knew that we had a third generation coming up that deserved at least a chance to be the third Smythe in control of hockey at the Gardens. After the war Stafford had coached the Junior Marlboros, with Ballard as manager; now they had made Tom manager of the Marlboros. I had confidence that he was on his way, the best young man I knew. None of us knew about the trouble that was going to dominate the next few years.

The first intimation was over a business deal that we had made about the time that I sold my controlling interest in the Gardens in 1961. In 1959 I had begun attempting to establish the best possible plan to handle my estate in event of my (sooner or later, I continued to hope later) death. My 52 per cent interest in C. Smythe Limited, the sand and gravel company, represented at the time about half my personal assets. The company had about three quarters of a million dollars in undistributed surplus which, if it was still undistributed at my death, would be subject to income tax as well as death tax, a strong motivation to reorganize the company in a way that would reduce the potential tax burden on my estate.

If the surplus had been distributed on the basis of share holdings (52 per cent to me, 30.8 per cent to Stafford, 16 per cent to Hap Day, and 1.2 per cent to Art Boyd) it would have been taxable as income, and the remainder subject to death duties. I naturally depended on financial advisers to suggest a better way. S. E. V. Smith of Price Waterhouse and Company worked on various plans. We had turned down one proposal late in 1961 by Greenshields Inc., stock brokers, because Mr. Smith advised that it would be "asking us to countenance some type of transaction . . . that might lead to the evasion of taxes (being charged against us) eventually." But he did recommend one plan as being within the laws of the land. It involved forming a new company, C. Smythe for Sand Ltd., which would take over the assets of C. Smythe Ltd. Then a series of share deals and other transactions with two Vancouver companies, which would buy all the shares of the old company, would release about $275,000 to us four shareholders that would not be taxable. We went ahead on the grounds that, by the best professional advice available to us, it did the job without breaking any laws. The amount involved was not huge, giving me $143,175 in cash, in a sense a tax-free bonus from the results of more than forty years of building a business from nothing but an old truck and a bedspring for sifting gravel; with $84,763 going to Stafford, $44,054 to Hap, and $3,344 to Art Boyd. All these transactions were reported on corporate tax returns as a matter of routine.

But if anyone thinks that any financial deal in this country is unassailable they should have been with me one morning late in May, 1966, when a registered letter arrived at my home from the Department of National Revenue. It was headed, 1961 Income Tax Return, and read:

Dear Sir:

On consideration of the transaction in 1961 involving the sale of the assets of C. Smythe Limited to C. Smythe for Sand Limited and the subsequent sale of your common shares to F. H. Cameron Limited and Dabne Investments Limited (the two Vancouver companies), it would appear that you thereby realized a dividend which constituted taxable income in your hands.

This dividend is now being included in the reassessment of your income for that year.

This was signed by L. Kesten, "for the chief assessor."

But that wasn't the worst of it. I was being assessed not for the amount of cash received, but for $378,899.04 – which would have been my share if we had distributed the entire surplus as dividends and had not gone through the entirely legal (or so we had been assured on the basis of similar transactions) estate-protecting exercise at all. My tax payable on that, they said, would be $203,205.18 plus interest of $49,277.25 for a grand total of $252,482.43. Considering I'd only got $143,175 on the deal to start with and that this was supposed to be a tax re-assessment, not a sentence to penitentiary, I figured this was rather a sensational way to do business and could not be typical of all government departments or the country either would be in a lot better shape financially, or all the taxpayers would have starved to death.

Stafford and Hap also were re-assessed on about three times as much as they received.

Late in June we filed notice of objection with the deputy minister of National Revenue. Then came what I thought was rather a strange development. A tax official telephoned S. E. V. Smith at Price Waterhouse and asked him to notify us that if we would drop the objection, we could settle the case by paying 16⅔ per cent of the dividends we were deemed to have received. In my case this would have meant paying $63,162 and change instead of more than a quarter of a million. But when Smith asked the tax official to put this in writing, the guy wouldn't. So who was hiding what? As it turned out, we would have saved a lot of court costs and legal fees just by knuckling under, but I wasn't going to. My lawyer, Ian Johnston, and the people at Price Waterhouse still insisted that our actions had been legal. So we went on with the objection. When we lost it in Exchequer Court a year later, the *Financial Post* story on the matter started out this way:

> With few exceptions our courts traditionally have clung to the rule that a man may organize his affairs in order to pay the least amount of tax possible so long as his actions are legal. However, a recent decision of Mr. Justice H. F. Gibson of the Exchequer Court of Canada . . . marks a notable departure from this principle.

And the last paragraph noted that "although there was no suggestion of any impropriety on the part of the Smythe group, and no question that the group's transactions were legally valid and effective," the government ruled that that wasn't good enough. The truth seemed to be that they were going to get tougher on estate planners and had started on us as a good retroactive case that would be popular enough, as a couple of Smythes were being soaked.

I just wonder who decided to make us the scapegoats? The entire case hit me where it hurt; implying that I had broken the law, when I have always insisted that anything I do is within the law. If I had been told in 1961 that the government could challenge our transaction, which admittedly was designed to help preserve my estate, I would have backed off.

Then, of course, we had to deal with sloppy reporting, as usual. The *Telegram* printed one retraction and apology for wrongful use of the term, "tax avoidance." But worse, the CBC actually broadcast on its National News that I was being sued by the government for non-payment of taxes! I'd been a big taxpayer, individually and in business, all my life. The CBC made a retraction, too, so-called. I wrote to Hap a few days later with a copy of the CBC "retraction" saying,

> Enclosed find a statement from the CBC which is about as accurate as the one they made originally. We have had many years together and know it is useless to try to get anyone in the news business to put out a story that is in any way correct. I see [by the CBC] that we sold the company for $400,000 which makes a tax of $400,000 for the three of us pretty high, I would think, but nothing to what is liable to happen if we keep Pearson in much longer.

As part of this game, I met the Finance Minister, Edgar Benson. Waste of time. Later we decided to go to the Supreme Court with an appeal against the decision of the Exchequer Court. Before that, after about one million news stories, letters, and articles in magazines (one writer suggested in the Canadian Chartered Accountant magazine that "if this judgment is upheld Canadians might as well throw in the towel and ask the Department of National Revenue just to invoice them"), we almost settled. I would have done it except that Stafford, on the fringe then of the deepest trouble of his life, refused to give me his proxy in working out a settlement, which had to be unanimous. I was unhappy about it but did not press him on it because he had greater concerns right then. I didn't know, at first, how great. Perhaps neither did he.

In October, 1968 – no one has ever told me what prompted this but it seems obvious that some informant must have – the Royal Canadian Mounted Police came to the Gardens' offices and removed some financial records. The Gardens' annual report written a few months later mentioned that some records had been seized as part of a special review of Maple Leaf Gardens Limited's income tax returns for the past few years. Stafford told one questioner that errors in invoicing by some contractors had resulted in the Gardens paying for some goods and services that should have been charged to individuals. He seemed almost casual about it, saying that if the tax department didn't accept the explanation they'd have to take it to court.

But it was worse than that. I don't have a diary of what went on behind the scenes, but nothing surprised me much. When the Gardens' directors found that their president and executive vice-president were going to be charged with income tax evasion, they were understandably concerned. Many headed or were connected with companies that did not wish their senior people tarred with the guilt-by-association brush. John Bassett was thinking of going public with his holdings at the time. Normally his shares in the Gardens would have been an attractive part of the package, but not, as he told a friend, "when I come back and find my partners with their hands in the till."

A hockey furore obscured the issue for a little while – Stafford fired Imlach minutes after Leafs had been knocked out of the playoffs by Boston in the spring of 1969. But the main event came in June that year, when Stafford and Ballard were among fifteen of the twenty-one Gardens' directors who met in the boardroom of Imperial Oil on St. Clair Avenue in a meeting called for one purpose: to ask Stafford and Ballard to resign.

At that time they had not been charged with anything. They refused. A motion to fire them was put to a vote and tied, seven for and seven against. Their buddy John Bassett cast the deciding vote to fire them. Whatever their faults, they had been mainly responsible in building his initial Gardens' investment of not quite $1 million into an estimated $5 million. It was a farce anyway. George Mara was the new president. There would be no new executive vice-president. Stafford would remain the NHL governor, meaning he would remain in charge of Leafs' hockey. Ballard would remain the alternate governor, and would run things from the same desk as before. But the purity of the other directors, the public washing of hands, had been done and that aspect satisfied. Two weeks later, charges of income tax evasion were laid, involving $278,920 for Stafford and $134,685 for Ballard.

It seemed an anti-climax when, in another three months, the Supreme Court of Canada denied our appeal on the old 1961 tax case and we paid our lawyer's bills, managed to get the 16⅔ per cent tax deal the department had been afraid to put in writing three years before, paid that, and tried to get on with living.

It wasn't easy, yet was infinitely easier for me than for Stafford and his family. After Irene's death Margaret Grose, who had been Irene's night nurse, told me that if I ever needed her again she would be glad to work for me. In a couple of years I took her up on that. From the late 1960's on she was my nurse and companion and apart from a certain amount of disagreement occasionally between her and Jessie it worked out fine. Because of my various wound-related conditions, I needed a nurse. The companion part was fine, too. They were a pair of good-looking women, Meg and Jessie, and when we sat in my box at the races together I knew some people were thinking, "What's that old goat got that we don't?" Let 'em think it. There were also those rumours from time to time that I was going to get married again, but I thought I had the best deal in the world – Meg and Jessie to look after me, but with more authority on my side than I'd ever have with a second wife!

Stafford and Ballard, meanwhile, were in more trouble than had been announced, and they knew it, as investigators worked away at Gardens' records. You could see the effect on Stafford more than Ballard. The probers were looking for more than income tax evasion. The time they were taking prompted rumours that the case was never going to come to court, snide remarks in the press about privilege. All the time those really in the know were telling me that it was going to be really bad. Stafford regained the presidency of the Gardens late in 1970, with Ballard getting his job back officially as well. And in June, 1971, Stafford and Ballard were arrested on charges of theft and fraud involving $146,000 in cash and securities, Stafford with an additional charge of defrauding the Gardens of $249,000 in the same period.

The trial was set for October 25 and the prosecution, headed by Joe Sedgwick, elected to proceed by indictment, a procedure which, unlike others open to the prosecution, carried with it a mandatory jail sentence of no less than two months, and a possible five years. In short, the intention plainly was to put Stafford and Ballard in jail.

Which maybe is where they should have gone, having betrayed their positions of public trust, but there are dozens of cases in which similar offences have been tried under a different method called summary conviction, which could lead to heavy financial punishment, but not jail terms.

I am not pleading the case of either of them. Sorry as I was, and hopeful as I was that Stafford's case would be well argued, I told him that when he broke the law he had to be prepared to take his punishment and I could not help him. But I did resent the way the government, and in a sense the media and the public, but especially the government, tried the case in advance and said: "Jail." A Liberal cabinet minister admitted to a friend of mine that the decision to proceed by indictment was taken after it had been discussed in cabinet. I do not know whether cabinet records would confirm this, but the minister had no reason to lie. My cabinet informant told me that the discussion among the ministers was on the political impact of a verdict that might find Stafford and Ballard guilty but would not send them to jail. The general opinion was thumbs down on that. The profiles were too high. If a guy was a relative unknown in Windsor or Saskatoon, he might get off with a fine (many have, before and since). But anyone with the name Smythe or Ballard getting off on such a charge, some Liberal ministers argued, would cause the government to be charged with favouring the rich and powerful. It definitely was a case of one law for the rich and one for the poor, but in this case reversed. The rich would get the book thrown at them.

Other people thought I should have fought tooth and nail to keep my son out, but I thought he should get what was coming to him. I still loved him, but he'd broken the rules, he'd broken the law, so why the hell shouldn't he suffer? But I didn't think they'd be so rotten to him. Ballard didn't seem to give a damn. That's fine. Stafford did. He had his wife and family, and showed what he thought of them. He told me once, "Dad, they will never put me in jail."

The press took delight, as usual, in kicking men when they are down. Of course, few reporters ever face pressures that would get them more than a parking ticket, but genuine humanity among them is rare. The photos and stories seemed somehow to relish the idea that the mighty were taking their lumps, as the two top men at Maple Leaf Gardens were taken to court and then released on $50,000 bail each.

That was June 18, 1971. The tax department gave us three weeks' grace, which was nice of them, and then struck again, on another front. I could hardly believe it when I read their next letter.

Four years earlier I had made a deal with Elgin Armstrong to sell 1,067 acres of Caledon. I was acting for C. Smythe for Sand Limited, he for Armstrong Holdings (Brampton) Limited. For a couple of years we'd been leasing to them, for $20,000 a year, most of the output from our pits. I wanted to sell and Elgin wanted to buy. Interest was never mentioned. I had never in my life charged interest on anything and in buying much of that Caledon land had not paid interest, either: I would put so much down and give non-interest bearing notes for the remainder. It might be old-fashioned of me, but I can quote from Exodus, Leviticus, Deuteronomy, Nehemiah, Psalms, Proverbs, and Ezekiel in support of not charging interest. It is also a principle recognized in government loans to some businesses, and to some other nations. Anyway, there were fifteen parcels of land involved. We settled on individual prices per acre, depending on how valuable the land was. These prices ranged from $9,000 an acre in some places to $400 an acre in others, and added up to $2,490,000, to be paid in fifteen instalments, without interest.

However, as I said before, maybe to work for the tax department you have to think everybody is a liar and a crook. The tax department informed me that a review had been made of the Caledon sale and that the department had decided a fair market value for the 1,067 acres was $1,350,000. They were ruling that the remaining $1,150,000 would be consider as interest for tax purposes and the C. Smythe for Sand Limited tax returns would be adjusted accordingly.

Well, for a while it appeared as if the tax department was not the only one that thought the case against us was strong. A few weeks later the tax department said it was prepared to drop the interest rate it was using from 12 per cent to 7 and make the pill easier to swallow. My advisers said maybe I should settle. In reply, I put my views into a letter to Price Waterhouse that I did not send, but passed on verbally. They were: "I have decided against your advice (to settle), which I think was predicated on my age and the effect this contest will have on my health rather than on the justice of the case, and would ask you to prepare to fight this case to a finish."

So we fought it. I'll go ahead a bit through reams of meetings, hearings, citing of prices paid for land in the area that were higher than I had charged. Finally nearly two years later we won although it cost more than $20,000 in legal fees to win a case that never should have been brought in the first place.

But the principal reason for mentioning it at all was that it started so soon, three weeks, after the arrest of Stafford and Ballard. The early stages of the Armstrong-Smythe tax case were being argued in the late summer of 1971 only a few weeks before Stafford was due to go on trial. I was seventy-six then and I have pictures of myself in which I look older than I did nine years later, when I was eighty-five. It was that kind of summer. Even on some beautiful mornings at the track I had difficulty in letting that peacefulness of watching good thoroughbreds soothe me.

Bassett bailed out in style on September 1, when Stafford and Ballard borrowed nearly six million dollars at the bank to buy the Bassett shares. Less than two months later they would be facing the first of seventy-three witnesses the crown had lined up. Stafford's case was to be tried first. He stuck it out, not looking well, through Leafs' training camp and into the first exhibition games. Asthma had bothered him all his life. Now he had something else, a stomach pain that nagged at him until one day he began to throw up blood and was admitted to Wellesley Hospital with a bleeding ulcer. That was a Wednesday, October 6, 1971. After surgery he seemed to be coming along well. His family was in to see him and so was I, over that weekend, but on Monday night, five days after his admittance, he suffered a massive hemorrhage of the esophagus. His condition was critical but he authorized his doctor, Bob Mitchell, to go ahead and do another operation. That time much of his stomach was removed. The doctor said Stafford put up a terrific fight but I have my own opinion about that. Early Wednesday morning, on the day Leafs were to play their first game of the season, he died.

I was with him near the end. I went in and stood by his bedside. He had his back to me but he turned and opened his eyes and said to me, "See, dad, I told you, they wouldn't put me in jail."

That moment has been with me ever since. I have thought about it and thought about it. I believe that he gave up the fight to live because that was the only way he could spare his family, his son and daughters and grandchildren, from the stigma of jailbird. Sometimes I wonder if I didn't imagine those last words he said. I know this is disjointed, a little, but I was not far off being seventy-seven years old the night this happened and my spirit was full to the brim with the pain of seeing my son go. For Patricia and Irene, death had been a blessed release, but for Stafford it was a tragic early end to a life that I believe would have been a great one in the end if he had lived.

Still, I wonder about the two men. Stafford, if he lost his will to live to save his family from disgrace, was taking one way out that did not lack courage. Ballard on the other hand stood his trial, went to penitentiary, did his time, paid his debt, and joked about it while he was doing it. How many people have gone to jail and come out and faced the world and got the media eating out of his hand right away, like he did, absolutely sure he could get his name in the paper any day of the week? He did good things and bad things, as before. But he went on, faced it all, and Stafford could not.

I have never been able to decide which one was right. The closest I can come is that each did what was right for him.

At his funeral on October 15, 1971, a headline read: *Business at standstill as hockey world pays tribute to memory of Stafford*

Smythe. Everybody in pro hockey was represented there. And I think a lot of them agreed with sentiments expressed in some letters I've seen that were sent to cabinet ministers protesting that Stafford, in spite of his shortcomings, had not been deserving of the fate he got. One mentioned that the death penalty, which had all but been abolished in Canada, had been revived in this case for tax evasion.

Stafford was buried under a natural rock tombstone in the graveyard of Christ Anglican Church, in Gregory, in the parish of Rosseau, Muskoka. It carried this inscription on a brass plate:

Here lies Conn Stafford Smythe, Lieut. RCNVR 1940-1944. He was dearly loved by his wife, children and many friends. He was persecuted to death by his enemies. Now he sleeps peacefully in the quiet north country that loved him for the person he truly was.

Born Toronto March 15, 1921. Died October 13, 1971.

A day or two after his funeral I inserted in the newspapers a card of thanks which read:

SMYTHE – To all my friends who have written in their sympathy many thanks, and to the friend who wrote that Stafford was brutalized by the press unnecessarily and unfairly, I would like to say those are my sentiments too. Conn Smythe.

Within a week, the directors met and chose Ballard as president of the Gardens and Hugh Smythe as vice-president. The stage was set then for an argument that persisted for a few months. At the time, because of stock splits, the share total had been increased and Ballard had the largest single block, about 264,000 shares. Stafford's estate and other Smythes had about 250,000. Hughie was prepared to get into battle with Ballard for control, looking for support among other shareholders. To do that, he would be going against a written agreement between Ballard and Stafford that if one died the survivor would have the right to vote the stock held by the other. Hughie offered to buy out Ballard's shares. One of his concerns was that Tom should have a chance to take his place as head man. People came to me about Hughie's intention to make a take-over fight. They said, "We'll put in the money if you say it's all right."

I said, "It's not all right, it's absolutely ridiculous. You would be taking a good doctor out of circulation and you wouldn't be sure how good a hockey man you were putting back in."

In the end, Ballard bought Stafford's shares early in 1972, before going to jail to begin his three-year sentence, which ended in parole after eighteen months. He ran the Gardens from Kingston through his son, Bill. Hughie agreed later that the outcome was not all bad, because in the medical profession a man can't be in only halfway, or take a few years off and then come back. He'd never catch up. But at the time, in some bitterness, Hughie made a decision never to go into the Gardens again, which he has kept.

Chaper Fourteen

The part of my life that I am going to miss most when I am gone is the horses. That is not a reflection on the people I love, or who may love me. Horses, hockey, and business, including the people I met in all of them, have been my life, apart from my family and the two wars.

A long time ago, making money stopped being a great challenge. I seemed to have an instinct for picking good investments, one of my best being something my broker said was garbage. My veterinarian, Murray Dudgeon, says I was psychic about horses; like one time I phoned him from Florida and told him I had a feeling he should go and check the feet of every horse on my farm. He thought I was crazy. I hadn't seen the horses for six weeks. But he found almost every one had some foot problems. Buying stocks, maybe I was sometimes psychic, too. Anyway, on a fairly average year when I was eighty-two or eighty-three, my dividends or maturing investments, which promptly would be reinvested, might exceed $400,000 a year. I enjoyed it and shared it. In charitable campaigns I think I was thought of as a good giver, and I made investments in the names of grandchildren and others, or gave cash bonuses to people who worked hard for me. I never thought of myself as being rich, because it was all going to charity at the end.

Hockey gave me my biggest push financially at first, but building great teams was the real kick I got out of it. Of course, if you win games you sell tickets, so one supported the other. When we had a six-team league, that was my kind of hockey. There was something worth watching every night. People knew not only every player on their home team, but every player in the league.

Isn't that worth something? Hockey is more saleable now, but you only see decent games in the playoffs. The rest of it stinks. Too many teams. Lately I would go every night, see the first period, and then usually say, "Let's get the hell out of here." Who on the Leafs now can show you what we had?

But the horses have never palled, good years or bad. Of course, breeding and racing thoroughbreds at my level was not like having a string of Secretariats or Nijinskys or Northern Dancers. Race writers called my stable modest. Compared to other owners such as George Gardiner, Jack Stafford, and E. P. Taylor, it was. I rarely had more than fifteen broodmares at my farm, compared to one hundred and thirty or one hundred and forty at Taylor establishments, and only on special occasions have I paid huge stud fees, preferring my own sires Bull Vic, Jammed Lucky, Major Flight, Bye and Near, Lucky Colonel S., and a few others. I ran the show. Taylor has had Joe Thomas for years to handle his racing operations, shrewdly matching fit horses to races they can win. At Gardiner's peak he had Lou Cavalaris, who was even better than Thomas at, as we used to say in the Air Force, hiding in cloud – meaning that both of them always seemed to be able to get better weights, better breaks, better races for their horses, at the racing secretary's office than most people strictly through knowing always what they were doing. Yet in 1979 when the Jockey Club listed leading stakes winning owners in Canada over the years, good old modest Smythe was second only to Taylor. His horses had won 171 stakes, including a few registered to Mrs. Taylor, their son Charles, and Cosgrave Stable. I had won 145, including the 41 as Smythe and Maloney. The list trailed down from there to the Seagrams, Jack Stafford, George Gardiner, the Beasleys, Jean-Louis Lévesque, and Lanson Farms (the Boylens). Nobody was close enough to crowd me out of second place for years, if ever.

One of the big advantages I had over a lot of people was that at the time I went back into racing in 1954, E. P. Taylor was in the midst of growing from an ordinary breeder, selling horses around an average of $8,000 to $10,000, to becoming a giant in the business. I was able to watch all his experiments. He had some stallions that weren't worth thirty cents and he threw them out at no expense to me. I give him a lot of credit. He has the courage of a lion. They talk about his Nijinsky and Northern Dancer being great horses, the greatest horse of them all was Taylor. He came through against everybody's arguments that he couldn't do this or couldn't do that to develop in Canada – in the frozen north where you're not supposed to be able to do it – the best horses in the world.

He did this partly by being a great salesman, too. I've often heard about people so good that they could make a living selling Eskimo Pies to Eskimos. He could make handsome living at that, if he had to. He's a terrific organizer. He does not fall in love with horses or with men. He knows that if you fall in love with some old nag, you're going down the drain. The same applies to an employee who's a nice fellow. If you give him a top job he can't do, but never fire him, that leads down the drain, too. Taylor has that toughness and he also learned early where the money is – in breeding. Any horse of his is for sale. He sold horses to me that weren't worth thirty cents and yet I'd always gladly pay the money, in fact beseeched him to sell me some horses. And I don't throw my money around.

People have often asked me what it takes to get into the thoroughbred racing business. There are nineteen ways to do it, from having seven partners, claiming something with three legs for $5,000, and getting Frankie Merrill to train it, to spending a million or more and still not being sure what you're doing. However, my way was to start buying mares in foal, or fillies, from the top thoroughbred lines. To find out which those were (I knew a lot, but no man can know enough in that business) I read everything I could find on the subject. I wanted to amass enough knowledge and confidence to make my own mistakes, as well as win my own victories. My idea was that if I started with the proper material, I would come out all right. If I bought a brood mare, I wanted her to have in her or at her side a foal with an excellent chance of being a stakes-winning filly or horse. I can illustrate that. I bought Broomflight with her Bunty Lawless foal from Jack Loughry's Maryvale Farm in 1955, for $3,000. She had eight foals. All won races. Four were stakes winners and two others placed in stakes. My other top mares like Eolia, Kitty Girl, Twice Shy, all worked out that way. If you get the blood lines, you're getting your own factory to manufacture your own horses.

To make sure you get those horses properly raised, you need a farm. I fell into mine by the back door, looking for gravel, but an awful lot of people are astute enough to know that if you buy a farm in the right place you'll make more money out of the real estate than out of the horses. E. P. Taylor, George Gardiner, Carr Hatch, Jim Boylen all have proved that. But there are other considerations – firm soil, good water, good grass, somewhere near a really old-fashioned country veterinarian who will look after your livestock. That is very important. Murray Dudgeon is mine. You've got to get a good farm manager so that the straw and hay are good and the fields rotated properly. You need a strong foreman in charge of your horses, men, and exercise people. The men and women there are as important as the horses. Even the way yearlings are broken can make or break a horse, and I always figured the start my yearlings got under Jim Torrance at Caledon was just as important as anything that happened later.

In training, I had these rules:

All horses to breeze two furlongs.
All horses to gallop or be ponied two and half miles.
All horses to be breezed no longer than six days before a race.
All horses unable to breeze or gallop to go to the farm.
All horses that breeze in 23 (seconds) or better can run.
All horses that breeze in better than 23, bet on.
All training and racing to be on safe tracks.

If you don't learn something in fifty years of owning horses you've been wasting your time. A trainer might tell me that this one can gallop only a mile and a half. I'd say, "If it can only go a mile and a half, you may as well shoot it."

The breezing two furlongs is for speed. They've got to have speed and they've got to have condition, that's all they need. If they can't breeze in 23 or better they can't win a race. If they can't gallop two miles they can't win a race.

Also, you let the horse tell you – which it always will – that it wants to run. When I tried to help deaf people in Ontario I found that they have their own ways of communicating, their own language. So do horses. You check the feed tub to make sure they're eating well, weigh them, take their temperatures, watch the way they act in training and the kind of training times they have. You'll know when they feel like running. If they don't, leave them in the barn.

About trainers, you have to watch out for those who spend more time training the owners than they do training the horses. I remember one time Gerry Lavigne won a Queen's Plate with Almoner. I went around to his barn the next morning to congratulate him and he wasn't there – he was out schooling some two-year-olds. That's a trainer.

My first, away back in 1930, was Bill Campbell. He was a big soft Scotchman, who smoked cigars all the time, and loved to sit and talk. He knew nothing about breeding, nothing about feet or shoeing, he just knew how to recognize a race that would suit his horse, and that was enough on the old half-mile tracks.

Emerson Davis, a real old Kentuckian, was the next trainer who trained Smythe. By then I had graduated into thinking that I knew something, that all I had to do was go down to Kentucky and buy some yearlings. So I went south and Emerson helped me pick horses like Shoeless Joe, Dedication, Second Helping, Skating Fool – I think I got nine for $9,000 and I thought I had it made. With Emerson Davis as my trainer, I won races and lost money every year until 1938, all over the United States, until I bought a horse on my own, Sir Marlborough, and won a little money in 1938 and 1939, then sold out in 1940 because of the war, and fourteen years later hooked up with Johnny Starr, for a very good run.

Still, there is so much goes into racing that is beyond that huge thrill of seeing a horse you believe in charging through the stretch in front. I am going to ramble a bit here. I remember the last year I won the Queen's Plate, 1967, the Jammed Lovely year, at year end I was going over the books and could illustrate another side from that year alone. In January that year, my ledger showed, I'd been overdrawn in my horse account, so I'd put in $10,000 from my own personal account to cover expenses like $1,700 for the month to the Florida farm where some of my horses were training, $1,340 to Ehrlich's for transporting horses, and other bills. By March I was overdrawn again, so in went another $10,000 of my own. I sold some horses for $15,000 at the Fort Erie Jockey Club sale, but that was eaten up by heavy expenses in April, $26,613. In May, the book showed, early purses started to come in, but the $14,070 total wasn't quite enough to handle even that month's training and transport expenses of more than $15,000. In June, my cheque from May purses was $17,140 so I could pay myself back $7,500 and leave a grand $367 in the account. In July, including the Queen's Plate win, my Jockey Club purse cheque was $81,000, but my own money in the horse account at that time (going back to the previous year) totalled $36,823.89. I was able to take all that out, along with $20,144 for Johnny Starr's Norstar stables, and still be solvent. Later in the year again the expenses started to overcome the receipts. By December the horse account was in the hole again. *Sic transit* something.

Another of my plus-horses in 1967 was one of my favourite horses, Bye and Near. He dated back with me to 1955 when I bought Broomflight with the Bunty Lawless foal, ten or twelve weeks old. The foal turned out to be a stakes winner, Bonnie Flight, but meanwhile I'd bred Broomflight back to Bunty Lawless and in 1957 got Bye Bye Bunty, a nice brown filly, but accident-prone. Once she was behind the gate for some reason, was never even put in, so never got into the race. Another time she was leading her first time on the turf course, but hadn't been jogged around to learn the layout and when she got to where the turf course crossed the main course she swerved into the gap obviously intending to beat everybody else back to the stable, being that smart a filly. But she was a big strong thing and in 1962 I bred her to Nearctic. I was one of the originals sending mares to Nearctic, two or three a season until the stud fee, which started about $2,000, got past $7,500 and out of my range.

In 1963 Bye Bye Bunty dropped the foal we called Bye and Near. But within a few weeks good old Bye Bye Bunty stepped on his heel somehow and broke a bone. We sent him to the horse hospital at the University of Guelph and got him fixed up, but that foot still bothered him. When he was a two-year-old he won a couple, then folded. Nobody even wanted to groom him. They thought he was just a big quitter. But the ankle was bothering him and he had a curb, a painful leg growth, as well.

So the soldiers at the farm, who often are the reason for success when things are going tough, worked all fall and winter on him. When we got him back to the track at three, in 1966, I ran him in a few allowance races but couldn't get one that was exactly right for him. I knew that he needed a win under his belt, so I entered him in a $7,500 claiming race. He just cakewalked. When you consider the horse he turned out to be, I could be criticized for running that horse in a claimer, taking a chance on losing him. But I got away with it and that was the start of his career, really. A man and a horse must be treated the same. If you have a man licked every time he competes, he'll never develop. He's got to get a couple of wins into him to make him feel good. A horse is just the same. If he doesn't win a race sometime and feel like a champion, he'll go down, down, down. Within weeks after that one victory Bye and Near won the Plate Trial, and ran second in the Queen's Plate to a top horse, Titled Hero; would have won it, I always thought, if Avelino Gomez on Titled Hero hadn't shut Bye and Near off in the stretch. In those days I never claimed foul.

Bye and Near just kept on getting better. He won the Mohawk Stakes three years in a row after that – at four, five, and six years old; the first two at a mile and five-sixteenths and the third one at a mile and an eighth.

The nice thing about the first of those Mohawk Stakes wins, in the fall of 1967, was that it was also the first stakes win for Donnie Walker, who had been assisting Johnny Starr for years and had taken over training my stable a couple of months before.

Why did I split with Johnny Starr, after all those years? A matter of principle. The horsemen were going to go on strike. The Jockey Club directors had a meeting and E. P. Taylor and the others said they were going to fight to a finish. I foolishly took them at their word. There were some good races coming up, however, and I asked Johnny Starr, "If there is a strike, what will you do?"

He said that he would have to stay with the Horsemen's Benevolent and Protective Association, because he was a director of that. It was a matter of split loyalties. I didn't want anyone working for me, even as good a man as Johnny Starr, whose first loyalty was to someone else. So I asked around among others in the stable to find out what they thought.

"Hell," they said, "the H.B.P.A. never did anything for us – we'll send your horses out."

Then the Jockey Club settled the dispute without a strike. Made a deal. I was the one, in effect, who fought to a finish – and found myself with a new trainer, as a result. Taylor tried to talk me into patching it up with Johnny. I told him next time he was going to fold in a fight to let me know before I bet too much on him. Too bad, but Johnny and I were through.

But before we get away from Bye and Near, there's one other decision I made that tells you what I thought of him. In 1969, he was six – and that spring the federal Post Office made a ruling on mailings for charitable purposes that cost the Ontario Society for

Crippled Children tens of thousands of dollars. That's the kind of government we don't deserve; they blow money on everything under the sun and get even by charging the crippled kids extra postage.

Pierre Trudeau had been elected in 1968 on the promise that he would bring a Just Society to Canada. I phoned a newspaperman that spring of 1969 and asked if he could get me a cartoon drawn that I could publish as an ad. "What I have in mind," I said, "is a crippled kid, you know, with the braces and the poor twisted limbs and all that, and crutches, struggling to walk while some guy labelled the Just Society is making him carry a great big bag labelled postal rates."

I didn't get it drawn, but I did have a hot correspondence for months with Trudeau and his Postmaster General, Eric Kierans, about how come we could spend $200,000 for a third-rate hockey team to go to Europe and get beaten, while he refused to give a break at the Post Office to all the charitable organizations that depended on the mail for soliciting funds. When I could see that I was talking to a couple of deaf men I announced that I would designate Bye and Near to run for the crippled kids, and donate all his winnings up to the amount, $27,000, needed to make up the extra postage the government was taking. His third Mohawk at Woodbine that fall brought his earnings for the year to $26,250. It wasn't long after that he took it over the top. Before I retired him to stud Bye and Near started 84 times, won 21, was second 27 times, and brought $202,040 into the barn. Not bad for a horse that always had a sore ankle from that accident when he was a foal.

To go back a bit, Johnny Starr landed on his feet every bit as well as I did, after we split. Jean-Louis Lévesque gave him a fine string of horses and Johnny has done well with them ever since. Anyway, one thing a man in the horse business must accept is loss. It might be a trainer who goes elsewhere, or a rider who decides to take another mount just when you need him most. Or a horse that breaks down on the track and has to be destroyed. The worst thing to me is a senseless loss. My office at Caledon has a window through which I can see what's going on in the paddocks, and many's the time I opened the window and roared at something I saw being done wrong. That's one thing that didn't weaken as I got older, my voice. But often I was not around when something happened, and then it always would fall to Murray Dudgeon to call and let me know, because he's the veterinarian at the farm both for routine and emergencies. I would ask what happened. I'd be angry enough to fire someone if it was an accident that could have been prevented. If a horse gets loose, as one did, runs into a fence and breaks its neck, someone is at fault but perhaps not wholly. I tried to be fair. But once one of my best mares, Kitty Girl, was in foal to Nearctic and due to foal soon, when someone stupidly let her out on an icy morning. She slipped, broke her pelvis, and died within minutes, was dead by the time Dr. Dudgeon could get there. We lost Famous Road, Bye Bye Bunty, Caledon Beau, Northern Minx, Bye and Near – heart attacks, ruptured blood vessels around foaling time – there are many ways, none of them easy to take.

The ones I really hated to lose were the good mares. I figured if you can't beat the opposition on the race track, you can beat 'em in the breeding shed. If I had a real good horse beaten by a filly I'd do anything I could to get that filly into my string. That's usually the only reason I would claim a horse. If there was a good filly or mare with bloodlines I liked, or a win over a good horse, I'd keep an eye open for the owner to make a mistake. Once in a while there'd be a little more than that to it. At one time Hal Waggoner from Hamilton, the former football player, claimed one from me, a half-sister to Kitty Girl. I waited three or four years. Finally one Waggoner had, named Twice Shy, who'd beaten a really good one of mine, had top bloodlines, and had won some stakes races, was dropped into a claiming race for $7,500. I claimed, meaning I got that high quality mare for almost nothing.

I sent Twice Shy down to the stud named Sailor and got a good filly named Sailor Take Care who placed in several stakes while winning about $42,000.

Next from Twice Shy we got Not Too Shy, a great example of the importance of the farm operation. This filly was big, too heavy for her joints and tendons, but I had up on my farm a married couple, Charlie and Ruth Woodcock. Ruth Woodcock is a magnificent rider, gentle, loves animals. Charlie is probably the best veterinarian who never qualified. He came from England and had rubbed some of the best horses in the world. He is very patient and when Not Too Shy showed signs of tendon trouble because of too much weight, we didn't race her much as a two-year-old. She won a maiden race in slow time, just running as fast as she had to, and in the fall she won another on the grass before we put her up for the winter.

They all worked on her at the farm. In the spring when she got back in training and the tendons filled up a little, we went easy. Charlie Woodcock spent tremendous time on her. In the 1969 Oaks she came second, but the Oaks is run in early June. With the cold and icy tracks of Canada in the spring it often is not possible to get a filly really strong that early, without pushing her too hard. I lost the Oaks twice with great fillies that could pull a farm wagon and still beat most of the others – Jammed Lovely and Not Too Shy. But they weren't fit because my men had enough brains not to force them and hurt them.

From then on Not Too Shy was a top filly, upset an odds-on favourite United States import Hail to Patsy in the Duchess Stakes that fall, and won 23 races and $189,441 before she was through at the track. Not bad for the get of a $7,500 mare. I was offered $150,000 for her as a three-year-old, a big price in those days, but that's the craziness of the tax system we have in this country. I figured if I sold her, I would have $37,500, the buyer would have Not Too Shy, the government would have $112,500, and the trainer and the Woodcocks at the farm and Stanley Parenteau, my little Indian groom who was so good with her, all would have felt that all they had done to help make this a great filly, one they would feel part of, was for what?

So I kept her and was glad I did. As a broodmare she produced Lucky Colonel S., which won $94,917 as a two-year-old, including being second by a nostril to Jack Stafford's great Overskate in the richest horse race in Canada for juveniles, the $158,340 Coronation. But Not Too Shy's 1978 foal, by Grey Dawn, came out backwards and the birth complications meant we had to send the mare to Guelph for surgery. When she came out of anesthetic, she threshed violently as horses sometimes do. In so doing she broke a leg and had to be destroyed. It's impossible to assess the real value of a good broodmare, but a few months earlier a breeder in the States had offered me $400,000 for her. Her line lives on in Lucky Colonel S., who went to stud for me eventually.

From 1968 to 1976, I refused to enter the winner's circle, no matter what kind of races my horses won. It was my own little protest, not supported by anybody, against the custom of making the "Official" sign at the end of a race official only for the gamblers and touts. For the owners, trainers, riders, grooms, and hot walkers, nothing was official for a couple of days until tests had been completed to make sure a winner didn't have any banned substance in its blood or urine. Racing has to be honest, but after Dancer's Image, trained by Lou Cavalaris, as honest a man as ever entered a backstretch, was disqualified because of a positive test two days after winning the Kentucky Derby, I made a stand. Official should mean official. If some banned substance (which can be from medicine used a week earlier) is discovered later, bar the person responsible from racing, fine him more than the purse, or whatever the situation warrants. But as long as I did not know each time a horse of mine won whether I was really going to get the purse or not, I refused to dignify (if that's the word) the winner's circle with my presence.

Once when I won a big stake a reporter asked me, "Why don't you go over this time, bury the hatchet?"

I replied, "Maybe I'll go over in a couple of days, when it's really official."

I only made the trip once in the eight years between 1968 and 1976. That was when Saul Wagman's Gentleman Conn won the Coronation Futurity in 1971. Saul had named the colt after me and urged me to cross the track with him when he accepted, so I went. But that was the only exception until 1976, when my beautiful filly Bye Bye Paris charged through the slop at Woodbine in June to win the Canadian Oaks. The Queen's representative, Ontario Lieutenant-Governor Pauline McGibbon, was on hand to make the presentation. When she requested me, on behalf of the Queen, to cross the track with her to the winner's circle, I went.

In a way again, it was to give the proper recognition to what my people had done to make Bye Bye Paris such a great filly. From the beginning she had been terrified of the gate, causing a lot of trouble in her two-year-old starts. The people at my farm worked with her patiently for more than a year to make her feel easier at the gate. Donnie Walker had brought her up to the race in perfect shape. Jeff Fell had given her a first-rate ride. I finally thought that to all of them belonged the right to see the owner go over and be a gentleman about it.

Besides, at eighty-one, I was jubilant; that win had put me into the money-winning lead among owners, something I didn't often enjoy with my "modest" stable. Incidentally, in the Queen's Plate itself, I made a sentimental gesture, in a way, putting Chris Rogers on Bye Bye Paris as an endorsement of how he had fought his way back from alcoholism. At fifty-one, he was still one of the shrewdest riders around. We didn't win, but when Rogers died of cancer a few months later he at least went with the knowledge that another non-drinker had had the faith to put him on that filly for the country's finest three-year-old race.

The Oaks win was one of our big early-season thrills in 1976. When the $101,770 Cup and Saucer came up in the fall I was within striking distance of leading all Canadian owners in earnings in a season for the very first time. My entry for that one was Lucky North Man, by Jammed Lucky out of Northern Minx. When I went into the paddock before the race I told Jeff Fell, who was only twenty, "Just ride him the way Fell can ride him." I've never believed in detailed instructions being more effective than putting a good rider on his mettle to do better than his best; a system that always worked with hockey players, too. Fell came from well back to wear down the odds-on favourite Sound Reason and win by a head. That gave us 31 wins for the year and purses of $415,912. In the next few weeks before racing ended for the season we won about $104,000 more and topped all the owners for the year. It was only the second time in Canada that an owner had won more than $500,000 (George Gardiner being the first).

That, as it turned out, was my peak year. When I picked a few horses to send to Florida that winter to train at St. Lucie, and flew down there myself with Jessie Watson and Margaret Grose, to keep warm like the horses, I was feeling my age. The long flight never used to bother me. Now it did. I had a good racing season behind me, but my eighty-second birthday was only a few weeks away, and I had had one disappointment in 1976 that bothered me – fund-raising for the Ontario Community Centre for the Deaf seemed to be going nowhere fast. As that might be my last big project, I didn't want to conk out before it was built.

Chapter Fifteen

As I became older, I was struck by the fact that just by reacting loudly all my life to things that I thought needed changing, doing, improving, or to be shot down in flames, I had developed a reputation that sometimes worked against me. For instance, I am sure that when I was nominated in 1980 for the Order of Canada, someone with a long memory or even a short one would put in a negative vote on behalf of Mackenzie King, who thought I should have been court martialled for daring to speak out against his policy of appeasing Quebec by not enforcing overseas conscription. I had differentiated publicly between good people I thought of as French Canadians – Sir Wilfrid Laurier, Louis St. Laurent, and many Quebeckers who thought of Canada first – and people I thought of as Frenchmen, who I claimed didn't rate the term Canadian because they were still fighting the British. Once I started a speech at a noisy NHL awards banquet in Montreal with the words, "Gentlemen, and Frenchmen," which I correctly figured would get their attention. Several times I told Pierre Trudeau, whom I liked personally, that he was ruining the country by imposing bilingualism – spending hundreds of millions on a program that more than half of Canada didn't want, taking away money from programs they did want. I told Mike Pearson that he was splitting the country by forcing adoption of a flag that ignored our British heritage.

When I blasted Ontario Attorney-General Roy McMurtry for interfering with hockey by laying assault charges, do-gooders thought my intention was to brutalize the game; actually, I was only standing up for what I knew, that hockey could manage itself, as it had since the game began, without government interference. When I fired a woman and told her to leave the house of mine that she was using at Caledon, because I did not approve of her having a live-in boy friend whom I had not hired and did not wish to help support, she took the case to the Human Rights Commission and tried to back up her case by saying that I had been living with an unmarried woman for years – Jessie Watson, our housekeeper, for goodness sake. Directors of the Jockey Club thought I was a cantankerous pest because I was always arguing for seven-days-a-week racing, a glassed-in box so that I could watch the races in comfort, and maintained in other ways that Woodbine had been built all wrong.

Even when the Ontario Society for Crippled Children threw a party for me on my eightieth birthday in 1975, and the Premier of Ontario, Bill Davis, was a surprise guest, part of his speech was to the effect that, "if any of you think editorial comment in the *Star*, *Globe* or *Sun* about what I do, or my government does, is devastating, try being Connie Smythe's member, as I am, and getting letters from him on what I'm doing wrong." And Brigadier A. R. McIntosh, president of the society, said that there were times when he would cheerfully have strangled the honorary president, me. He felt he had to say that even while announcing establishment by the society of the Conn Smythe Research Foundation to co-ordinate and develop research into the physical disabilities of children, better methods of treatment, and so on.

I had trouble realizing that I was eighty. I had just got used to being in my seventies. But that night of my eightieth birthday I could also look out on hockey people, newspaper people, people I'd worked with for various charities, and figure that with all my faults, which I knew better than anyone, including some no one else had noticed, somehow I had come out with a lot of friends. I liked better, to tell the truth, a family birthday dinner at the Royal York's Imperial Room when they announced from the stage that I was there, and it was my eightieth birthday. Everybody in the room stood up and sang happy birthday and cheered, without starting off by telling me what a terrible man I was.

Somehow being eighty bothered me. Later that year I often felt depressed and uncertain about things I was doing, and had done, until something happened that made the next few years among my best and happiest. The horses were part of it, of course, our success at the track, but the most important thing, something that lifted me and made me think I still had something to contribute, was when we finally got underway in plans for building the Ontario Community Centre for the Deaf.

My connection with the deaf began almost ten years earlier. We were looking for someone to do an important job at the Crippled Children's Society and people kept saying, "We should get someone like Reverend Bob Rumball." After I'd heard that a few times I said, "Look, if he's that good, we should not get somebody *like* Reverend Bob Rumball, but get Reverend Bob Rumball."

My friend Bert Telford, a pillar of the society, knew Rumball and went to find out if he'd be interested. Bert came back to say that he wasn't. I insisted, "He has a price tag." Bert said, "No price tag." I thought every man had his price, not always in money but in challenge, the satisfaction of taking on a job that needed to be done. Finally I went to see Bob Rumball myself, both to see what made him so great, and to figure out what we had to do to get him with us.

I was impressed. He had been a lay preacher when he played football and basketball for the University of Toronto, then pro football with Ottawa and the Argos. One time when the Argos had a request for a player to attend a gathering of young people at a church for the deaf, someone's finger had travelled down the roster and stopped at Rumball. As Milt Dunnell of the *Star* wrote, "whoever selected Rumball that day couldn't have done a more important job if he'd selected a quarterback who could win the Grey Cup." In his first contact with the deaf he had found his vocation and set out immediately to learn the sign language.

I found a fit, athletic looking man who was built like a middleweight fighter. Before going full-time with the deaf, he had graduated from a Baptist seminary in Chicago with a Bachelor of Divinity degree. Then he joined the Ontario Mission of the Deaf, and began preaching at the Evangelical Church of the Deaf in Toronto.

The day I met him, my aim was to persuade him to come to the Society for Crippled Children. Instead, he wound up convincing me not only that the job he had was so important to him that he would not leave it, but also that I could help him. Instead of me telling him about crippled children, he told me how the deaf were discriminated against in education. Naturally most of them couldn't attend regular schools and the Department of Education would not allow schools of their own where they could be taught by deaf teachers. All Ontario Schools for the Deaf had to be staffed by teachers who could hear. No matter how good they were, those teachers did not face the same handicap as their students so they were not able, in Rumball's opinion, to do a first-rate job in fitting deaf children to cope in a society where almost everyone else could hear. Some deaf children were finishing their schooling with the equivalent of a Grade Five education.

He was trying to get support, he said, for a pilot project – one classroom where the deaf could be taught by deaf teachers. I said, "How much would that take?"

He said, "Ten thousand dollars."

I said, "If you can raise five, I'll put in the other five."

In ten days he raised the five. I put in mine. He said publicly later that the classroom changed the whole course of deaf education in the province and influenced it elsewhere. And I came to think of him as about the closest thing I have ever met to a true apostle. He was dedicating his life to a cause, not only his church services for the deaf in the Toronto area, but in courtrooms where he acted as a translator and in thousands of miles a year he travelled helping the deaf throughout the country. He scrounged everywhere for names and addresses of deaf people, and in the Maritimes found some who never had been to a church service that they could understand.

As the years went on, through my tax troubles, Stafford's death, and the rest, we kept in touch. Sometimes he talked to me about a dream he had – a community centre where deaf persons of all ages from children to senior citizens, and multi-handicapped people (deaf and blind, deaf and without speech, deaf and cerebral palsy) could live, learn trades, play games in their own gymnasium, present plays, hold meetings, swim, play cards; community centre, I guess, says it all. He wasn't just sitting and dreaming about it. Looking for a central site, he had been in touch for a while with my old Army friend, General Bruce Matthews, and his wife, and had made an offer to buy the Matthews estate, Stonedene, on Bayview Avenue across from the Granite Club, a Toronto haven for the well-off. It was perfect, a little more than six well-treed acres with room for outdoor facilities, the pool and tennis courts, as well as for buildings to house other elements, from specially-designed living quarters for the profoundly deaf, to lecture and dining halls, a sanctuary, craft rooms, vocational training. But a hitch had developed in plans being made by the deaf community so negotiations had broken off. I bugged Bill Davis to make some land available, as George Drew had made available the land for Variety Village School more than twenty-five years earlier. The premier kept saying it was not that easy. Finally we went back to Bruce Matthews and made progress. At first, he agreed to an offer of $600,000 but then, because the estate was in his wife's name, legal advice was that it would have to be appraised. The appraisal set the price at $900,000. I said, "Okay, Bruce, we'll take it. But if you'll put in $50,000 as a contribution I'll match it, and that will bring the price down."

Meanwhile, Rumball had done a fair amount of planning. His original idea was to build in stages, expanding in future years as funds became available. I encouraged him on all but one thing, building in stages. "Build it all at once," I said. "See what you can get from governments, and in mortgages, and then get the rest all in one big fund drive. Building isn't going to get any cheaper. Do it now."

In the early months of 1976 things began to take shape, because by then we had our site assured and the deaf community itself had raised the $900,000 needed to get started. Part of this had come from selling the Deaf Mission's headquarters' property in downtown Toronto. We had plans drawn estimating the final cost at around six million dollars. I contracted Jacques Pigott of Pigott Construction because of the way he had treated us in building the Crippled Children's Centre in 1959. And in June, 1976, about a week or so before Bye Bye Paris won the Oaks for me, we called a luncheon at Sutton Place to lay out the plans and ask for public support.

I was honorary campaign chairman. Bud Turner, president of MacLaren Advertising, had grown up on our street. So I knew him well enough to call him that spring and say, "Bud, I'm going to be honorary chairman of the fund raising campaign for the deaf centre."

"Yes?" he said.

"And you're going to be the chairman," I said.

"Oh," he said.

. Gordon Bell, vice president of the Bank of Nova Scotia, agreed to be treasurer. At the kickoff luncheon, I did some of the talking, Bud did some, and Bob Rumball the rest. We had about $1.5

million assured, we said, and were going to be beating the bushes to find the rest. I think we all made an impression. Some media people came, I think, to make sure I was still alive, because the main theme in a lot of stories the next day was that, yes, I was. However it happened, every important columnist in the city wrote about it the next day and we thought we were off to a booming start. But somehow the money didn't come in that year from private donors, big companies, or the public, the way I thought it should have. There was a big boost in December when Premier Davis came to see me with word that the government would grant $835,000 to help with construction, from the Ministry of Community and Social Services. Another $435,000 would come from Wintario funds for recreational facilities. But in Florida that winter I worried about the slow progress of private-sector fund raising. When I came back in the spring I had decided that within a few months we were going to be over the top in money or pledges, if it killed me.

It almost did. At least, Margaret Grose and Jessie Watson told me later that they were worried for my health, I seemed so obsessed with getting completion of what might be the last big project of my life.

Bob Rumball and I made a lot of calls together, as we had the previous summer and fall. I enjoyed it. I hadn't been involved in anything big for years, and I liked going in and meeting the young fellows running big companies. Bob later told me he had been warned that he would be embarrassed by me in these fund raising calls, that I would be too tough on people, get their backs up. The reputation again. But I can talk to bank presidents or hot-walkers, they are all the same to me. Bob soon relaxed. I remember one time we visited the president of a big company. I told him what we were there for. Immediately he wanted to talk hockey. That went on and on. We had other calls to make that day. Finally I said to Rumball, "I thought you told me there were only eight thousand deaf people in Ontario."

He said, "That's right."

"Well, here's another one," I said pointing across the desk. "Apparently he didn't hear a word we said about what we're here for."

The man then reached for his chequebook.

Bud Turner had a good idea that a lot of the areas and facilities be sponsored by individuals, companies, or foundations. We put a price tag on everything. I would show someone on the plan of the main building something he could donate, and have his name on for, say, $60,000. He'd say, "Haven't you got something cheaper?"

I'd say, "Well, there's something here for nineteen thousand . . ." And then I'd hear from him, or not. The big donors, for the four corners of the main building, were two foundations and two individuals, which I think is a good mix. One of the corners came through the efforts of Mrs. Hindmarsh, daughter of Joe Atkinson, the founder of the *Star*. She came to lunch with me one day, a lovely lady. That lunch cost the Atkinson Charitable Foundation about $180,000. Beland Honderich, the *Star*'s president, later told me Mrs. Hindmarsh lobbied carefully to get the foundation to donate for what would be the Atkinson Lounge, in memory of Joseph E. Atkinson.

For another corner, I remember the day we went to see John Fraser of the Samuel McLaughlin Foundation. He was in his late nineties at the time. "What do you kids want?" he asked. We went out of there with his pledge of more than $250,000 for the combined gymnasium and auditorium, called the McLaughlin Gymnatorium.

Besides the sanctuary I had named in Stafford's memory, a lovely chapel with a nursery attached, I had one area dedicated to Bay Arnoldi, my boyhood benefactor. I went to Harold Ballard one day and showed him the floor plan. "McLaughlin, Atkinson, and Smythe have three of the corners," I said. "There's one left. Here's a chance for you to do good." He just reached for a cheque and the Harold E. Ballard and Maple Leaf Gardens dining area was paid for, the final corner.

In all, I think there are twenty-seven plaques on special facilities or areas throughout the centre. The one on the sanctuary and chapel bears this message: "This area dedicated to the memory of C. Stafford Smythe, president of the Toronto Maple Leaf hockey team. World champions 1961-62, 62-63, 63-64, and 66-67." A big photo of Stafford stands outside.

One visit I made that spring was to Ken Thomson, who had taken over the Thomson publishing and other companies after his father died. "Tell me exactly why I should contribute to the deaf centre," he said. I did the best I could, getting a little hot about it. He said he would think about it.

That was in April of 1977. A day or two later Meg and I spent a nice warm spring day at Caledon. We swam and had a good time but I was still adding up government grants and mortgages and all the rest in my head and thinking and talking about the half-million or so that we still had to get from private donors. Our mailings to ordinary citizens had brought a good response, more than $50,000 in a matter of weeks, and some of the big ones had come through as well. But a lot of rich people seemed to have their money tied up. I'd had a lot of turndowns in trying to get that last half-million, which we needed to get started that summer if we were to open late in 1978, as planned.

Mike Walsh was driving us down Highway 10 from Caledon that day, April 20. I was going over who I could call that hadn't already been called, when suddenly I became violently sick. I didn't know it then, but I was having a heart attack. Meg did know. She got Mike to pull in to the nearest place, a little restaurant. By then I was a mess. I had thrown up all over everything. I've admired that restaurant man ever since. When a guy staggers in all covered with vomit, the average restaurant man would think, "He's drunk." He didn't. He helped get the Peel Memorial Hospital at Brampton on the phone. Meg took over from there with the arrangements. Later Jessie said I wouldn't have lived through it, if it hadn't been for Meg. She stayed with me all that night, made sure I was never left alone, and insisted on nurses around the clock to look after me.

I just remember being ashamed of myself, for shooting my bird. The thing was, I hadn't exerted myself that day, or anything. Meg and I sometimes argued and she'd yell at me when I wasn't obeying medical orders. That day had been just nice and quiet. But nature can show us once in a while that we'd better look out, and that was one of those times for me.

After eight days I was well enough to write to my secretary, Una Potter, giving her the wording of notes of acknowledgement to all the letters I got while I was in the hospital. That note, which I read again the other day, sounded as if I was fine: "Here's to some more wins and good times at the old Office of Various Affairs. Let's meet at the head of the stretch some day soon . . ."

I also phoned Donnie Walker to see what was doing with the horses.

I almost gummed up, however, thinking I knew more than the doctors. I'd been told somewhere that a man shouldn't move around after a heart attack, so I refused to move, and got worse. When that became obvious, Hughie told me staying still was the worst thing I could do because of blood clots forming. As soon as I started to move around, I felt better.

The cards and letters and flowers that started arriving at Peel Memorial kept coming when I was moved to Wellesley. When I could talk, one call was from Ken Thomson. He said he hoped that the hard time he'd given me – I'd got quite heated that day – hadn't brought on my heart attack! He also told me he was sending a handsome donation. That gave me an idea. I got someone to call the papers and say that I'd been inundated with flowers and would prefer another form of tribute – contributions to the deaf centre. That did happen.

I still can read, if I need cheering up, the hundreds of letters and cards I received in the few weeks I was sick. I couldn't begin to list all the people who wrote to me, hundreds I didn't know, and some I did – Ward Pitfield, E. P. Taylor, my grandchildren, and many old friends. Charles Bronfman of the Montreal Expos and other concerns, wrote, "You pioneered great things in Canadian sport which . . . make those of us who are involved in the same endeavours regard you as our dean." It sounded like an obit to me.

Another came from Stephen Clarke, a messenger with Imperial Oil who'd been a tank driver in the war, much different: "Come on, Conn, get well and get out of that bed. We need you, the handicapped need you, and there is plenty of work left undone . . ." He must have been a horse player because he added, "Your good horse Be Near Me won on Saturday. You are surrounded by fighters and can't lose . . ." There was a letter from a couple named John and Maude Spence, who said, "You won't remember us, but we purchased this house in February, 1946 . . ." The house was one I'd built on East Drive near the sand pit for returned men and they said in their happy lives since "you share a portion of our heart strings."

Pauline McGibbon said she'd see me at the Queen's Plate. Bob Bridger, one of my old 30th Battery men who was my farm manager at Caledon, wrote to say, "Don't worry about anything here at the farm . . . Not For All foaled at 6:00 a.m. this morning, dark bay filly, doing very good." He signed it Bridger Here, which we used to call him because he answered the phone that way.

United States horse owner Peter Fuller kidded, "I hear you are temporarily in a restful position. Knowing you, in a few days you'll be back officiating in the winner's circle, as usual." Peter, who owned Dancer's Image, disqualified after winning the Kentucky Derby, knew how to make me smile with that reference to the winner's circle.

A wire came from Bill Torrey of the Islanders, a note from Joe Primeau, others from politicians and friends, and one I liked from Mort Greenberg, the TV film cameraman I often saw at the track and the Gardens: "I was at the track yesterday, major, and a casual enquiry regarding your whereabouts had a dismaying effect on me. I have always admired you. For those who are hard to convince, I say, 'What's irascibility?' There perhaps have been those who would cap that certain flare, that internal combustibility of yours . . . For me, you have been a beacon showing not only direction, but exuding a certain kind of warmth."

Perhaps this kind of praise and, yes, love, should not be for me to print, but what the hell: Indulge an old man. Those letters and the others kept buoying me up, every day. Never think that when someone you know or even know of, is sick, he'll be getting all the letters he needs without yours. Every one counts. The strength flowing out to me through all these friends I knew or didn't know began to form an idea in my mind: I'm going back to the track four weeks from when I had my heart attack.

Which I did. That day, May 18, I had four horses running at Woodbine. I had been discharged from the hospital two days before, and had gone to Caledon. Meg was worried about me getting excited at the races. I was supposed to take it easy, stay in the car. The idea was to park it close enough to the rail to see what was going on. When I got there, I just couldn't stay in the car. I got out and went to the rail. Then a sort of funny thing happened. Lucky Colonel S., a good two-year-old, was in a five-furlong race. I was excited. I had to urinate. Suddenly. Couldn't control it. So I just got Meg and Mike to crowd in close to me along the fence. I peed through it. I don't think anybody else knew what was going on. It was a steel mesh fence. For a long time after that, every time I went past that spot I would smile to see the little rust streak running down the steel mesh. I must have had strong stuff in me that day.

When Lucky Colonel S. won, the groom, Caesar Hamy, led him over to the rail where I was. Track photographer Mike Burns took a picture showing Caesar Hamy and C. Smythe gripping hands and grinning, while the colt pricked his ears at what was going on.

Oddly enough, my heart attack had an effect of sorts on the campaign for the deaf centre. Of all the things that have been said about me, nobody ever accused me of not knowing how to use publicity. Every story about my heart attack and recovery, my return to the track, everything else, mentioned the deaf centre, sometimes on front pages. Others in the campaign committee were carrying the ball. But in the newspapers reporters writing stories about my recovery all said, one way or another, that uppermost in my mind was the Ontario Centre for the Deaf, and "we only need $400,000 more to meet our $6 million goal, and we can begin to build."

It all helped. In September that year, less than five months after my heart attack, Pauline McGibbon and I put our hands on a shovel to turn the first sod. Construction was delayed some, but in April, 1979, when we had collected 98 per cent of the money we needed, Premier Davis came to open the centre – and let slip something about his early involvement. Rumball had gone to see him years before to plead for a better deal for the deaf. Davis had said, "Blast me and the government in the papers, Bob. Spell it out, the second-rate education, everything else. That'll get things started." Only a politician would know that kind of shortcut.

Another funny thing: the Granite Club of Toronto, across the road from the centre, had been trying for years to get a stop light so its members could turn into the club without getting creamed. They couldn't get the stop light, but we did – and the Granite Club rebuilt its parking lot entrance to take advantage of the light. Some media people called the centre, which cost $7,300,000 in the end, "The Miracle on Bayview Avenue." I call it the Deaf Granite Club.

In the time since it opened, people from many parts of North America have come to visit – and marvel at the spread of services it provides, from the little deaf kids in the day care centre to the old or sorely handicapped people in the apartments, and basketball games where there are no whistles, but the referee flashes a light to stop play. There is no voice intercom in the centre, but closed-circuit television to give visual signals. Other facilities for the deaf in the world have parts of what we have, but none has it all in one place and we do.

As a member of the special advisory committee, I raised hell now and again. I promised the people I got money from that their donations would be spent in a manner that would please them, and I wasn't letting anybody forget that. Bob Rumball and I had our arguments. He's a tough guy too. But that doesn't diminish at all the deep personal satisfaction I got from working to help him fulfil his dream. I also liked it when I heard he had said, "We could not have done this without Conn Smythe." Nobody is indispensable, but it is a more or less harmless pleasure once in a while to think we are.

Chapter Sixteen

When I passed my eighty-fifth birthday I was in Florida. I still stayed busy because if you sit in your chair, you're going to die. If you don't use your brain, you can't think. I have seen men stop working and just fade away. I kept in touch with the farm at Caledon by phone and sometimes went to the training establishment at St. Lucie to look at the few horses I had training there. Jessie and Meg and I went to the track with Florida friends, and sometimes with visitors from Toronto. I had had to quit playing golf after my heart attack because sometimes I was a little shaky on my pins. I swam twice a day, though, and when we returned to Toronto and Caledon I started swimming again as soon as we could get the Caledon pool warm enough for me.

Late in April I started organizing material and putting my memories on tape for this book. Royalties from it will go to my personal charitable foundation. One day in May or June my co-author told me that the publisher's first payment would be made in January, 1982.

At no other time had I said to anyone that I was sure my days were not numbered in high numbers any more, but I said to him, "I'd like to be around when it happens, and I'll be in the box by 1982." He made a phone call and arranged for payments to begin in 1981 after the book was published. I didn't want an advance, never have for a job not yet done.

I was feeling lousy a lot of the time. Taping the book helped. It made me feel young again to go back over so many good times as well as the times not so good. But when a session was over I often felt weak. At night I would sleep only a few minutes at a time because of the endless pain in my leg. The doctors changed medication once and asked me to make a note each time I woke during the night, each time I went to the bathroom, and so on. My scrawls of 1:15 a.m., 1:27 a.m. sometimes would be no more than fifteen or twenty minutes apart for most of the night. After watching the news one night I fell going to the bathroom. Jessie heard the thump and came running. She tried to help me up. She was straining and I was trying, but suddenly I had to laugh.

She stood back astonished and said, "Mr. Smythe!"

I said, "It's just so ridiculous." I couldn't even roll over to help push myself up.

I was losing weight, down below 130, part of it shrinking through age. A year earlier when I had put on my grey morning coat to go to the Queen's Plate Jessie had told me it looked big on me and would have to be taken in to do another year, but I had forgotten. There was more to think about that day than a too-big coat when my colt Ram Good, the long shot in the 1979 Plate at about 59-1, came charging in the stretch to take the third-place purse of better than $16,000.

When the Plate got near in 1980 Jessie reminded me about having the morning coat altered. I refused. Meg made an issue of it. I got more stubborn. With Meg and Jessie cajoling, eventually we did have it fixed. I badly wanted to win one more Plate and if I did I might as well do it in a coat that fitted.

I was lucky in the people who looked after me, all in different ways. Meg was strict, Jessie wasn't, and Mike Walsh, my driver, just had one aim in life (like the others), to look after me. I was going to the track in the mornings less and less, sometimes I just couldn't get going, but on some mornings I did go to watch Bye Bye Tony and some of the good two-year-olds I had, like Muskoka Weekend and Regal Stafford. Mike would pick me up early and drive me to the grandstand side. I would sit in the stands and clock the works myself with my trainer, C. C. Hopmans, beside me. At the end of the 1978 season Donnie Walker had decided he wanted to work more with his own theories of training horses than with mine, which I insisted on. I could see his point, but was sorry to lose him. I had taken on C. C. because he was young enough, not yet twenty-five, that I thought I could teach him some of what I knew. Maybe I did. He says I taught him a lot. In my orneryness, he took a lot from me, I know that.

I thought I had a good chance in the 1980 Plate. My colt Bye Bye

Tony was named after a good groom I had, Tony Kuzma, who died about the time the colt was foaled. Tony, as we called the colt, had gone ten races without being worse than third – four wins, four seconds, two thirds. In the Plate Trial, a week or so before the main event, he was well in front in the stretch. I thought the rider Gary Stahlbaum, went to sleep on him – thought he had the race won when all the time Driving Home was making a hell of a move that nipped Tony in the last few yards.

Something happened on Plate Day that showed what kind of shape I was in. I had a mild form of diabetes, according to the doctors. That meant I was supposed to keep away from sweet stuff. Meg made sure I did when she was around. But I had been eating candy and chocolate and fruit cake all my life for quick energy. I really missed it in times of stress. As the early races went on that day, I was in trouble with what I used to call playoff fever, but worse. Jessie told me later that I was stuttering a bit, jigging my bad leg, drumming my fingers a lot. Those were signs she could read several seats away. I usually kept the seat next to me clear for certain people, my trainer or my grandson Tommy. Just before the Plate horses were due in the paddock, that seat was empty. Jessie came and slipped into it. She always carried a piece of chocolate in her purse, had for years, in case I needed it. Discussing something on the program with me, she slipped me the chocolate. When we went down toward the walking ring, for a minute I was beside Jessie. "Thanks," I said. "That saved my life."

Then I was able to stand in the walking ring with the crowd gathered around the fence and my family around me; Hugh and Bernice, Miriam and Jack, Dorothea, Tommy and some of my grandchildren. One of them, Mary Swatuk, came up when we were leaving the ring and kissed me and whispered, "Good luck, Grandpa." Then, with someone holding my arm to steady me, excited as hell, I went back to the box and saw Tony run a nothing race. He was never in it. Later I found he had lost some weight and had a fever, so his last ten races when he'd never been worse than third didn't mean much that day.

Jessie, incidentally, also got mad at me from time to time. A week or two earlier she'd hardly spoken to me for a day after I named a new-born filly for Joan Sutton, the *Star* columnist. "Who's Joan Sutton to get a nice filly like that named after her?" she demanded. But with me, it was business. I like Joan Sutton.

but mainly I knew it would get some publicity, help get people interested in my horses. When I died and my stable was sold, with the money to my charitable foundation, a little extra interest might produce some extra funds for good causes.

So the summer went on. I went to the races when I had one running, especially Muskoka Weekend and Regal Stafford. I would have Meg and Jessie with me. Sometimes Tommy would be there, too. If I had two horses entered a few races apart, I would send my crowd to the Director's Lounge, then Mike would drive me to the backstretch. There I would sit in the shade of a tree and talk to backstretch people, my favourite people at the track. There were too many phoneys in the Directors' Lounge. Not all, of course, but too many.

One day I remember also. My old friend from Jarvis and the Crippled Children, Reg Hopper, had died. I was at the funeral home paying my respects when Irene's old close friend Elsie Ridpath came up. "What are you doing here?" she asked.

"Getting measured for a box, what do you think?" I replied. Ask a silly question.

That summer of 1980, the little comforts counted for so much. We would usually drive to Caledon from the races for a couple of days of checking what was going on. When Meg wasn't there, Jessie would make a pumpkin pie out of real pumpkins. I thought I had earned such small compensations. Every time I had eaten the small piece Jessie would allow me of the forbidden pie, she would ask, "Have you had sufficient?"

"No," I would say.

"Would you like another piece of pie?"

"Certainly."

"I don't think I should give you any."

And I would agree, knowing that was the direction it was going in, all along.

But life was getting to be a lot harder to take day by day, with the pains in my legs, the pills I didn't like taking because each new prescription did something different to me, and so much that I liked ruled out of my diet. Nights were the worst time, but I've covered that. I kept losing weight. Meg and the doctors wanted me to take some blood tests to see why I was losing weight. I fought them. I knew why I was losing weight; I wasn't getting enough to eat. But finally I gave in, in August. They took me to Peel

Memorial in Brampton for tests. Once the decision was made, I didn't worry. The hospital people, 90 per cent of them, do everything they can to help you. While I was in there, Hughie and others phoned or came to visit, and I read my usual things, like the *New Yorker*, and Meg would be there a lot. She read passages to me from books I liked, *The Lonely*, by Paul Gallico, and *The White Cliffs*, by Alice Duer Miller. I'd met Gallico long ago in Detroit when he was a sportswriter and I was only in my thirties. They gave me X-rays and tests and put me on a strict diet, but still I felt there wasn't anything the matter with me that hadn't been the matter for a long time.

I got out, eventually, and went back to what I'd been doing. We were at the races on Labour Day. Mike drove us from there up to Caledon. It was a lovely day and we were all going to go swimming. I felt tired, however, and thought I would lie down first for a while on the bed I have in the pool house. Meg told me it was time for me to take some of the new pills I had. I refused. We had a fight about it. I knew she was doing exactly what she was supposed to be doing, but I still refused. Jessie had said she was going to have her swim first and then get supper while we were swimming, so she was swimming when we were arguing. Finally Meg yelled at me, "Why do you have to be so stubborn?" and stormed out to go to the house.

At the time, Jessie was almost back to the house in her swimming robe. She had dropped her bathing suit, which we always did, to be dried in the pool house. Jessie came back over and asked me if there was anything she could do. I said no, I was going to have my swim. She was watching me when she saw that as I got into the deep end I started moving very slowly. One arm just fell into the water and stayed there, and then the other.

I don't remember any of this; just that suddenly I felt very weak, and then felt nothing. Jessie told me later what happened in the next minute or two. She ran along the side of the pool yelling at me, and then just dropped her robe and jumped in and grabbed me as I went under. Luckily I was completely limp, unconscious, which might have been a good thing, she said, because if I'd been fighting her maybe she wouldn't have been able to handle me. She held my head up and got me over to the side, but we were still several feet from the ladder. I didn't know a thing but she tried to get my hand up so I could hold on to the side. It would just fall down. The next thing I knew was coming to, hazily, to hear her voice as if at a great distance screaming, "Mr. Smythe! Mr. Smythe!" My eyes rolled open and I was aware that she was trying to get me to the ladder.

"You move your hands every time I give you a little boost," she said.

She had her arms circling me, holding on to the sides of the pool herself and supporting me there. Every time she would give me a shove toward the ladder, I would move my hands. I could just do that. But at the ladder I didn't have the strength to climb. She told me to hold on to the ladder. Then she just put her head under my bare backside and shoved while she climbed, and the two of us fell out of the pool.

It had only taken a minute or two. She had been too busy to yell. Anyway the pool house is too far away from the house for Meg to hear. She got me up but I couldn't stand by myself, so she eased me along the side of the pool to the open end where she got my arms around the flagpole and said, "Now you stand there and hold on while I get help."

Suddenly I couldn't control myself. I was throwing up, I had diarrhoea, I was an unholy mess standing there skin and bones when Jessie and Meg ran to throw towels around me. Then they cleaned me up and got me to bed. That would have been the end of my life, if Jessie hadn't saved me.

I knew then that I didn't have much time. My will made sure that the people who had looked after me so well would be comfortable, in some cases for life, as my thanks for all they had done for me. Jessie was to stay on at Baby Point for a year, if she wished, and then it would be sold. She could use Caledon as much as she wanted, and at the end it would go to Hugh and Bernice. For years Jessie had had a house in her name, and also would get all my silver trays and trophies, because she kept them so clean. Meg, Mike, and others would be looked after for helping me live surrounded by people who loved me, to the end.

I talked to Miriam, Hugh, Hap Day, and my grandson, Tom, and told them what I wanted done with the Conn Smythe Charitable Foundation when I was gone. For one thing, I wanted Tom to have the final say on what the foundation would support. That was a new decision, but had been growing for months. I did not think it would be fair to ask Hughie to do it, because he was already terribly busy as a leading specialist in rheumatology, one of the best in that line anywhere. Inevitably there might be a conflict of interest with things he was professionally interested in. He agreed. He hardly had an hour to himself most days as it was. As he got older, someone else would have to take it over anyway. Hugh and Hap would consult with Tom on everything the foundation was asked to support, but he would have the final say.

I enjoyed myself through the next few weeks, seeing the leaves turning and sometimes going to the paddocks or to the race track to see my horses. I tried to keep the routine as usual – on the weekends go from the track directly to Caledon, keep in touch by telephone with my young secretary Stella Konstantopolos in my Gardens office, talk to C. C. Hopmans every day about training matters. I also did a lot of thinking about my life.

After my heart attack in 1977 I had done a few things I had been thinking of for years, writing several letters like one that went to my half-sister, Moira, Mrs. T. W. Davis, in Ottawa just before Christmas, 1978, telling her that,

> going through my will, I was wondering if perhaps it might be better to give some of my money away now when I can give it paying a gift tax which is a somewhat smaller amount than the tax would be if I waited until I die. If you are interested, I will send you $15,000 in January, 1979, it being understood that this is to take the place of anything I would leave to you, and there would be no further money coming to you at my death. I would appreciate your letting me know your answer to this so that I can make the appropriate plans.

They all jumped at it. It was a benefit for me, too. I know that they got their money. With the kind of idiots we have running this country, I didn't know what the law was going to be on inheritances, and whether there would be anything left. Also, it cleaned things up, because apart from the few people I wanted to look after, it would all go to charity when I died.

Am I being unduly harsh in what I say about the people running the country? I don't think so. I have some beliefs that are out of fashion now, but I have them anyway. Like changing the law on capital punishment. Why the hell should we pay to look after a guy who has murdered somebody, until after fifteen years or so they let him out maybe to murder someone else. The absolute worst that can happen to a criminal these days is to get free room and board for life.

And why, when half the time I couldn't get people to work at the farm for me, should anybody be paid more than a hundred a week by Unemployment Insurance, not to work? If you're going to pay him not to work, why should he work? Worse, you teach young people to get all they can without working. That is 100 per cent wrong.

I also have some unpopular ideas that stem from what I did in breeding thoroughbreds. My main purpose each time was to get an animal physically and mentally better than what went before. Humans approach the problem in exactly the opposite way; the poorer they are, the more unable to cope with life, the more children they have, and we pay them bonuses for doing it. There's a great wave going on now through the world that the weak should be looked after and the strong can look after themselves, so if a man does well, soak him. If a man has the inclination to go into the north, take all the hardships, make an honest dollar, don't give him a prize like they did for explorers in the old days, saying, "Well done, good and faithful servant," put 'em down – make them pay taxes as heavy as anyone else's and more for groceries, clothes, rent. But let's get behind the poor weak people, the homosexuals, the drunks, the dope artists, all the rest. Society today is like the kind of a crowd you get at a hockey game – out of 15,000 people, 14,900 are yelling, cheering, enjoying themselves, but when the other hundred make a noise it's treated as a bigger noise than the 14,900 enjoying themselves. It should be reversed. I have never been in favour of the squeaky wheel getting the grease.

I also believe in something that our new Ontario Lieutenant-Governor, John Aird, said when he gave up a lot of his career to take the job: "I happen to think the successful man puts more into life than he takes out."

I'm sometimes wrong for the right reasons, or right for the wrong reasons. People I like, I like. One night at Caledon there was a knock at the door. Jessie answered and a tough looking guy was standing there. It scared her.

"Is Mr. Smythe in?" he asked. "I'm Tiger Williams."

When I heard that I called, "Ask him in!" I'd never met him and he'd never met me, but things he had heard about me he liked, and things I had heard about him – except his goals against average – I liked. He had his wife and two kids with him. They came in. Jessie got cookies and stuff and I realized that here was a man with spirit and loyalty, a natural man. Punch Imlach never should have got rid of him in 1980. Leafs needed team men then, and there wasn't anyone who thought more of the team than Tiger. Even the captain, Darryl Sittler, thought more of his agent than he did of the team – or sometimes seemed to.

I was against anybody going to the Olympics from the countries that boycotted, but when it was over I knew I was wrong – because those two Englishmen, Coe and Ovett, said to hell with the boycott and went in there and showed the Russians and everybody else that England can still produce the best. I'm glad they went, although I would like to see the Olympics stop being phoney and political. The competition should be open to all, pro and amateur, and should be held every year in Greece on a permanent Olympic site supported by all nations.

One of the things I stressed to Tommy was that no money should be paid out of my foundation to any organization that took expenses for volunteers out of general funds. That's something I've been fighting for years. Some people think I'm wrong. Even my lawyer thinks so. "When the Red Cross calls a meeting in Winnipeg why should a man have to dig into his own pocket for expenses?" he asked.

My answer to that is, why is he in the Red Cross?

That little old lady who sends in a dollar bill to help a cause, why should it help pay expenses for a guy to come from Sudbury to Toronto for a meeting? Why should Terry Fox go out and suffer great pain to raise millions of dollars for the Cancer Society, part of which will go to pay some expenses of running the society that have nothing to do with stopping cancer? All these outfits have to do is raise a special fund for expenses. Let rich people put in to the special expense fund and everybody else's money go for the good of the crippled children, cancer research, or whatever. Not one cent will go from my foundation to pay expenses for people who are supposed to be volunteers.

In October, Meg and I made a six-day trip to the Gaspé. It seemed a good time to go and we enjoyed it but it took a lot out of me. When we returned I went to bed and some days I couldn't even sit up. Tommy came to see me twice a day, morning and evening, on his way to and from work. I had a lot of things boiling around in my head about arrangements for my funeral. Many times I would come right to the point of mentioning these concerns to him but would draw back, right at the brink. This went on for nearly a week.

One night when he was sitting by my bed and his wife, Anne, was downstairs with Meg and Jessie, he said quietly, "Grampa, is there anything you want done, any plans we should make?"

I suddenly felt better. He had realized. "I guess I'm not going to get better this time, am I?" I asked.

"Well, maybe not, grampa."

It was as if the dam broke. We talked of many things, not only funeral arrangements. Hours passed. He said he had always felt that his father wanted to talk, but held back, and then never did get said what he wanted to say at the end. Tom had not wanted that to happen to me.

That night all the funeral arrangements were made. It was Tom who suggested the sanctuary at the Deaf Centre, named for Stafford, as the place where my friends could come to pay their last respects.

"That would be exactly right," I said. But I hadn't thought of it.

"How about pallbearers?" he asked.

I said the ones I'd like were either dead or couldn't do the job any more. He suggested we have honorary pallbearers representing the various areas of activity in my life, and ask Toronto Maple Leaf captains to be the active pallbearers. I agreed to that too. When it was all done, I felt a great weight had been lifted.

Near midnight I said, "Having these things settled calls for a celebration. Get Meg and Jessie and Anne up here and we'll open a bottle of champagne."

It turned out there was none in the house. Anne drove home for a bottle. I even felt well enough to sit up in bed. First time in days. We poured champagne for everyone but Tom, who doesn't drink.

It was a pleasant evening, my best for a long time. I was at peace. Before going to sleep that night I thought a long way back into my life. A few months earlier I had written out something for my co-author, asking him to keep in mind what I saw as the essentials: that this was the life "of a blue-eyed, fair-haired Canadian boy, poor as the proverbial church mouse, who had other assets including being sired by a Protestant Theosophical Irish father and born to a warm fun-loving English mother. Was taught early to practise the Golden Rule, to do unto others as you would have them do unto you, that as you sowed so would you reap and the absolute truth that if you cast your bread on the waters it would sure come back many fold. He has lived eighty-five years and with the help of hundreds of people and certainly a nudge in the right direction from The Man Upstairs, now sits at the end of the rainbow, well satisfied with what's in the pot."

Postscript: Conn Smythe died in his room at Baby Point near 5:00 in the afternoon of November 18, 1980. Those with him, Meg and Tommy, said that during his last hour or so he had been restlessly moving his arms under the cover, apparently not strong enough to get them free without help. They were then placed outside the cover. At the instant of death, they said, a big smile came over his face and he reached out with both arms as if to embrace what those present could not see.

INDEX